# Mamphela Ramphele

"The joy of Ramphele's autobiography lies ... in its richly anecdotal content and the intelligence of its frank atmosphere. Carrying all the hallmarks of Ramphele the maverick, *A Life* takes swipes apparently at the holy sages of doctrinaire wisdom on all sides. But she doesn't let herself off lightly either."
Charlotte Bauer, *Sunday Times*

"This challenging critique of South Africa today ... makes this publication not only a very readable autobiography but also vital for anyone involved in the transition of South Africa."
Barry Streek, *Cape Times*

"Opsommend is *A Life* nie net 'n teksboek vir vroue wat 'n rolmodel soek nie, maar ook noodsaaklik vir almal wat wil leer hoe ons onlangse geskiedenis één uitsonderlike vrou se lewe geraak het. En op die koop toe, baie leesbaar."
Madeleine van Biljon, *Die Burger*

# Mamphela Ramphele

# A Life

SECOND EDITION

## DAVID PHILIP
Cape Town & Johannesburg

First published in 1995 by David Philip Publishers (Pty) Ltd,
208 Werdmuller Centre, Claremont 7700, South Africa

Second edition 1996

ISBN 0-86486-316-0

Printed by Clyson Printers (Pty) Ltd, 11th Avenue, Maitland, South Africa

# Contents

# Preface

One is always ambivalent about telling one's story. Critics may charge that one is being self-seeking or ask whether one is as true to one's demons as to one's angels. The issue of selective memory also rears its head: it is so easy to rewrite history for one's own benefit.

Among those who inspired me to tell my story was Mrs Albertina Sisulu. She has said: 'We are required to walk our own road – and then stop, assess what we have learned and share it with others. It is only in this way that the next generation can learn from those who have walked before them ... We can do no more than tell our story. They must do with it what they will.'*

Story-telling is a historical imperative. We cannot successfully navigate uncharted waters without some script to guide us. This is particularly so for women, especially black women. Women have to find a script, a narrative to live by, because all other scripts are likely to depict them in roles that fit the conventional stereotypes.

Story-telling is also an urgent project for black women in post-apartheid South Africa where so much forgetfulness is willed upon people. It is much more convenient to forget the past than to recall its ugly face. Today hardly anyone is willing to acknowledge the support once given to the iniquitous system of apartheid, which caused so much pain to so many. With the formal death of apartheid, its former supporters have disappeared.

All the same, the temerity of writing one's biography in one's forties still needs to be explained. It is a foolish act by any description. Why should one make oneself so vulnerable? There are mitigating factors for this foolish act. I believe that growing up under apartheid promoted premature ageing. One's childhood, adolescence and young adulthood were knocked out of one very rudely. One either

* C. Villa-Vicencio, *Spirit of Hope* (Johannesburg, 1993), p. 259.

grew up and survived, or was destroyed along the way.

I have other inspirations for my story-telling. The important women in my life have shaped my life through texts that have come my way in the form of praise poetry (some of which is captured in my narrative). They chanted and ululated at occasions where celebration was called for, and also had the courage to sing the praises of fallen heroes. I cannot match their elegance, but in transforming their stories into the written word, I am paying my dues for the rich milk I drank from them.

I have other more pressing reasons to tell my story. It is a story of loss. The many losses I have suffered in my short lifespan have forced me into greater self-reflection. Other people's stories have also aided my own personal growth and made me more conscious of the interconnectedness of pain and human suffering. The loss of country, the loss of innocence, of space for creativity, personal freedom and one's loved ones are important themes in this book. Storytelling is part of the struggle to transcend loss. This struggle for transcendence is a major theme of my narrative, as well as a historical imperative for our deeply wounded society. The past cannot be undone: it has to be transcended.

I must also acknowledge my hope that if I make myself vulnerable in this narrative there will be less reason for women in general to be seen as 'transgressives'. If this story helps to make women feel good about who they are, and turns what is seen as abnormal for women into everyday practice, then I would have managed to intimate another possible female destiny* – a destiny worth living and dying for. But greater will be my joy when the sons and daughters of South Africa see this alternative female destiny as mainstream and desirable. Only then shall we be truly free to reach for the sky.

---

* C. Heilbrun, *Writing a Woman's Life* (New York, 1988).

# Acknowledgements

I would like to acknowledge with grateful thanks:

Makgatla Mangena, without whom parenting would have been an intolerable burden.

All the friends who supported me through the tough years of my life.

Fr Thomas Duane, Fr Ted King and Archbishop Desmond Tutu for the spiritual sustenance they continue to provide for me.

Amina Jacobs, my Personal Assistant, who holds my life together.

The Carnegie Corporation of New York, who funded the sabbatical during which this book was written.

*For my late father, my mother and my sons*

*Left:* My father, Pitsi Eliphaz Ramphele, born July 1916.

*Below:* My maternal grandparents, Sethiba Michael Mahlaela, an evangelist of the Dutch Reformed Church, and Matlala Aletta (Mamphela) née Masekela.

*Above:* My paternal grandparents.

*Below:* My mother in front of our family home at Uitkyk.

The doctor in charge at Zanempilo Community Health Centre.

*Above*: The opening ceremony at Zanempilo Community Health Centre in 1975. In the centre of the procession is Bishop Zulu.

*Below*: Crowds celebrating the opening of Zanempilo.

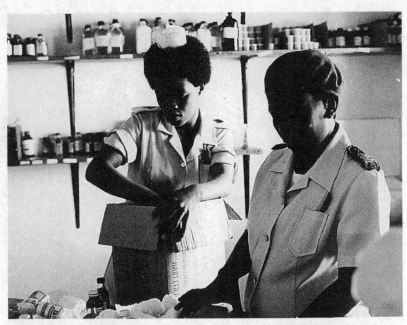

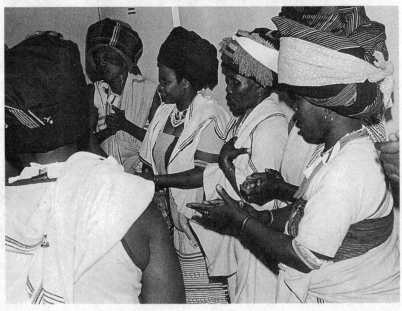

*Left top:* Nurses working in the dispensary at Zanempilo.

*Left bottom:* Local women at my farewell function when I left Zanempilo.

*Right:* Saying goodbye to Zanempilo.

*Below:* Father Aelred Stubbs CR.

*Above:* Barney and Dimza Pityana, in exile in England, 1984.

*Below:* Three student leaders at the Abe Bailey Centre, UCT, 1971. From left to right: Johan Fick of the ASB, Steve Biko of SASO and Neville Curtis of NUSAS. ·

Steve and I outside the East London magistrates' courts: one of Steve's many appearances to answer charges of breaking his banning order.

A painting done by a South African artist in detention just after Steve's death in 1977.

Steve Biko

*Above:* The doctor in charge of the Ithuseng Community Health Centre.

*Right top:* Ithuseng staff members with the visiting Rev. Bennie Witbooi.

*Right bottom:* Frank Thomas, President of Ford Foundation, on a visit to Ithuseng.

Some of the people of Tickeyline village among whom I worked at Ithuseng.

*Above:* With Hlumelo (aged 6) and Malusi (aged 1).
*Below:* With Hlumelo in Basel, 1984.

*Above:* With Walter Sisulu at a youth conference, 1991.

*Below:* Sheila van der Horst, myself and Francis Wilson celebrating Sheila's work as an academic on black labour, in 1992 at UCT.

*Above:* With President Nelson Mandela and Mr Clive Menell at the launch of the Nelson Mandela Children's Fund in Pretoria, 1994.

*Below:* Presiding as Deputy Vice-Chancellor at a graduation ceremony at UCT, 1993.

Deputy Vice-Chancellor, UCT

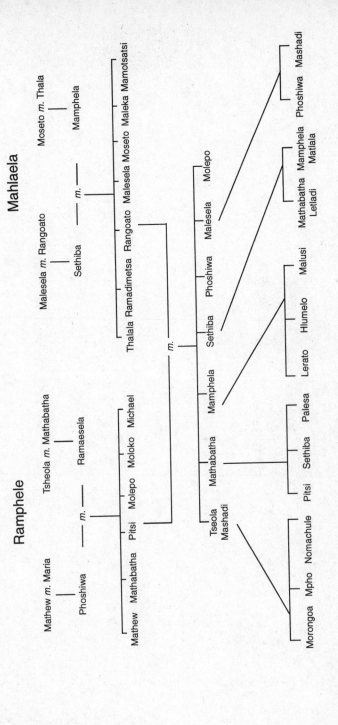

# 1

# My Roots

Helen Frantz Hospital in the Bochum district of the northern Transvaal is a desolate set of buildings, most of which are hidden from the lazy gaze of passing motorists by thornbush. A lethargic stream which more often than not struggles to justify its status because of the perennial droughts, trickles across the road under a narrow bridge, a few metres from the hospital. It is here that I was born at two o'clock on the afternoon of 28 December 1947, having inconvenienced my mother in no small measure.

A pregnancy in the heat of the northern Transvaal summer was no small feat. The Bochum district has a harsh climate and only hardy species survive. The vegetation tells the story of repeated long droughts. Sparse thornbush and an abundance of marula trees cover the flat countryside, and villages provide the only relief from the monotony of the landscape, which stretches all the way towards the Botswana border. There is hardly a wild animal that thrives here: only occasionally would one see a frightened hare scurry across the gravel road at night. Temperatures range from the upper thirties at the height of summer to the lower teens in mid-winter. Late December and January present the greatest challenges.

My mother had more than simply the burden of pregnancy to deal with. For a woman to be able to deliver in Helen Frantz Hospital during those days of poor transport and communication, one had to book in as an expectant mother and manage under difficult conditions, catering for oneself in the antenatal section for a few weeks until one went into labour. My mother had to forgo Christmas celebrations to ensure the safe delivery in hospital of her third child.

Both my parents were primary schoolteachers – a position of relative privilege in their social environment at the time, which placed me in a better position to survive and thrive than most of my contemporaries. My mother had no reason to anticipate the problems which lay ahead. The midwife who attended to her at my birth was, according to my mother, most unhelpful. She disparaged any request from my mother for help during labour as the cry of a spoilt schoolteacher seeking special attention. As a result my mother delivered me without any assistance from the midwife. She only came in later to cut the umbilical cord, heaping more scorn as she tidied up. I was to bleed heavily from the improperly tied stump of cord that night and, according to my mother, nearly died over the next few days from a combination of neonatal jaundice and the after-effects of blood loss.

But my mother was not an ordinary schoolteacher. Born on 19 February 1919, the third in a family of nine, she leaned more towards her own mother in both looks and personality. Her father, Sethiba Michael Mahlaela, born in 1885, was a tobacco and corn farmer who was also an evangelist of the Dutch Reformed Church. He was a short gentle man with soft keen eyes and a sharp intellect. His wife Matlala Aletta, born Masekela in 1887, was a remarkable woman, tall and beautiful with an incredible intellect. She was better known by her praise name, Mamphela.*

Mamphela was a teacher before her marriage. Her extraordinary memory was an asset to the largely illiterate people among whom she lived, for in those days births and deaths were not registered by any authority. She was a mobile archive for the region. She could recall most birthdays, deaths and other important events in the life of the people of her village and surrounding areas. Children born in the locality used to come to her to find out when they were born, before going to register at school. She would enquire who their parents were, where they lived, and would make a connection with some event and say, 'Oh, you are so-and-so's child, you were born on this or that date, because I remember that this or that happened just before you were born.'

Mamphela's talents were numerous: a facility for communication and organisation, traditional healing learned from her mother, and efficient management of the household supported by many practical skills. She mastered the art of roasting pork and preserving it in its own fat for up to three months – a useful skill in an environment where there was no refrigeration. Her own personality balanced the kindness of her husband, whom unscrupulous people often took

*Praise names are important linkages with one's clan and are used both as endearments and as a mark of respect amongst Sotho-speaking people in the northern Transvaal.

advantage of. She called him *kgwebeane*, the easy one to cheat. She spoke her mind openly, sometimes to the embarrassment of her kindly husband. She was aware of her capabilities and was full of self-confidence. Her most determined statements were always prefixed by *Rare Serogole*, a reference to her father's praise name (Serogole). She did not suffer fools easily.

My mother, Rangoato Rahab, has fond memories of her childhood on a communal farm in the Moletsi district, about thirty kilometres due west of Pietersburg. They lived in a seven-roomed house with a corrugated-iron roof, the first in the area. Both her father's and her mother's relatives lived within walking distance, and it was accepted that she could stay in the homes of other family members whenever she wanted to. This multiplicity of abodes came in handy. Whenever she had been naughty at home she could escape punishment by going off somewhere else to avoid repercussions.

Naughty she was indeed. For example, she remembers an incident which took place when she was about ten. She climbed a very tall bluegum tree in search of birds' eggs, a feat which was the preserve of boys who used it to test their climbing skills. My mother was not one to be outdone by anybody, boy or girl. A particularly small bird known in the area as *lentshwarelele* had made its nest right at the top of the tallest tree. My mother climbed the tree to get to the nest, but lost her nerve once she reached the top and could not summon the courage to climb down. Her younger brother, Malesela Thomas, went to call for help. Her father came and put a long ladder against the tree and gently coaxed her down. Her mother, *Koko*\* Mamphela, was not one to let a child get away so easily. As soon as she stepped down, my grandmother went at her with a stick which had been got ready during the anxious moments before her descent – a tension-breaking tactic my mother used regularly at our expense as we grew up.

Shortly after this incident, my mother was bitten by a spider whilst searching for birds' eggs. She had taken her baby brother, Moseto Moses, to be breastfed by their mother, who was doing the family laundry by the river. As she carried the baby home and shepherded Malesela, she saw a bird's nest on the side of the footpath. She sat the baby down on the path and went over to get the eggs. It happened suddenly: a bite and then immediate swelling of the hand, face and every part of the upper body. My mother put Moseto

---

\* *Koko* is the North Sotho designation for grandmother; and *Rakgolo*, for grandfather.

on her back and hurried Malesela along, crying all the way back to their mother at the river. My grandmother rushed her to an old man who was a healer, known as *Rakgolo* Ngwanamorena (Son of the king) to all the children. He gave her a mixture to drink, incised her swollen blue finger and sprinkled some permanganate of potash, or *makgonatsohle* (cure for all ailments), onto the wound. She felt rapid relief.

My mother's passion for independence bordered on stubbornness. She recalls an occasion when she was beaten, pinched and abused verbally by older girls, mostly cousins of hers, with whom she was playing *kgole*. This is a game similar to hockey, but it is played over long distances, hence the name *kgole*, which means 'far'. The device used as a ball was a rounded, polished piece of wood. On this particular occasion the older girls were using my mother's ball, which one of her male cousins had made for her. She became frustrated at losing repeatedly, and just before the seniors could score another goal, she grabbed the ball, sat down and held it tightly between her legs, refusing to budge. Her concerned elder sister, Ramadimetsa Salphy, a much gentler soul, pleaded with her, but to no avail. In the end they all gave up, to my mother's delight. She often reminds people that it is not insignificant that an extension of her praise name is *Nkgakgathu nama moshifa* (The tough one who is like the ligament supporting the neck muscles of a beast).

My parents owe their meeting, courtship and eventual marriage to Bethesda Normal College, where they both trained as teachers in the late 1930s. Her eyes still sparkle as she recalls the time she first set her eyes on Pitsi Eliphaz. He was smashingly handsome, tall and strongly built, with well-proportioned facial features. She was envied by all her friends for having captured his attentions. Pitsi was the top student at the college and a crafty soccer player, Columbia being his cheer name. My mother remembers him as a quiet, reserved and shy person at College. Pitsi was born in July 1916 at Stofberg Bible School in the Free State, where his parents, Phoshiwa Nicodemus and Ramaesela Christina Ramphele, were living at the time to enable Phoshiwa to complete his training as an evangelist of the Dutch Reformed Church. Pitsi was his parents' third son in a family of six boys. Coincidentally, I share with both my parents place number three in terms of order of birth – a not insignificant factor in shaping one's life path.

The Ramphele family was supported during the three years of

Phoshiwa's training by Ramaesela's widowed mother, Ramaesela Ruth Tsheola, who had also been married to a Ramphele. After her husband's death she was left to fend for herself and only daughter. She took up employment as a domestic for a white farmer in the district of Moletsi. She also farmed on her own account and could regularly send corn, beans, dried meat, spinach and other food for the upkeep of her daughter's family while my grandfather trained at Stofberg Bible School.

My great-grandmother was illiterate. In order to send the produce to her daughter, and undaunted by the obstacles placed in her way, she would catch a ride on an ox cart, known as *sephumamagapu* (breaker of watermelons) because of the bumpiness of the ride, and get to Pietersburg railway station. Here she would request the officials to help her fill in the requisite forms for railage.

She told my mother a story which best demonstrates her resourcefulness. Early one morning she was on her way to work when she came upon a big trunk, which must have fallen from a passing ox-wagon. Having made sure that there was no one in sight, she decided to push it off the road and conceal it under some bushes. She spent an anxious day wondering if her employers would mention that some traveller had made enquiries about lost property, or fearing someone else would come upon her treasure. At the end of the day, she deliberately finished her chores later than the other staff members to secure the privacy she needed for the task ahead. Under cover of darkness she carried the heavy trunk on her head all the way home. Once there she found that it contained clothes for a whole family. What a gift from the gods for her needy daughter's family! She buried the trunk in her backyard, having satisfied herself that the owners were unlikely to reclaim it, selected some clothing for both her grandchildren and their parents, and sent them off in the usual way. At intervals she returned to the treasure chest, which remained in its hide-out, and sent instalments of clothing to her family until the trunk was empty. By this time she was confident enough to use it for storing her own personal effects.

My grandfather completed his training at Stofberg and was posted by the church to Uitkyk as an evangelist. He was a strong leader of his church and was sought after for his wisdom. He established himself as an important member of the local community of peasant farmers, and made a comfortable living for himself and his family.

When my parents married in 1942, my great-grandmother, *Koko*

Tsheola, was assigned as a baby-sitter for my father's children. In 1945 she moved from Uitkyk No. 1, the communal Ramphele home, to join my parents at Kranspoort Mission Station, which nestled comfortably at the foot of the Soutpansberg range of mountains, about fifty kilometres from Louis Trichardt in the northern Transvaal. The Soutpansberg district stood in stark contrast to Bochum. Besides the beauty of the landscape with its rugged mountains and gentle valleys, the lush vegetation bore witness to the abundant rainfall, and the gurgling streams and rich variety of birdlife sang the praises of mother nature.

My father had been transferred from his home village to this area in 1944 on promotion to become the principal of the Stephanus Hofmeyer School. My great-grandmother looked after all of us except Molepo, the last born, *'n laat lammetjie*, who arrived on 10 October 1961. *Koko* Tsheola died in 1964, then over a hundred years old, according to the estimates of my maternal grandmother, *Koko* Mamphela, the mobile archive. The two knew each other well as they were distant cousins. I remember *Koko* Tsheola as a kindly old woman with a face etched by a pattern of firmly set wrinkles and graced by her kindly soft eyes, which were given to watering. My memory of her dates back to 1953 when she supervised me in my role as caretaker of my younger brother Phoshiwa, born on 25 May 1952, thereby enabling my mother to resume her teaching post at the local school. I was six then. *Koko* Tsheola carried out a great number of household chores for her age. She walked with a slight shuffle, supported by a walking-stick. The shuffle became more pronounced as she got older. She meticulously swept the mud floor of our three-bedroomed house and its surroundings, and washed dishes and pots. My responsibility was to mind the baby and to play with my toddler brother, Sethiba. I carried Phoshiwa on my back to encourage him to sleep, which then freed me to play.

*Koko* Tsheola spoiled us rotten as children. She was the embodiment of a fairy godmother, though with limited means to cater for our childhood fantasies. She divided up between us most of her old-age pension, which amounted then to a little less than £5 per quarter, starting with my eldest sister, Mashadi Ramaesela Ruth, born on 27 March 1943. Mashadi, who was named after her, was her favourite great-grandchild. The next allocation would go to my elder brother, Mathabatha Alfred, born on 6 February 1945. I was the third in line and would get an allocation to suit my status. Next would be my younger brother, Sethiba Michael, born on 28 March 1950. We used our spoils to buy sweets at a local store run by an Indian man, known as Makana, who had a large family living on the property. The only unpleasant memory I have of my great-grandmother was of the pinching she once gave me because I had not responded to her repeated calls to go on an errand for her. She told us stories about her childhood as well as many riddles and folktales in the warmth of our kitchen, in which stood my mother's efficient black coal stove with the proud label 'Welcome Dover'.

There is more to names in our family tree than a casual observer might notice. Naming of children amongst the North Sotho people, where my roots lie, is a major part of the process of incorporating new arrivals into the extended family. The name one is given also signifies one's position within the lineage, which has major implications for access to scarce resources. One's namesake often looks after one's interests in vital ways. Women play an important role in this system as partners to their brothers, who are the heirs in the family. Women partners are regarded as female husbands (*borakgadi*) and without them important rituals in their partner brothers' families cannot be carried out successfully.

Central to these rituals is the naming ceremony, which takes place at the end of a wedding feast. The bride is introduced to the ancestors by the presiding female husband as *Ma-So-and-so* (Mother of So-and-so), according to the line of succession. For example, the wife of the first-born son is given the responsibility of perpetuating the name of her father-in-law, and therefore receives a title with his praise name attached, such as Matlou, Matshwene or Mangwoatshipa. Her own first-born son will then be known by the father-in-law's name but, given the reverence attached to it, women are only allowed to use the praise name. If the first-born child is a girl, she is named after the mother of the man, unless special arrangements are made by the woman's family to 'ask for a name' (*go kgopela leina*). Such an 'asked-for name' was customarily that of the woman's mother.

Sons other than first-borns name their own first-born sons after their immediate elder brothers. If the first-born is a girl, she is named after the partner female husband unless the latter indicates otherwise, as when another family name is in danger of becoming extinct, because of a couple's infertility or some other unforeseen circumstance. The next son has to keep his immediate elder brother's name alive, and so on down the line. If there are more than two children, then alternate children are named after members of the maternal family, starting with the mother's parents, then her siblings and other important relatives.

The names of children in an extended family within this system are not only predictable, but also pregnant with meaning and pulsate with the tensions embedded within each patrilineage. With knowledge of the naming system one can deduce the family tree from a set of names. Children born out of wedlock can also be easily identified by their names, which are out of kilter with the system, unless some agreement is reached between the two families to adopt the child ritually 'who has come with his mother'. In most cases such children are adopted by their mothers' brothers and brought up in their households to avoid the conflicts which often occur in families with children 'who came with their mothers'.

My mother is Matlou, thus my elder brother's praise name is Tlou, as he is named after my father's immediate elder brother Mathabatha, with the same praise name. My sister, Mashadi Ramaesela Ruth, being the eldest daughter, was named after an important female in the Ramphele lineage. Because he had no sisters my father had greater freedom in naming her, so he chose his grandmother's name, Ramaesela. Mashadi, her middle name, was given to her by my maternal grandmother, *Koko* Mamphela, in honour of the German woman who was the founder and matron of Helen Frantz Hospital at the time of her birth. Helen Frantz was given the name Mashadi by the locals, because she could not pronounce the Sotho word for 'women' (*basadi*), referring to them instead as *mashadi*.

The European names which occur in my family deserve comment. They embody the legacy of the missionaries, who saw it as their duty to give Africans 'Christian' names as part of the sacrament of baptism. African names were regarded as heathen and unacceptable to God. Considerations of convenience were thus turned into a theodicy – for most whites did not, and still are unwilling to, learn African names, some of which are tongue-twisters for foreigners. The ease with which most whites shrug off attempts to pronounce African names is a logical consequence of the low status accorded Africans historically: there were no incentives to learn to pronounce their names properly nor sanctions in the event of failure. Thus even those Africans who were not baptised were given 'slave names' by white employers for their convenience.

Negotiating extended family relations can be a tricky process. The fifty kilometres which separated Uitkyk No. 1, my father's parents' home, and our own home in Kranspoort in the Mara district did not pose any threat to the closely knit extended family network, and yet gave our nuclear family sufficient distance to develop its distinctive lifestyle. My mother's parents were also within reach in their home in Krantzplaas, twenty kilometres due west of Uitkyk, where they had moved in December 1942.

Family ties were strengthened by regular school-holiday visits to my father's home in Uitkyk. These trips were great occasions for all. There was never any need for my father to announce our intended arrival: there was mutual understanding that specificities such as dates were unimportant in the flow of communication within the extended family. People did not have to keep diaries – there was always time for everything, and no need to be uptight about schedules. Everyone relaxed in the knowledge that the visits would happen during the course of the school vacations.

My recollection of these visits dates back to the beginning of December 1953. Our mode of transport – the envy of the locals at the time – was a mule wagon. My father owned a span of six mules, which were a source of much family pride. Mules combine the elegance and beauty of horses with the sedateness of donkeys. My father's mules were handsome animals: all but Japie had shiny black-haired skins. The journey to Uitkyk was an exciting day-long trip. We set off early in the morning laden with provisions. My cousin Oupa Phoshiwa, my father's eldest brother's son, whom he adopted after his own father had died in a car accident, took great delight in being in charge of the mule wagon. He loved speed and would ensure that we arrived at our destination early in the afternoon.

My brothers and sister and I enjoyed playing a game of spotting interesting things on the way, particularly the infrequent cars which passed us by on the gravel road, throwing clouds of dust at us. As we drew nearer to Uitkyk, we vied with each other in identifying members of our family as they milled around the homestead oblivious of our impending arrival.

The welcome opened with loud praise-singing by my grandmother who sang the family praise song as well as our individual praises. This was high-class theatre with my paternal grandmother as the lead actor generating a pulsating emotional atmosphere. She would emerge from the nearby fields, and occupy the centre stage, elegantly strutting about as she shrilly proclaimed:

Ke bana ba sebešo segolo sa Bashita-Meetse, Bakwena, ba gaModubu wa mela nokeng dikala tša okama madiba, bana ba kgomo e tšhweu Mathabatha. Ke Phjatla-dihlaka-tsetsepa tsa mogatša' Moganwa wa gaBosega. Lena methepa le yang mashemong le ntlele nyoba ya nkgopo le a mpona ke Letladi ke kgopame.

Ke bana ba Phoshiwa Madumetsa rangwane wa Sekgopetšane, Matšhoša, ba ga Mahlo-mahwibidu a gaMathabatha a hwibila a etšwa go Ramphele, Mohlaloga. Phoshiwa ka mekgolodi ya marumo. Ke Matšhoša-dibata, Ramathiba-tsebe wa bo Mafepeng o ntše leweng la nkwe o ntše a shitisa nkwe go bopa. Mokgoši wa gabo Mmaselaelo o hlabja o lebana le Mmatšhwaana. Ke batho wa ga boMafoša ntsikitsiki kua moseo le kua monyako.

Ke bana ba Pitsi ya boMmatlala a bo Noko. Ke phoofolo ya mabalabala, Mamongwangwai wa mabaka, mesela ke metshanyelo, melomo ke metloutlo. Ke Lesetša Rabotse o tšwa badimong. Ke Motšhishi gatoga dinose dilo tša botse ga di gatiwe otla roba mamapo. Ke papago Lehlaba o thopa di ile go fula Moeketsi, ya sakeng a thopela kgosi ke mang? Nna ke thopile gaManyoba-Tsokotlana kgomo yešu e sa retiwa Moletši'a Raphuti. Ke Seya-nokeng-ka-legata Lesetša, a be a pega ka seatla sa monna wa kua gaManangana. Ke motho wa gabo Molepo ke Matshwana' Boshega, Tlou-setumula megala. Ke ditlogolo tša Kgetsi ya go rwala bana ba Lesetsa e subela nabo Mmedike ga gabo Letlatsa.

Ke ba gaNhloma-Marumo, ba gaRamphele wa Tswetla, Mohlaloga, batho ba tšwang Bodupe ba gaMmathepe-a-Polokwane. Bodupe wee-ba-gaMmangwako-a-Molobe!!

The rules of equity demanded that she incorporate the praise song of the Mahlaelas, her son's in-laws, as an acknowledgement of their part in perpetuating the Ramphele lineage through the gift of their fertile daughter:

Ke ditlogolo tšă Mahlaela-a-Mmutele'ntotoma. Ba gaRamotse wa kgang ga o dulwe e ka motse wa mashoboro. Ke ba gaSekata-ka-pitsi wa ga boSefagwana sa boMatsiri. Ke bana ba Sethiba-dipata-tšă-makgowa, Sethiba a hlabiwa mogolo batho ba dikobo ba tletšě gona a be a lamolela Moloto kua Madikoti, thaba ya maaka, thaba e phaswa ka morago. Ke Phatola-motag-wana. Ke phatela kua Maribišeng. Maribišeng go hlomilwe folaga ya go iletšă ditoro. Ditoro di na le bjala ba bogale ba go taga boMatshere a

boDinonyana.
Ke motho wa ga boMakgatša-ka-patla wa ga boRaisibe. Ba re o rile o kgatša ka patla wa ekiša mang le mogwera wa gago o saka wa mo tseba. Ke Lefalaolo la gaPhahla-nkgori, le le rileng kgomo, la re motho. Ke batho ba tšwang Dikgabong. Ke Matebele Makwankwane a hloka kgomo a ja motho. Ke Ditlou, phoofolo tše dikgolo. Ke batho ba tšwang Kgobadi, gaNyedimane-a-Tlokwa.
Ke bana ba Rangoato wa ga boMalesela, sa naga sa lešoka. Ke motho wa ga boMoseto, Setlogolo sa Mmankwana-a-modumo le bo Malekola a sena tšhemo Moroko wa jwala wa boMautšana. Ke ditlogolo tša boMasekela-a-Molobare, Bakwena Baroka-meetse-a-pula. Ke tše dithlaba-tša-gaMabolesa, bare ga dia ripelwa bokwala, direpetšwe go hlaba tše dingwe. Ke bana ba Mamphela wa gabo dikgoši, monnyana wa gaRamothopo, kgaetšedi wa boSefadima sa boMontsho-ke-fifetše. Ke ditlogolo tša Raisibe, Thalala-a-tsoku, wa topa yena o humile le dinala. Ke ditlogolo tša boMaleka a dutse, Moraswi Letebele, batho ba ga boSanaga sa lešoka.

Never one known for false modesty, my grandmother always ended the praise-singing by acknowledging her own central role in the extended family, as a 'jack' that lifted all implements, large and small:

Ke batlogolo ba Jack, tshipi ya go rwa'a tše dingwe. Shate-shatee!! Wo a sareng moshate o llela dilo, ore nkabe ele tša gabo! Bodupe wee--!! BaMmangwako!*

The electric atmosphere thus generated was enhanced by the ululating and dancing which went with every phrase, even the neighbours coming to join in. As Harold Scheub has correctly observed, African oral tradition in this form is able to distil the essence of the human experience and offer it in memorable form to help shape future relations and action.†

My grandmother was a true artist, adept at recasting family narratives into poetic language. The heroes of my family were for the most part predictably identified as the males in both my paternal and maternal family lines. The namesakes of Phoshiwa (my paternal grandfather), Pitsi (my father) and Sethiba (my maternal grandfather) were singled out as brave men who took on challenges in spite of the considerable odds against them. Phoshiwa's bravery

* Praise songs are difficult, if not impossible, to translate. The substance of my grandmother's words is given in the following pages.
† H. Scheub,*The Xhosa Ntsomi* (Oxford, 1975), p. 1.

silenced even tigers (*o dutše leweng la nkwe ontše a shitiša nkwe go bopa*). Pitsi was the warrior who went to capture enemy livestock and carried home with him trophies in the form of a human skull, which he used as a water container, and a human hand as a balancing mechanism within the skull to prevent spillage as he carried the water home (*seya nokeng ka legata la motho a be a pega ka seatla sa monna wa kua gaManangana*). Sethiba, on the other hand, was a handsome only child, a leader and warrior who blocked the white settlers' way, and was killed in the process, whilst ugly cowards stood by (*Sethiba dipata tša makgowa, Sethiba a hlabiwa mogolo batho ba dikobo ba tletse*).

But some significant women received honourable mention as important sisters of the heroes, or as co-actors: Thalala, Mamphela, Kgetsi, Rangoato, and Jack (my paternal grandmother's nick-name). She had great admiration for her own mother, who saved her from an unwanted marriage at puberty to a local chief in their village. Her beauty had attracted the elders of the village. *Koko* Tsheola, realising that the net was closing in, had to flee and live in a different area where her daughter was much safer.

My family's heroes moved to the boundaries of their communities. Both my paternal and maternal grandfathers took the risk to part with traditional lifestyles and elected to become evangelists of the Dutch Reformed Church. My maternal grandfather, Sethiba, had the advantage that his own father had converted to Christianity whereas my paternal grandfather, Phoshiwa, was a pioneer in his family. It came as no surprise that my father would move even farther outwards – taking up a teaching position and physically moving to the Soutpansberg district (*Mmedike a boLetlatsa*). My paternal grandmother's creativity is demonstrated by her extension of the family praise song to incorporate new images etched by transitions into new historical realities. She expanded her text by transforming old tales, and infused them with contemporary imagery and themes.

Elaborate formal greetings of each relative, young and old, followed the emotional praise-singing, and cooled the air. These formal greetings were confusing for us children. Some adults insisted on being kissed, while others expected us to clap our hands and hold them in a clasped position for them to be kissed by the adult through the mediation of their own hands in a style intended to show deference towards adults. One was never sure what to expect.

The offloading of the provisions provided the next exciting moment for the welcoming party. The fresh fruit and vegetables which we brought from the better-endowed Soutpansberg district were a treat for the residents of Uitkyk. Young and old would tuck into the fruit as they carried the provisions from the wagon into one of the many huts around the homestead.

My father's natal homestead was a large one consisting of a corrugated-iron-roofed house together with several rondavels situated round an enclosed courtyard, or *lapa*. There were other buildings on the periphery: two rondavels, one the private room of my grandparents and the other for *Koko* Tsheola, and a three-roomed thatched mud house which belonged to one of my father's brothers. A one-roomed flat on one wing of the central house belonged to my father, and this we used during our visits. The size of the homestead signified my grandfather's success as a patriarch, blessed as he was with sons and grandchildren, and with the material means to sustain a coherent extended family.

My grandfather was a tall, strikingly handsome man, strongly built with a well-proportioned body. He was generally a stern man with strong views on many matters. His face would, however, light up when he was in a good mood. He was fond of telling us stories of his youth heavily peppered with jokes, which he told at his own or other people's expense. As he told them he would literally roll around in fits of laughter on a goatskin under a large shady tree: this served as a gathering place for the family's midday meals and afternoon rest away from the blistering summer heat.

Like most of his contemporaries, my grandfather was an authoritarian patriarch. He ruled his family with a firm hand. To underline his control over his descendants, he issued an edict that all his grandchildren were to refer to him as *Papa* and his wife as *Mma*, whereas their own parents were to be called *Brother* and *Sister*. This was a major symbolic statement about the lines of authority within the family. But my mother would have none of it. As a compromise, my father suggested the use of *Daddy* and *Mommy* – an interesting way of diverting patriarchal tensions through flight into another language. But my mother stood her ground. We thus grew up calling my grandfather *Papa*, my grandmother as *Mma-o-mogolo* (Big mother), and my father *Daddy*. Having been successfully challenged by my mother, the edict was sufficiently weakened to allow my father's younger brothers flexibility in their own family relations.

My mother fought many battles within this patriarchal family system. She walked a tightrope as she carved out space for herself to live with dignity within the extended family. She established a delicate balance between challenging those aspects of the many rigid rules about gender roles, lines of authority and the conduct of relations that violated her dignity, and avoiding actions that would undermine the system and thus create anxiety and instability. She faithfully fulfilled her responsibilities as a *ngwetsi* and a *lethari* (newly married and young woman in the village) – no mean feat – but she would not be bullied by anyone. Young married women were often reminded that *mosadi ke tšhwene o lewa mabogo*, a woman's only real value lies in the fruits of her labour, including her reproductive labour.

Newly married women had to establish their credentials as hard workers from the very first day after their wedding. The luxuries of a honeymoon were not for them. But even an authoritarian system as tough as this patriarchy recognised the limits of human endurance – a wise step in ensuring its perpetuation. It was customary for the newly married woman to go back to her natal home after two weeks, *go tsholla bongwetši* (literally, to pour out one's newly married status). This was an opportunity for her to have a break from the hard work, to share experiences with her old friends and relatives, and to get useful advice about how to tackle some of the challenges of her new life. One could look upon it as a retreat of sorts.

Upon her return to her in-laws, the bride was expected to fit into the routine of her new family, and demonstrate her capacity to produce goods and services for her new family, as well as to reproduce. Any undue delay in falling pregnant tended to set tongues wagging about possible problems of infertility. Given the level of physical exertion, one wonders how the newly weds ever managed to make love, let alone conceive. Most women did.

My mother survived the punishing schedule of a young married woman through a combination of creativity, hard work and courage in standing up for her rights. She established boundaries beyond which she would not allow anyone to go. She tackled her brothers-in-law on many levels to let them know that she was not at their beck and call, but should be treated with respect if they expected respect from her. They were quick to blame her attitude on her professional status, for none of them had married a professional woman.

A major bone of contention was the holy of holies – slaughtering of animals, from which women were excluded because their potential for pollution was thought to pose a threat to the generative capacity of livestock. Whenever a beast was slaughtered, the men were in the habit of delaying the process – keeping women waiting being part of the whole exercise of power by men over women. Slaughtering after sunset was quite common. This caused enormous frustration amongst the women, who had to wait for the meat which was to be prepared for supper. The men had little incentive to change this practice. They chose certain tender parts such as the liver, heart and spleen to cook for themselves on a makeshift fireplace, thus ensuring that their needs were catered for. They had scant concern for the children falling asleep before food was ready – it was the women's responsibility to feed the children.

On one occasion my mother decided that the critical boundary had been crossed. She calmly walked up to the men's fireplace and carried away the pot containing the meat with tender portions which was ready for consumption. She dished it out together with the porridge which the women had prepared. My father was placed in an invidious position – he was torn between loyalty to his brothers and the compelling logic of his wife's actions. In the end he decided to stay out of it. His brothers were stunned! No woman had ever dared to touch a pot cooked by men. The other women, including my grandmother, were jubilant that the spell had been broken. From then on there was greater cooperation between men and women with the slaughtering. The men were still allowed to roast some liver over open coals, but gave the women more control over the rest of the meat. My mother's transgressive act had liberated both men and women in the extended family from an archaic custom.

My mother also challenged the iniquitous practice of compelling daughters-in-law to return to domestic chores three days after delivery of their babies. After delivering her second child, she simply told her mother-in-law that she was going to stay put in her bedroom for the next ten days. My grandmother was appalled by the prospect of being laughed at by her friends in the village, who would notice that she was fetching water, cooking and doing other domestic chores, whilst her daughter-in-law enjoyed the luxury of post-natal recuperation. Grudgingly, the older woman came to terms with it and even defended her daughter-in-law's position in the village.

My mother was a survivor. She endeared herself to everyone through her hard work, skilled housekeeping and, above all, her delicious cooking. Her father-in-law was particularly proud of her in this regard, denigrating other daughters-in-law who were less competent. The way into my grandfather's heart was through special attention to his palate – a truism my mother always kept in mind. My grandfather's favourite treats were freshly baked bread, *vetkoek* (deep fried cakes) and piping hot tea, or *mafisa-molomo* (burner of lips). He would sing my mother's praises as he drank one cup after another and munched the accompaniments. Because of her special culinary skills my mother was spared the discomfort of working in the fields.

Our visits to Uitkyk were mixed blessings. Whilst we enjoyed catching up with family and the novelty of visiting the area, we found the extended family arrangements very taxing. The rigid boundaries between male and female roles separated me from my younger brothers during our vacations. I missed them terribly, and they in turn missed the warmth of the nuclear family.

Water had to be carried from a windmill about a kilometre away by female members of the household for all domestic purposes. This was hard water, which took some getting accustomed to for those of us used to fresh water from sparkling mountain streams. My mother spent most of her time with the other women in the household cooking and feeding the multitudes, including villagers who took advantage of our presence as visitors to share in the windfall. There is a saying in North Sotho, *Moeng etla ka gešo, re je ka wena* (Visitor, come to our home so that we can eat through you). And how! It was not unusual for my mother to feed up to twenty-five people each meal. We found the custom of feeding men first, elderly women next and children last, very frustrating, because sometimes food would run out. We were also not used to eating out of a communal dish with so many other children, who were quite adept at tucking the food away quickly.

Children were also sent around a lot. It seemed that some adults could not bear the sight of children playing happily – it was seen as idleness, which called for action. My father's youngest brother was the worst offender on this score. He made us pick up gravel stones in the hot December sun and stash them along the fence around the large homestead. One was not expected to argue or question such instructions. After all, children were regarded as part of the family estate – property to be handled as one pleased. It did not take long for all of us to long for our own home.

The nuclear family home stood in sharp contrast to that of my extended family. My memory of my childhood goes back to a rainy day at the beginning of 1953 when we were moving house from one end of Kranspoort to another. We used a mule-drawn cart to transport the household furniture and personal effects. It was a confusing day for me as a little girl who could contribute nothing to the process, though I was made to understand very clearly that I had to keep out of the way of the busy adults. It was strange to sleep in a new house, which was to become my home for the next twelve years.

The notion of home as more than the physical structure one inhabits took on a special meaning for me as a little girl. Our new home was a mud-brick house with a mud floor which had to be smeared with cow dung at least once a fortnight by my mother. The floor itself had to be strengthened and smoothed over with specially prepared mud mixed with dung (*go dila le go ritela*) at least once a year. The house had three bedrooms, a kitchen, a pantry, and a living-room which served both as a dining and a relaxation area. Children were explicitly discouraged from using the living-room. It was reserved for adult use, and had to be kept in good shape for the entertainment of visitors who dropped by quite often. There was a front *stoep* (veranda) and an enclosed mud-floored space (*lapa*) at the back of the house which was used most frequently by the family, particularly in the afternoons when the sun hid its hot rays behind the Soutpansberg. We often sat on floor mats made of goatskin and straw. The few chairs which we had were mainly used by visitors, and women and children deferred to men in this respect.

The house had a large garden with flowers in the front, and vegetables and fruit trees on the rest of the property. A pig-sty and fowl-run stood at the farthest end of our backyard next to a pit latrine. I can still remember the characteristic smells around our house – a mixture of fresh flowers, dry earth and a whiff of tobacco from my father's pipe.

The village in which we lived was well planned with three main streets: Bloed, Mahomed and Church streets as well as two semi-developed ones on the outskirts. Each street had an irrigation furrow which was used by residents to water their gardens in turn. There was one tap for the hundred or so households. Refuse removal was the responsibility of individual householders, as was the cleanliness of streets. Most households used the open veld on the other side of the gravel main road as a public toilet. This patch of veld (*pho-moshene*, derived from the word 'permission') was polluted beyond description by human excreta, but it was strategically hidden away by thornbush.

Kranspoort was a tidy village. Villagers were proud owners of flower and vegetable gardens and numerous fruit trees. Great effort went into maintaining their houses. There were only two families other than the dominee's with cement houses. One belonged to a well-to-do builder* and the other to a teacher who headed a school in the Soekmekaar area. The teacher's wife, Mrs Pauline Moshakga, was my mother's great friend.

The laundry was done at the river every week. Huge bundles of laundry were carried on women's heads to the river. Washing clothes provided an occasion for village women to meet and share the latest news and concerns. I picked up a lot from the unrestrained talk of the women, who treated us children as part of the open environment and spoke their minds quite frankly on many issues including troubled marriages, family feuds and general village politics.

I had hoped to be able to start school in 1953, having just turned five in December 1952. I found staying at home very boring. But I was given no choice by my parents, as I had to look after my younger brother, Phoshiwa, then seven months old, because my great-grandmother was getting on in years and could not cope alone with a baby. I cried bitterly on the day school opened, but had to come to terms with the finality of the decision adults had made. I subsequently spent many happy days playing with my two baby brothers, Sethiba and Phoshiwa, in our house and yard, particularly amongst the fruit trees. I learnt to climb the orange trees which were closest to the house, but was discouraged from this activity by my great-grandmother, who feared for my safety. She also said that it was inappropriate for a girl to be climbing trees. I was later to pay the price of an injury to the back of my right thigh, which has left a permanent linear scar.

Our household in Kranspoort was organised for maximum efficiency by my mother, who had to juggle her roles as wife, mother to seven children and schoolteacher without the benefit of domestic help. She was a tough marshal and expected every one of us to make a contribution to the smooth running of the house. We woke up at set times and had specific tasks allocated to each of us which had to be

*Our family moved into this house in 1964.

done before and after school. There was a division of labour between the boys and the girls, but it was not rigid. My brothers had to fetch water from the village tap just as we did, but they had the benefit of using a wheelbarrow, which could carry two twenty-litre containers. They also shared in the making of endless cups of tea for my mother and her occasional guests. They made their own beds, and later when both my sister and I were away at boarding school or working, the younger ones learned to cook, bake, iron and so on. My mother was a pragmatist. Traditional gender roles were cast aside to make room for survival.

My father was a great provider for his family. We were the best-fed children in the area. He often came home unexpectedly with a goat or sheep for slaughter. If none of my brothers were home at the time, he would encourage me to help him slaughter the beast. Those were the most tender of our moments together. He never referred to me by name, except in class where he was my teacher. He always called me *Mommy*, because I was named after his mother-in-law. We had great fun skinning the beast and opening it up, and finally eating the liver roasted on the coals as a reward.

My father was also a generous man. He believed in sharing scarce resources with those less fortunate than us. We always had children from needy families in the district living with us, so that they could attend school. Such decisions he would make on the spur of the moment whenever he identified a needy child, much to my mother's frustration. We were not wealthy, but by local standards we were well off. We slept on floor-beds until the 1960s when we began to share beds in the children's rooms. To make our floor-beds we spread either straw mats or goatskins on the mud floor with a blanket placed on top. My mother made soft feather pillows (from carefully selected and preserved chicken feathers) for each of us, and we had enough warm blankets to cover ourselves even during the cold winter months.

My mother was a strict disciplinarian. She was intolerant of any naughtiness on our part, and also ruthless in punishing any misdeed. I received many beatings for breaking things, which made me even more nervous and thus led to further losses. I remember an occasion in 1959 when she had gone to a Mothers' Union church conference in Meadowlands Township in Soweto, and we had been left in the care of my father. It was dusk, and I was wiping the glass cover of our paraffin lamp, from which we derived reflected prestige, when it fell from my hands. What a disaster! I put the pieces together and knelt down and prayed: 'God, nothing is impossible for you. Please put together what has been broken and save me from the inevitable.' Disappointment awaited me when I opened my eyes. I hid the lamp away and lit a candle. My father, who was at the time lying on his bed and reading, did not comment on the candle when he came out to have his supper, but after two days, he called me. I burst out crying, expecting the worst. He embraced me, wiped my tears and sent me off to the shop to buy another one. I could not believe his response. I still cherish that touch of softness.

We were nonetheless deeply appreciative of my mother's domestic competence. We enjoyed treats which many children in the village had no idea about: freshly baked bread, dumplings, soup on cold days, pancakes, canned fruit, jam, cakes and puddings. Our greatest regret was that we could never have enough of the treats, particularly pancakes, which were my father's favourite and of which he was given the lion's share. I learnt to cook and bake quite early in life, because I enjoyed being near my mother and watching what she was doing. I promised myself that when I was old enough I would make myself a plateful of pancakes and eat them to my heart's content – a promise I kept years later, in 1974, when I was expecting my first child.

My father kept aloof from many family concerns. He kept to his room in his favourite position – horizontal – with a book in his hand. We longed to get to know him better, but were not rewarded much. We would delight in taking tea in for him, and in doing whatever would give an opportunity for direct contact. When occasionally he came into the kitchen, where most of the family spent their time, it would be like Christmas! We would giggle at each one of his few jokes and hang on to whatever he had to say. But these were brief and rare occasions.

When my father became angry or grumpy, we would be quite scared. He would fly into a rage over a mistake one of us had made some days before, which we would have even forgotten about by then. Perhaps one of my brothers had been careless with tools or livestock, or had not performed his domestic chores properly. On other occasions it would be complaints about the way my mother and we girls ran the household, which did not meet his high standards. Those were painful days, and unless *Koko* Tsheola intervened timeously, we would end up being beaten. I can only surmise that he bore grudges, and that he was inhibited by his shyness from expressing his feelings. Alcohol released him from these inhibitions.

His role as both father and teacher to his children was also not uncomplicated. So too his relationship with his wife, who had to negotiate the tensions of collegiality at work and a marriage partnership. He was always punctual and could not tolerate anything less from others. This was infuriating for my mother, who had to attend to his domestic needs and still be on time at school. He was a wonderful teacher who enthused his pupils with the joy of learning. Although he was supposed to teach us through the medium of North Sotho, as was required by Bantu Education at the time, he quietly insisted on teaching us in English during the course of the year, and would only drill us in North Sotho for examination purposes. I still remember some of the ridiculous words such as *okosijeni* (oxygen) which we had to learn in science. He also departed from the official syllabus, which had a heavy ideological content, though he would caution us to produce what was required for the external examination at the end of Standard 6.

I was a naughty pupil, because I got easily bored in class. I was rarely challenged intellectually. My father tried to keep me disciplined by seating me next to boys, in the vain hope that I would be shy and quieten down. I soon found a way of amusing myself, in most cases at the expense of the boy I was sitting next to. One such boy used to be so frightened when asked questions in class that he would wet himself as soon as his name was called out. I would draw the attention of the whole class to this poor boy's pants by turning around to gaze at the wet patch.

I had problems reconciling my father's role as my teacher and parent. He would appear to treat me so indifferently in class that I was saddened. Although I was his best student, few if any words of praise would come my way. He expected me to do well, and would show disappointment if I got anything wrong. He also seemed to be much stricter on me than on other children. Any mistake would unleash severe punishment. I had to be perfect.

My father had a sizeable library to feed his love for books. I had access to the full range of Shakespeare's plays, the *Encyclopaedia Britannica* and many English novels and books of general interest to my father's generation, which I read through as soon as I could. I remember many conversations between adults in my presence, to which I was not supposed to be privy, but which I perfectly understood in my own way.

My childhood social world was complex in its own way. Our neighbours across the street were the family of a widowed woman who worked as a domestic in Louis Trichardt, fifty kilometres away, leaving her children in the care of her kindly mother-in-law, *Koko* Sanie Seko. The second oldest girl, Rebecca, was a very aggressive person, a street fighter known for her toughness. On the few occasions we played with them, we ended up with a disagreement or even a fight. We thus tended to play on our own and avoid the street.

These neighbours resented our position of relative comfort. My mother's generosity in sharing left-over food with those less fortunate did not placate them. Their mother also became sulky and moody towards my mother on the few occasions she was home over weekends or on leave. It became so bad that we stopped having anything to do with them. The last straw was when one of my mother's large black pigs, fattened for the next winter slaughter, was found dead. A post-mortem revealed that someone had pierced it with a piece of wire, which was left *in situ* – a more agonising death the poor pig could not have experienced. The carcass, which had signs of sepsis, was not fit for human consumption and was used to make soap for the household. Rumours abounded about who could have been responsible, but we never got to know the truth.

There were other neighbours who were part of my childhood world. *Koko* Mma-Abinere Tau (Mother of Abner) was a large woman whose property adjoined the back of ours. She liked sitting on the veranda of her house and surveying all passers-by. She got the latest news from casual conversations with those who cared to stop for a chat across the fence. Her house was dark, poorly ventilated and untidy. She also liked eating meat that was off, which she claimed was tastier than fresh meat. Her house had an unpleasant odour. She came in handy whenever my mother needed to dispose of unwanted meat which had gone off. She was a stingy woman, known as the Jew, because people in this village perceived Jews as particularly stingy people. A story was often told of her putting a steaming hot teapot between her legs to conceal it from passers-by who she feared would have been tempted to drop by for a cup of tea – a not unfounded fear, given the practice of the time. She demanded being greeted by children passing by and would clear her throat audibly to attract attention; if that failed, she would resort to scolding those she labelled as disrespectful.

Showing respect for adults was an important attribute sought and nurtured in children. I remember being reduced to tears by a cruel comment from a woman, known as Setlotlo, who lived in our street. I had greeted her and her guests in the customary way, *Realotsha!* (Greetings!), but she was engaged in a conversation with other adults on her veranda and did not hear me. Those who heard me responded in a loving way, but she turned and scolded me fiercely for being disrespectful and not greeting. I was rescued from this verbal abuse by the others, but even then she did not apologise. Children's feelings were frequently hurt in this manner.

*Koko* Mma-Abinere had redeeming features too. She had a beautiful soprano voice, which she put to good use as a church choir member and Sunday school teacher. She also had a good sense of humour and an ability to laugh at herself. Her husband had deserted her and was rumoured to be having an affair with Setlotlo, who had at one stage burned her severely by pouring boiling water with caustic soda over her back. She spent many months at Elim Hospital. She often joked about the fact that her beauty transcended the scars occasioned by that traumatic experience.

Kranspoort had a friendly village atmosphere where personal safety was not at risk. We grew up with a deep sense of physical security. There were tight social networks in this closely knit community. The residents felt bound together by the common identity of being believers (Christians) in contrast to 'the heathens' (non-believers), also referred to as *ba gaLosta* (lost ones), who lived on surrounding farms and who were regarded as inferior. The term 'heathen' was used quite unconsciously in conversations about 'the other', and was also a rebuke for those residents failing to behave 'properly'. It was partly this 'insider' versus 'outsider' approach which led to the break-up of the mission station in 1956 over a dispute to bury an 'outsider', who was mother of one of the residents, as I shall detail later.

Social networks revolved around kith and kin. Many households had extended family members living in different parts of the village and, because of its small size, most kept in almost daily contact with one another. There were also close friendships which involved parents and children from particular households. These friendships evolved into close reciprocal relationships which approximated kinships. It was the custom in this village to address others respectfully using the same terms normally reserved for relatives, such as 'uncle', 'aunt', 'sister', 'brother', 'granny' and so on. It was thus sometimes difficult to distinguish between kinships and friendships, unless one knew the family histories of those involved.

Support flowed along the contours of social networks. Those well connected were protected from the harsh realities of poverty and the disruptive effects of migrant labour, which were a common experience of most households. Households shared and borrowed necessities from one another as part of life. Food was the most common item of such exchanges, though the natural fertility of the area and the bountiful fruit and vegetables also ensured that few people ever went hungry.

Emotional and other forms of social support were also an important aspect of village life. Many women had to raise their children alone because their men were migrant workers. Most of the affected households functioned reasonably well, aided by regular remittances and annual visits from the migrants. That the experience of absent husbands was common reduced the pain of separation. Similarly affected women rallied together for mutual support.

There were also a few women migrants, such as our neighbour whom I have referred to, who were single parents or widows and had to leave their children in the care of others to seek employment to support their households. Some children ended up living at home without any adult present, but relying on neighbours for adult support in times of need.

I developed some understanding of the remittance patterns of several households because my father handled the village mail as one of his responsibilities as school principal. The mail arrived twice a week on the railway bus, which passed through Kranspoort on its way to and from Alldays, farther west along the foot of the Soutpansberg. The mailbag had to be fetched at about 10.30 a.m. by one of the schoolboys and brought to the school for sorting. The post was then distributed at the end of the school assembly when names of recipients of letters were called out, and their children or neighbours' children collected and delivered them. Registered letters were treated differently. Once notified, children were asked to alert their parents or neighbours, who had to come personally and sign for their registered items. The same applied to parcels. It was clearly a system based on trust, but sensibly tempered with safeguards.

We often had people come to our home after school to collect their registered mail which my father kept for them. Some came to enquire about possible parcels even if they had not received notification. These were the desperate women whose men were not regular remitters. My mother often gave them food on the quiet as they left our house.

Households who lived on the margins of supportive networks experienced abject poverty. These households tended to be on the outskirts of the village, and were in most cases relatively new arrivals. Their properties were also not as well endowed with fruit trees and were less fertile, providing little opportunity for growing vegetables. The irrigation water which flowed along the street furrows reached them last, and often when it was too late and too dark to water properly.

Pain and joy were shared by residents. People supported one another in times of illness or loss through death. Funerals were communal responsibilities: at these times every member of the community played a supportive role. News of death was spread by word of mouth and people rallied to the bereaved household. A few old women would immediately move into the household to provide support, and remain there until some days after the funeral. Younger women helped with the practicalities of keeping the household clean, fed and comfortable.

Women were also responsible for preparing a meal for all those attending the funeral. A beast, commonly an ox for a grown-up man or a cow for a woman, was often slaughtered the night before the funeral. It was in some cases an expensive affair, but fellow villagers brought food and other goods as well as monetary contributions to help the affected family.

Children were not allowed to go to funerals, except those of close relatives, but we often watched processions as they passed by, and clandestinely listened to the conversations of adults around these issues. Death remained a mystery to us. Our curiosity was not seen as legitimate by adults, so we could not ask direct questions. There was an uneasy silence around death.

My closest encounter with death in my childhood was in 1955 when my mother gave birth to a baby boy on a Saturday afternoon (although I remember the day vividly, I don't remember the date). It was a home birth assisted by the local midwife, Sister Nteta. We were shown the child after it was bathed, and were excited. Birth was another mystery – an area of silence which children had no right to explore. My paternal grandmother had come a few weeks before the birth to help support my mother during this period. Early on the Sunday morning my grandmother called my sister, elder brother and me, and told us that the baby was no more. The child had died during the course of its first night. I did not understand how this was possible, but from my sister's reaction, I understood that its death was a reality. Her tears were infectious. We were later asked to go to the Sebatis, my mother's relatives, for the day.

I still remember seeing my father outside the kitchen window, just before we left, digging what must have been the baby's grave, in an enclosure (*lapa*) on the side of the house. He was assisted by one or two other men. We came home that afternoon to find a freshly smeared mud patch which my great-grandmother, *Koko* Tsheola, looked after and to which she repeatedly applied a mixture of cow dung and soil for the next few months until it faded into the rest of the *lapa*. It was customary for newborn babies and stillborns to be buried within the homestead – they were not regarded as fully developed, independent persons to be interred in the public grave-yard. We were not given the opportunity to share this loss with my mother, whom we hardly saw for the next few days, as she was confined to bed. This silence was very confusing to me as a child.

Sharing festivities was also part of life in Kranspoort. The residents knew how to celebrate in style. Weddings were elaborate, as were Christmas and New Year celebrations, which were particularly valued as times for family reunions and sharing of treats brought home by the *makarapa* (returning migrants). Almost all children were bought new clothes, and, for the fortunate few, new shoes were included. Homes were decorated with fresh colourful mud and cow-dung applications, as well as decorative paper ribbons and balloons for those who could afford such luxuries. Most people strung strips of colourful left-over material, and hung them on doorways. There were no Christmas trees, nor did anyone expect Father Christmas to come with presents or a stocking full of goodies down non-existent chimneys. People shared food and drink and the joy of life in song and dance.

On Christmas day children walked in groups from house to house asking for 'Christmas', rather like the 'trick-or-treat' which American children indulge in on Halloween. Towards late afternoon, groups of children from different street choirs assembled in strategic places for friendly singing competitions. Good dancers displayed their talents. My most embarrassing moments came when I was pressured by my friends to join in the dancing. I was a typical wall-flower. I was shy and tended to hide behind others, or bolted when I sensed that the net was closing in. Nonetheless I enjoyed the carnival atmosphere with all the streets brightened with colour, laughter and song.

I was never really a sociable child outside the family setting. I preferred my mother's company to that of children my age. So I took on myself the role of a human pram and made myself useful by carrying my brothers on my back, thus relieving my over-worked mother from the task. I also went around visiting with her on Sunday afternoons – the only time off she enjoyed. My presence enabled her to socialise with her friends in the secure knowledge that my baby brothers were in good hands.

In addition to Christmas and New Year, weddings were also wonderful occasions, and preparations for them were elaborate. Food and song were central to successful wedding feasts. There was often fierce competition between the bride's and groom's entourages in capturing the attention of the crowds through song and dance. White weddings were the norm. Wedding dresses were of varying degrees of sophistication depending on the means of the households involved. No expense was spared by parents on such occasions. It was an honour for young girls to be chosen as bridesmaids.

The wedding started with a procession to the church, for the marriage to be solemnised by the Dominee. An even more vigorous parade with singing and dancing took place back to the bride's home, where there would be more singing before the main meal was served to all the guests. After the meal the couple changed into another set of clothes, normally smart formal suits, and paraded along the street before retracing their steps back home. After an interval of an hour or two of continuous singing, the couple were seated in full view of the public in the household's *lapa* where they were given advice about how to make their marriage a success, *go laiwa*. The parents of the bride or bridegroom, whichever was the case, started off the advice session, each pep talk being accompanied by a gift for the couple. After all the relatives had their turn, the general public joined in for their penny's worth. These sessions often lasted into the late evening, with songs interspersed between the speeches.

The general tone of the advice was that marriage was difficult and that tolerance was the key to success. The woman was the focus for most of the advice. On her shoulders rested enormous responsibilities to create a new home, and to care for her husband and his family – indeed, to immerse herself in his family and to lose her maiden identity. Her child-bearing responsibilities were also stressed: heaven forbid that a woman should shun this duty or be unable to discharge it. It was not surprising that most brides spent the entire session sobbing uncontrollably. But it was also expected that the bride weep to show her sadness at having to leave the natal home, or else she was seen as being too eager for marriage. Such eagerness was regarded as a bad omen for the future of the couple. The groom's family celebrated the marriage in a manner they saw fit, but in general the same ceremony was repeated.

My introduction to politics was a silent one. I remember my parents discussing politics in hushed tones, particularly after my aunt Ramadimetsa's husband had been detained under the 90-days detention clause which the Nationalist government introduced to deal with rebellion against their authoritarian rule. At this time the anti-pass campaign organised by the Pan Africanist Congress (PAC), and later strengthened by the involvement of the African National Congress (ANC), was gaining momentum on the Witwatersrand and farther afield. My uncle Solly Mogomotsi was a member of the ANC and had been a member of the South African Communist Party (SACP) before it was banned in 1950. The SACP affiliation could be traced back to his active union membership in the boiler-making industry. My aunt spent many anxious weeks searching for her husband while he was detained, with no assistance from the authorities.

My own elder sister, Mashadi, was expelled from high school in her final matriculation year because she had participated in a demonstration against the celebrations of South Africa's becoming a Republic in 1961. All schoolchildren were handed miniature South African flags, which we carried high as we paraded around the school under the watchful eyes of our teachers. I remember the day vividly, though we did not know what the occasion was about. I wonder how much of the symbolic weight of that day impinged on the teachers, and how much, if any, discussion took place about the significance of the day's events.

My sister and her classmates refused to celebrate what they understood to be a worsening situation of oppression for black South Africans. They were summarily expelled, and put on homebound trains with the help of police. It was a bitter disappointment for my father, who was a strong believer in education as an essential part of a child's development and an escape route out of poverty. He was, however, wise enough not to make my sister feel too guilty about her stance. He took it in his stride and expected everybody else to do so. It was not a matter for discussion with us children. We understood that we were not to ask any questions about it.

My sister's expulsion was not an uncomplicated event for my father as principal of Stephanus Hofmeyer School, which was also part of Afrikaner hegemony. My father was expected to be an active member of the local Dutch Reformed Church: conducting Sunday school, being a church warden, the church choirmaster, as well as interpreter for the local Dominee. The Reverend Lukas van der Merwe was certainly not an easy person to work with. He was a bully, a racist, a chauvinist of the worst kind. It is difficult to remember a redeeming feature in him. His wife was a gentle woman who endured many abuses, some of them public, from her ill-tempered husband. She was a kindly woman who was a source of great comfort and assistance to many local women, especially in matters of health. She saved many lives in a place far from medical facilities and with poor means of transport. According to my mother, I owe my own life to her. I contracted severe whooping-cough at the age of three months. It was the advice given by Mrs Van der Merwe, together with the remedies she bought from Louis Trichardt to dampen the cough, which my mother is convinced saved my life.

As pupils from the local school, one of our responsibilities was to keep the Dominee's house and yard clean. This entailed sweeping the open spaces between the fruit trees around his house with makeshift brooms fashioned from local bushes. We were not allowed to touch any of the delicious-looking fruit on the trees. It took extraordinary discipline for children our age to do so, but the alternative was too ghastly to contemplate. The Dominee was a merciless man.

He ruled his congregation at the Kranspoort Mission Station like a farmer presiding over his property. He took over the communal mission fruit farm, employed his parishioners at starvation wages and denigrated them in the most racist way. He had a peculiar sense of morality which he applied to blacks under his charge. They were not to drink alcohol of any kind, on pain of expulsion from the mission, or suspension from the church sacraments for three months. This prohibition was a puritanical version of the liquor laws of the time, which prohibited Africans from buying and consuming 'European' alcohol. He also decreed that any unmarried woman who became pregnant faced immediate expulsion from the mission – being given a *trekpas* (dismissal) as the practice was referred to, no different from the sanctions racist farmers used against 'stubborn natives'. He was himself not a teetotaller, nor did we know enough about his morality to be convinced that he was the puritan he insisted others should be.

A particularly painful memory I have is of a classmate of mine who fell pregnant during her first year at boarding school at the age of about fourteen. She had one of those 'one-night affairs' with an older boy from the village whose father was a trusted assistant to the Dominee as the chief *koster* (church bell-ringer and usher). She came from one of the poorest families, her mother having been abandoned by her father, who married another woman and left her without any means of support except charity from locals. The girl was cast out in her pathetic pregnant state. After giving birth to a sickly child, she was not allowed to come home to whatever emotional support her mother could have provided. The death of her miserable child almost a year later released her from her agony. She came back to the village and was assisted by her elder sister to return to high school, and later qualified as a primary school teacher.

My father negotiated a fine line between obedience to and defiance of this racist tyrant. He understood that he was in the belly of the beast, but was not prepared to sacrifice his human dignity in the process of surviving. He enjoyed his beer and other alcoholic beverages with a 'Coloured' friend of his, Mr Philip Bekker, who lived in a neighbouring 'Coloured' village. The Dominee knew all about this aspect of my father's life, but never raised it. He probably sensed the limits which my father had set in their relations.

I remember my mother proudly relating to her friends how much the Dominee respected my father, in spite of his racism. She said that whenever my father accompanied the Dominee on district parish visits, they would be invited by his Afrikaner friends for lunch. They would set a *separate* table for my father in the same dining-room! That was an honour in the 1960s in rural racist South Africa.

The authoritarianism and high-handedness of this man eventually led to a mass expulsion of two-thirds of the mission villagers between 1955 and 1956. The events were the product of local and national grievances coinciding and igniting into open rebellion against racist tyranny. It was a significant development involving people who had hitherto been compliant and docile. Most of the men in the village were migrant workers, a significant proportion of whom were working as labourers on the Witwatersrand. The Defiance Campaign of the 1950s, the Kliptown Congress of the People of 1955, and the anti-pass campaign triggered by the extension of the pass laws to women, kindled a rebellious spirit in many of these migrants, who in turn influenced their relatives in Kranspoort. It required only a small spark to set the mission village alight. This spark was provided by the Dominee when he refused to allow an old woman, who was mother of a resident of the village, to be buried in the mission graveyard, because she was a 'heathen' (someone who had not converted to Christianity). This old woman used to live on a farm in the mountains above the mission village and had been brought to her daughter's home for nursing in the twilight of her life.

The battle for the right to have her buried was a fierce and sad one. I have only a vague recollection of it, because I was then only seven years old. I must rely on my mother's recollection of the events. The village was divided between those who supported the Dominee's ruling, referred to as *boDaza*, and those defying it, the *boSofasonke* (We will die together). It is noteworthy that in the 1950s there was a strong following of the Sofasonke party in the poorest parts of Soweto, and some of the migrant workers may have brought the name back with them for this local struggle. The old woman was defiantly buried in the mission graveyard with the church bells rung by the rebels, who physically took control of the church grounds. Police were called in to protect the Dominee. He was beside himself with anger after being humiliated by the public defiance, which included some militant women poking their fingers at his face and calling him 'Lukas' (his first name) instead of the usual respectful *Moruti* (Preacher).

The conflict raged on for months after that episode. The rebellious residents were arrested under various excuses by security policemen and beaten. But they would not give in. A massive removal was then executed with the support of the police. People known to be part of the Sofasonke were given short notice to pack and go. There was no compensation for the property they lost. Many also lost household effects and personal clothing in the rush to leave before the deadline. They left their houses standing, some with furniture, which was later stolen or destroyed by the elements. Only about a third of the village residents remained. These were largely families of civil servants or other people who kept out of the conflict for fear of repercussions. There were bitter feuds between the two groups, and physical and other forms of violence were traded between them regularly.

My father in his usual quiet way successfully walked the tightrope between remaining a loyal civil servant and not antagonising those who were up in arms against the Dominee. It was not easy. He took advantage of my mother's seventh pregnancy to send the vulnerable members of his family away at the beginning of 1956 to his natal home in Uitkyk. My mother and my younger brother, Phoshiwa, went to live at my mother's family home in Krantzplaas, where she could receive prenatal care from a nearby clinic. There were no clinics in Uitkyk at the time.

Sethiba, my younger brother, and I were left in the care of my paternal grandparents. My elder sister, Mashadi, was placed in the care of my mother's cousin's family, the Mahapas; while my elder brother, Mathabatha, remained at Kranspoort with my father. It was the first family separation, and it was not easy for us at all. The only reason I can now think of why all the children did not go with my mother was that my paternal grandparents would not have approved of 'their grandchildren' being looked after at my mother's natal home. We were naturally not consulted in the matter. The separation from both parents for the sake of keeping the peace between the Rampheles and the Mahlaelas was traumatic for us. We resented it and cried a lot over it.

Sethiba was then in Sub A, and attended a nearby local school which catered for only Sub A and B. I had to go to G. H. Frantz Secondary School, some three kilometres from my grandparents' home. Fortunately an older cousin of mine, Mbatha, attended high school there and could give me a lift on his bicycle. But I had to walk home from school on those occasions when he had afternoon activities. I found that hard, not only because of the long distance for my eight-year-old frame, but particularly because hunger was a constant companion. There was no lunch packed for me nor was I given pocket money to buy snacks from the village shop. I was regularly rescued by my mother's cousin, who was teaching at the same school and living near by. She would give me food during the school break.

Breakfast in my grandparents' household was mainly tea and dry stale bread bought from the local store. There was often no food

waiting for us when we got home after school. We would then have
to make do with whatever left-overs were available from the previous day's supper. Sethiba was even more miserable. He was expected to herd my grandfather's sheep and goats after school, often
without any food in his stomach. He also bore the full brunt of my
grandfather's authoritarianism and harsh approach to child-rearing.
His six-year-old body was subjected to hunger and hard work for
most of the nine months of our stay there. I was protected by the relative gentleness with which both my grandparents treated me. My
tears, which flowed very readily each time I was hurt or miserable,
were a useful lever for obtaining greater and gentler care. In contrast,
Sethiba was under pressure to respond to my father's edict that
*moshimane ke draad, ga a lle ge a e kwa bohloko* (a boy is like a piece of
wire and should not cry).

I saw my parents only once during the entire nine-month period.
Given the distances involved, my father could only afford to come
and see us during the June school holidays, and later took us to visit
my mother. We had to be torn away from her at the end of the visit.
Release came one Sunday morning in September whilst we were
waiting with my grandmother to depart on a church trip to another
parish twenty kilometres away. Someone came to tell my grandmother that my mother had just arrived with her new baby. I jumped
for joy and ran all the way home. Sethiba could hardly recognise his
mother. As she got off the donkey cart that brought her, he thought
to himself: That woman with the baby looks like my mother. But he
was not sure until my mother called out to him and hugged him. The
joy of reunion was indescribable for the two of us. We giggled and
danced to the music within our deprived hearts. Our family was
finally reunited.

The innocence of my childhood was brought to an abrupt end one
Wednesday evening late in 1960 just before I went to the weekly
evening prayer service. I was twelve years old. I ran to the toilet to
relieve myself, only to be confronted by a bloody panty. I had no idea
what was happening to me. I quickly changed and ran to church. My
special prayer was for the Lord to make the blood go back to where
it came from. It was one of my many unsuccessful pleas for God to
intervene directly in my life. The blood continued to flow for four or
five days.

Fortunately, Miriam Mokgadi Kutumela, one of the many young

people who used to stay with us, noticed my bewilderment and offered advice and practical suggestions about appropriate hygienic measures. She also explained what it meant in terms of the development of my sexuality, pregnancy and matters relating to childbirth. She had got to know all these 'facts of life' from the initiation she underwent at puberty in her village. Ironically, the embracing of 'Christian ways' deprived us of such an exposure, whilst not creating other mechanisms to provide information about human development for young people. One had the worst of all worlds in this regard.

It never occurred to me to tell my mother even though I was close to her in many other ways. The silence which existed between children and adults around sexuality was absolute. I sensed that this was not a matter to raise with her. It took my mother almost a year before she found out that I had reached puberty. Even then she did not talk to me directly about it. She asked her best friend, Mrs Moshakga, to speak to me. Mrs Moshakga was in turn very indirect in her explanation of what puberty was about and said very little which satisfied my curiosity. She simply said, 'This monthly flow of blood signals that you are now a woman. You should not sleep with boys, because you will then have a baby.' But how could I be a woman at the age of twelve? What did sleeping with boys mean? And what was the connection between that and babies? I had to rely on Miriam to respond in detail to my questions, and to interpret some of the innuendoes. My father's encyclopaedias also came in handy: I could read and follow the biological explanations with the aid of the diagrams.

It is interesting how little the discourse of sexuality between parents and their children has changed over the years, particularly amongst working-class folk in South Africa. In my work with adolescents in the Western Cape townships I still come across the same silences, and the unwillingness of parents to be open to their children about sexuality and their growing bodies. Many young people still have to rely on friends for information about this vital area of life. It is a measure of how deeply entrenched are the mystique of the human body and the ambivalences we seem to have about sexuality as part of the human condition. Some researchers have suggested that the incest taboo may have something to do with this silence. Talking about sex may itself be regarded as a sexual activity.

# 2

# An Unlikely
# Career Choice

I do not remember playing the fantasy games of 'when I grow up I will be this, that or the other'. Nor do I remember being asked by adults in their usual condescending way what I thought I would become later in life. It may well be that my distance from my peers had a lot to do with my unconcern about a career. But it may also have had to do with the fact that most people in our village assumed that one automatically became a teacher or nurse if one did well at school, or a policeman or labourer if one did not. Given my academic abilities and the fact that my parents could afford to educate me, my choice of career didn't invite questions from curious adults. I was destined to become a teacher.

Charles Dickens could well have set his bleaker social novels in South Africa and, specifically, in one of the most important secondary educational institutions in the northern Transvaal. Bethesda was a teacher training college which was started by Dutch Reformed Church missionaries in the 1930s. It was situated about fifty kilometres west of Pietersburg in a mission station known as Rita, which nestles under a beautiful, sharply defined *koppie* (hillock) whose name it shares. It had an enrolment of about three hundred students, most of whom were in the secondary school section. There were about three boys to each girl, and the boys' and girls' residences lay on either side of the school's teaching and administrative blocks.

Like many of my contemporaries, I arrived with great expectations in January 1962 at what I anticipated would be a place of higher learning. It was a major step in our lives. Childhood was finally behind us (even though I was only fourteen years old). We were on the road to preparing ourselves for the world of work. But on arrival I was taken aback at the state of the institution.

I did not have the chance to articulate my views of Bethesda, until a golden opportunity presented itself early in 1964. After all, teachers did not expect one to have views on these matters. I pounced on the first available chance, which came about when our English teacher asked us to write a letter to a friend, telling her about our school and encouraging her to apply for admission. I took off.

Bethesda Normal School
P.O. Kalkbank
Pietersburg
3/4/1964

Dear Friend,

I heard from a mutual friend that you intend to come to this school for your secondary level education. I feel it is only fair that I should give you a sense of what you would be letting yourself in for.

It has been a remarkable last two and a quarter years for me. My romantic vision of boarding school has been dented severely by my experiences here. I shall only focus on a few areas to illustrate my point. First, the dormitories we are housed in are in an appalling state of disrepair. There are bedbugs everywhere, particularly in the hot summer months. The authorities order fumigations only after repeated complaints, and even then the problem gets merely contained for a few months, only to resurface with greater vengeance.

The second major problem area, probably the most important one for young growing bodies such as ours, is the quality of the food. I cannot understand how any responsible adult can expect young people to live on a diet which consists of mainly carbohydrates, occasional meat (often rotten), and little fresh fruit and vegetables. The unchanging and unappetising weekly menu is as follows:

Breakfast – Soft porridge, cooked the night before, often served cold, without any milk, except on Sunday mornings when a quarter loaf of bread with a spoon of jam is served in addition.

Lunch – Hard porridge served with either boiled potato or over-cooked cabbage, and twice a week with meat (often off in the hot summer months due to lack of refrigerating facilities).

Supper – Hard porridge served with a cup of cocoa with no milk added to it. A quarter loaf of dry bread is served only on Saturday evenings.

It is hardly surprising that the majority of the students, particularly the girls, end up with severe pellagra (a vitamin B complex deficiency). What is even more infuriating, though, is the attitude of the matron. She blames the skin manifestation of the vitamin deficiency disease on the girls themselves. She emphatically denies that it has anything to do with the quality of the food, but claims that it results from the use of skin-lightening creams. Her assertions fly in the face of the diagnosis of the visiting general practitioner,

Dr Makunyane, whose opinions she completely ignores.

. The quality of education is itself not bad. Most of the teachers are keenly interested in the success of their students. I particularly like my arithmetic and biology teachers, who encourage me to excel. The latter two subjects are my favourites.

Social relations between the students and most of the teachers are a problem area. All our teachers, except those teaching North Sotho, are white people, all Afrikaans speaking except our Standard 6 and 7 English teacher. The latter is a kindly old man in his late sixties, Mr Erckels, who lives on his farm, less than ten kilometres from the school. He refers to Serolong* as his mother tongue, because he grew up in the western Transvaal. We are often taken aback when he says with perfect intonation: *Ka se haheso re re ke lengoele* (In my language we say it is a knee). Mr Erckels is an exceptionally caring teacher.

The majority of the teachers maintain a 'them and us' attitude. This is manifested in a variety of ways: no handshakes, separate entrances even in the local church which we are compelled to attend every Sunday, racist comments particularly from the spouses of the teachers. There is an invisible wall between students and teachers which is very disturbing, particularly from those teachers whom I really like, and whom I would like to learn to know a bit more.

You have to make your own decision in the end, but I would discourage you from coming to this school. Explore other possibilities. I am planning to go to Setotolwane High School next year for my matriculation years, and am already impatient with the slow passage of time. I will certainly not miss this place.

I wish you all the best.

Yours sincerely,
Aletta[†] Ramphele

Mr Le Roux, our Standard 8 English teacher, was appalled. How could I misuse a class assignment to complain about school conditions? An interesting question which begs the issue. Would he have complained if I had used the assignment to praise the school? He gave me 50 per cent for it, a marked departure from my average in other assignments and tests of 80 per cent and above. The message was clear. But I was not perturbed in the least, because I had given a true account of life at the school as I experienced it. I was also confident that my exceptionally good academic standing would protect

*Serolong is a dialect of Setswana, spoken in the northwestern part of the country.

[†]I used Aletta as my first name until my third year at Medical School when the Black Consciousness Movement challenged us to revert to our indigenous names.

me against further repercussions. It was good to know that the school could not afford to expel me.

The social distance between students and teachers was exacerbated by the system of *huiswerk* (Afrikaans for 'housework'), which was a form of forced labour intended to remind students that education was not an escape route from the inferior position blacks were 'destined' to occupy. Each student was allocated to a staff member one afternoon a week for about two hours. Most were asked to do the most menial of domestic chores, such as sweeping the ground around the house, washing pots, scrubbing floors and ironing – a peculiar way to promote good relations between staff and students.

Some of the staff were more pleasant to work for than others. So too they differed in generosity. While several gave food at the end of the afternoon, others remained quite indifferent to the hunger that was a constant companion of the boarders. The principal's wife, Mrs Grütter, who was also our music teacher, was the most unpleasant of all. She often reminded those students who seemed to her unenthusiastic in their tasks: 'You were born to work for us.' But there was a positive side even to this racist. It is to Mrs Grütter that I owe my interest in classical music. She was a pianist who taught music with great enthusiasm.

But how is one to explain that my parents, who had trained at Bethesda in the late thirties, and had had the same experiences, let me make the decision to follow in their footsteps? My mother's recollection of their life as students at this school differed only marginally from my own experience: the dormitories infested with bedbugs, the poor-quality food, the attitudes of 'them and us'. The whole ambience of the place did not seem to have undergone much change over the intervening decades. But why then did she not discourage me from making this choice?

Part of the explanation lies in the limited choices available to Africans: there were few boarding schools of quality at the time. There was also a strong conservative ethos which constrained my parents from exploring even the few alternatives open to us. I could have gone to Setotolwane High School from the very beginning of secondary school, but that would have been trail-blazing for a little girl and my parents would have found it difficult to accept. Setotolwane was formerly known as Diocesan College, having been founded by missionaries of the Anglican Church, and its religious ethos reflected its origins. With their conservative Dutch Reformed background my parents would have found it hard to send me there. On top of that, the authoritarian Dominee Van der Merwe at Kranspoort would not have made their lives any easier for letting their daughter 'go astray' and be lost to another denomination. It was assumed that children from Dutch Reformed missions would retain their denominational allegiances and go to Bethesda Normal College or Emmarentia High School, a course both my elder sister and brother followed. So the question of a different choice of school did not even arise.

The first few weeks of the 1962 school year were traumatic for me. Initiation was still alive and well at Bethesda in the 1960s, and we were humiliated in every possible way, as part of the ritual. The intimidating atmosphere became evident from the time we got onto the steam train at Mara Station where we joined students from Messina. We were assaulted with shouts of *mesela* (tails), to indicate that we were the last to come into the institution. It was also my first train ride. I had occasionally seen the passenger train pull off from Mara Station on its way to or from Pietersburg, but had never been on it until January 1962. The novelty of the experiences unfolding around me proved overwhelming. My heart was pounding in my tiny chest all the way. What an introduction to leaving home!

The same insecurity and sense of impending doom pervaded our arrival at Bethesda. No effort was made by either the school or fellow students to put us at ease, and make us feel welcome. Any senior student could order a *mosela* to run errands or engage in demeaning acts at any time. This 'treatment' lasted for about one and a half weeks, ending on the night of a belated welcome concert given by the school in the main hall. The last lap on this gruelling initiation track was running as fast as our frightened legs could carry us to our room immediately after the concert. Here we were at last free. The week and a half were the longest in my adolescent life. I cried myself to sleep during those first nights.

Mathabatha, my elder brother, who attended the same school at the time, was my only source of support and continuity with the protective family life I had left behind. He took the risk of breaking the rules during my first week at boarding school to check on me and to reassure me – an offence punishable by expulsion. He came to stand outside our classroom window before the classes started, and caught the attention of a fellow student, who then called me to the window. The minute I saw him I burst out crying. I had never felt so far from my family before, and I was miserable. He just stood there and comforted me.

Networks of support were critical in this environment. Homegirls were the most important people, particularly in the first few months of boarding school life, before one had made friends with girls from other parts of the country. Homegirls protected one from gross abuse during initiation, even though they could not completely shield one from the humiliation of the entire process. One of my homegirls was assigned to keep watch over me and to intervene where appropriate. Sometimes serious fights broke out between seniors about the reasonableness of the 'treatment' meted out to a particular *mosela*. Those unfortunate enough to be outside this protective network were often grossly abused.

Networks of support were also vital in enabling one to survive the inadequacy of even the bare necessities of life that were supplied. The school provided an iron spring bed with a coir mattress for each student. There were dormitories ranging from four beds each for seniors, to ones with twenty beds or so. There were neither lockers nor desks. One had to bring one's own blankets, pillows and linen. Our personal effects were held in locked tin trunks kept in the locker room adjacent to each dormitory, and supervised by a prefect.

We had to rely heavily on our own resources to supplement the inadequate food supplied in the boarding school. From home at the beginning of term we brought scones, chicken, rusks, tinned food, dried meat and vegetables, biscuits, and a variety of preserved food. The resourcefulness of one's family was severely tested. Homegirl groups, varying in size from two to ten, tended to share their provisions, as well as the occasional food parcel sent from home, and we bought as well from the store at Kalkbank once a week.

My brother and I had to learn to make do with one pound ten shillings each per quarter, which our father sent us as pocket money. It was barely enough to cover basic necessities, including toiletries. Mashadi, my elder sister, who was then working as an assistant in a fish and chips shop in Soweto, played an important part in rescuing me from total despair. I used to jump for joy each time I received a parcel from her, because I knew that there would be treats: biscuits, sweets, tinned beef and fish, toiletries and, occasionally, a pair of stockings or a handkerchief. One really learned to appreciate such small tokens of love from one's family.

The custom of sharing had its drawbacks. There were wide differences among students in the quality of provisions brought from home, the regularity and amount of pocket money, and the number of parcels sent from home during term. Tensions also developed around the amount of communal food each devoured. Small eaters were at a decided disadvantage. There was also difficulty in catering for different tastes. Some people with less delicate palates ate whatever came their way, and thus paid little attention to the needs of others in preparing food.

Survival is a stronger force than the fear of offending others. After the first year of sharing with about eight homegirls, I took the plunge. I felt that having complete control over my supplies would enable me to budget better, and spread my resources over a longer period. I had also learned to bake biscuits, and my mother loaded me with provisions, which used to last me until just before the end of term. My severe weight loss during the first year also prompted more regular pocket money and food parcels from home.

I had suffered a lot during the first year from near-starvation. As I could not bring myself to eat what I considered food unfit for human consumption, I often had to survive from Monday to Friday drinking only cocoa at supper time, with sugar water during the day. My small frame took severe punishment, but my will not to be reduced to an animal kept me going. So when I decided to eat alone, homegirls were dismayed but let me go. Thereafter I occasionally shared some food with them, but it stopped being an obligation.

Bethesda Normal College was like an island of Protestant morality in the Bushveld. The location of boarding schools in remote rural areas had its benefits and drawbacks. The isolated and barren rural setting offered few cultural, intellectual and leisure opportunities. Some adults, however, felt that it was an appropriate environment for taming restless adolescents. The fewer the 'distractions' from the learning process, or so it was felt, the better the outcome. Most of these schools also obliged by laying down highly rigid rules enforced by autocratic matrons or boarding masters. Bethesda was no exception.

Most of the male students spent their weekends loitering near the school and in the village of Rita. Some of the younger ones were responsible for looking after the herd of cattle upon which the school relied for its meat supply. Fridays and Mondays were slaughter days. The beasts were usually shot by one of the teachers, and the older male students were responsible for skinning, cutting up the meat, and storing it away. The meat was kept in large bath tubs for a day or two without any refrigeration – with predictable consequences in summer.

Female students were under stricter rules. One could only go to the Kalkbank shopping centre if one had permission from the head prefect, who had to be given a list of potential shoppers by midweek for the Saturday morning outing. Numbers were strictly controlled – not more than twenty at a time were allowed. A prefect had to accompany the shoppers. The four-kilometre walk was quite hard for younger, frailer persons like me, but it was fun and a welcome change from the dull surroundings of the boarding house.

Sundays were strictly observed as days of compulsory worship. A morning service was held at the local Dutch Reformed Church conducted in Afrikaans with North Sotho interpretation for the local villagers. Racial segregation was entrenched in both the entrance points and the seating – after all, it was God's law to keep blacks and whites apart, and one had to be even stricter in His house in this regard. Men and women also sat separately, presumably to reduce the temptation of being attracted to someone of the opposite sex. We had to be protected from ourselves.

Activities organised by the Student Christian Movement (SCM) and Mokgatlo wa Ba Bacha (MBB) dominated Sunday afternoons and evenings. Varying degrees of charismatic religiosity were in evidence particularly amongst women students. These tendencies were encouraged by the school authorities, who saw religion as the cornerstone of good behaviour. I found some solace in the various religious activities, particularly the singing, which was a major part of them, and I became a full member of the MBB.

In spite of the gloomy picture I have painted, the school had its warm and enjoyable sides too. We developed close friendships amongst ourselves. I became very friendly with a group of three girls in my class: Moloko Laka (a homegirl) with a tall beautiful body, dry wit and a stutter, Mphika Molokoane (from Messina in the northern Transvaal) who was the shortest of the foursome with a perfect baby face, gentle nature and softly spoken manner, and finally Greta Mogooane (from Natalspruit, on the East Rand), to whom I was closest. Greta's attributes stood out as gentleness, neatness, and generosity of spirit. She was also physically attractive and petite. She did not keep the unwritten rule which held amongst urban students, namely, not to befriend country bumpkins like myself.

Students from rural areas also kept to themselves, and viewed any association with those from urban areas as potentially destabilising and polluting, in view of the widely held belief at the time that cities had a corrupting influence on young people. *Bana be South ba tla go lahletša* (Children from the South – a metaphor for the Witwatersrand area – will lead you astray) were the words of caution uttered by one's senior homegirls. Boundaries between town and country were evident, and reinforced in social relations at the school.

As a foursome, we operated on the margins of all conventions. We enjoyed sitting next to one another in class, sharing jokes and gossip, helping one another with school work, and occasionally sharing treats, which were few and far between. We were all very different personalities, but enjoyed each other's company, and complemented each other's strengths. We referred to one another as 'Penkop' or 'Pennie', from an Afrikaans setbook we were reading at the time; this was the story of a group of mischievous young people who were given the same nickname.

It was hard to part from my friends at the end of our Standard 8, when I moved to Setotolwane High School for my matriculation. The class farewell party we organised at the end of 1964 was a great success. Food was in abundance, a rare event indeed. We celebrated our years together, and shared the hope of new beginnings. I was not sad about leaving Bethesda; my only regret was having to leave my friends behind. We kept up a brisk flow of correspondence for the rest of our school days, but lost contact later.

Gender stereotyping in career choices was deeply entrenched in those years. All but one of my female classmates chose to proceed to teacher training. Some saw teacher training as a strategy for securing a career before attempting matriculation, whilst others saw teaching as their final career choice. There was at the time a widely held view that only bright pupils should attempt matric. 'Matriculation is not a mattress' was the popular saying, which reminded one that only hard work would ensure success. I was one of only two girls amongst a handful of boys in my class who opted for matric. The other exceptional girl was Hester Motau from Belfast in the eastern Transvaal, who was older than I and came from a family of teachers that had high expectations of their daughter.

Not only were the three years at Bethesda difficult socially, but I felt intellectually under-stimulated most of the time. Although I came top of my class in every subject, I did not have to exert myself at all. On the contrary, I was bored most of the time, and tended to make careless mistakes. My arithmetic teacher, Mr Henning, used to be frustrated by these mistakes, because he was convinced that I could easily not drop any marks at all in his subject if I put my mind to it. With hindsight, I think he should have attempted to teach me mathematics instead of the mechanical arithmetic I found so boring, but Bethesda was not concerned with teaching blacks mathematics. They took very seriously Dr Verwoerd's words which he had used in motivating the introduction of the Bantu Education Act of 1953: 'Bantu' children should not be shown green pastures where they would never be allowed to graze.

Career guidance was non-existent during our school days. This was in part a reflection of the limited career options open to blacks at the time, but also the reason for such limited options. One's horizons were not widened beyond the known. The few positive role models for us were confined to the traditional professions of teaching and nursing. There was almost a sense of inevitability about replicating the known from one generation to the next.

The decision to follow a non-teaching career was perfectly logical to me. I had never entertained the thought of becoming a teacher even though, or perhaps because, both my parents were in the profession. I just knew that I had to do something else. But it was not clear at first what that would be. I was strongly attracted to science and the world of numbers, but could see no career prospect short of becoming a high-school science teacher. I had seen enough discrimination against black teachers even at a higher level not to be attracted to the profession. I also knew from my mother's experience, as well as those of my own teachers, that women teachers had even greater barriers to overcome.

What about nursing? My sister Mashadi started training as a nurse at Baragwanath Hospital in 1964. I did not like what I heard from her accounts of the nursing profession either. The authoritarian rule of seniors over juniors, and the role of both as handmaidens of the doctors, did not appeal to me. The little I had heard about doctors suggested that medicine could offer me the greatest professional freedom and satisfaction. It was not the desire to serve which influenced my career choice, but the passion for freedom to be my own mistress in a society in which being black and woman defined the boundaries within which one could legitimately operate.

My career choice was not easily accepted by others. My father had good reason to dissuade me. He was, unbeknown to me then, suffering from a fatal illness, cancer of the oesophagus, and knew that he would not be able to support my ambitious choice. His suggestion was that I choose teaching as a quick route to earning an income in order that I might help my mother support the rest of my siblings. I argued that if I were to follow my own chosen career, I would in the long run be of greater assistance to my mother. But where was the money to come from? he asked. 'The Lord will provide,' I said, with childish confidence. He looked at me sadly, and gave me his blessing.

It was customary at Kranspoort for all the boarding-school students to present themselves to the Dominee at the beginning of the school holidays, and bid him goodbye – an odd custom, given the lack of interest he had shown in us. It was more a means of symbolising the feudal relationship which existed between him and the community, a subtle mechanism of control which enabled him to keep tabs on his 'flock'. It was not for one to question, but to obey.

In January 1965 I accordingly went to pay my respects before departing for Setotolwane High School. Dominee Van der Merwe was appalled when he heard what my plans were. He dismissed them as a pipe dream. How could I – a woman, a black person and poor at that – ever expect to become a medical doctor? He told me that his own daughter had had to give up a similar ambition and settle for being a nurse. What hope did I have? He must have read defiance in my face, so he delivered the final blow: 'Your father is dying of cancer. Who is going to finance your education anyway?' Although I was aware that my father was seriously ill, I had up to then kept hoping he would be cured. It was cruel for a seventeen-year-old to be told this painful news with such insensitivity. I was devastated.

Although I wept on my way home, I did not tell my mother about the Dominee's remarks because I didn't want to add to what I then knew was an intolerable burden of pain, anxiety and fear of her impending loss. I decided that the best way forward would be to prove the Dominee wrong. But the path to a medical career had a number of major hurdles.

My easy pass through Standard 8 with a distinction, and topping the whole cohort of black students of 1964, was soured by my lack of training in mathematics. I spent the first two weeks in Standard 9 trying anxiously to understand how one could add and subtract alphabetical letters, much more divide and multiply them. Fortunately, the principal of our new school had been my biology teacher at Bethesda, and I felt confident enough to approach him with my problem. Special extra classes were arranged for the five or so of us who were in the same boat. Our mathematics teacher was an elderly retired person from the white education system. He was a dedicated teacher who patiently took us through the basic principles of mathematics. At the end of the first term I was more confident, but it was a struggle to work out all the configurations.

In contrast, I fell in love with physical science, and understood the principles with ease. I was challenged by Mr Gouws, our science teacher, who promised me a prize of R50 if I gained a distinction in physical science in my matric examinations. That R50 turned out to be the only cash I had at the beginning of my university career in 1967. I bought myself a pretty pink dress which fitted me perfectly. It was to be my only fancy dress for many years.

The generosity of Mr Gouws and his friend Mr Bowman, the English teacher, sustained me throughout my matric years. Mr Bowman found me to be too thin, and insisted that I should take multivitamins, which he personally supplied. The political affiliations of both these teachers did not stop them from liking me as an person. Mr Bowman even adorned me with a National Party badge in one of his enthusiastic moments. My political naïveté at the time prevented me from taking in the full symbolic significance of such an adornment.

It was the lack of access to information – the embodiment of the powerlessness of most poor rural communities – that nearly cost me my medical career. I had no idea that to gain entrance to a university one had to apply near the beginning of the second term for the following academic year. By the time I applied to Natal University, the only Medical School at the time which took African students without seeking permission from government, it was too late for the 1967 academic year. Mr Gouws advised me to go to the University of the North to do my pre-medical courses, and then to proceed to Natal in 1968.

I did not have a bursary nor did I know how one applied for financial assistance. I decided to present myself as I was – penniless. At the University of the North I was advised by the admission officers to fill in forms for a state loan of R100, which was sufficient to cover most of the tuition fees, and permitted me to be registered. I had no money for stationery or set books. I borrowed from friends, and was fortunate enough to have a generous boyfriend, Dick Mmabane, who supported me financially and emotionally during those difficult years. I lived on the hope that somehow the money problem would be resolved even though I did not have the faintest clue how.

A bigger challenge to my plans lay ahead, though. In order to qualify for admission to the second year of study at Natal Medical School the following year, I had to pass all four subjects which were prerequisites: Chemistry, Physics, Botany and Zoology. I had no difficulties with the last three, but Chemistry proved to be a problem. Professor De Villiers, then head of the Department of Chemistry, made it plain to our first-year class at the beginning of term that we were going to have a hard time. He made no bones about his displeasure at the size of our class. He told us that it was not possible for 73 'Bantus' to pass Chemistry 1. There was no doubt in his mind that 'Bantus' could not master Chemistry, and he made it his mission to prove this.

He would breeze into the classroom – his cold blue eyes not making contact with anyone, but emitting sparks of hatred whenever one attracted his attention and dared to ask a question. In his own section of the work, Organic Chemistry, he made learning almost impossible. He lectured from old scraps of notes which were visibly yellowing from age. He wrote some of the difficult formulae on the board, with a duster in one hand, and as soon as he got to the end of a long formula, he would begin to erase what he had written last, relishing the anxiety he read in our faces. He prescribed no textbook, nor suggested any reference works. We relied on notes from senior students who had in turn pieced them together from their seniors' disjointed notebooks.

A greater anti-educationist one could not find. He was the talk of the University and a law unto himself. There were many students in our class who were attempting Chemistry 1 for the third or fourth time, because it was a compulsory minor for B.Sc. He held the key to the successful completion of a university education for all students who wanted to make science a career – a powerful position, which he savoured openly.

I was fortunate to scrape through with a D symbol, the only one with a D amongst the handful of people who passed the final-year examination at the first attempt in 1967. I was horrified by this first D symbol in my academic career, but was grateful for small mercies, because failure would have endangered my admission to Natal Medical School. In contrast, I got a B aggregate for the other courses. My good performance in the other three subjects during the first half of the year prompted the Dean of Science to review my matriculation results, and to offer me a full-cost bursary, which solved my financial problems for 1967.

The death of my father on 21 May 1967 introduced me to the reality of the pain of loss. The fact that he had been ill since 1963 with cancer of the oesophagus, and that he showed all the signs of suffering from an incurable illness, did not prevent me from praying for a miracle to heal him. Indeed my childish prayers were for such a miracle to occur. I could not see why an omnipotent and loving God could refuse me. It was to be my third major disappointment with God.

Because my father had been a distant parent for most of my childhood, every intimate moment we shared was very special. Our last moment of closeness took place during the Easter holidays of 1967, a few weeks before his death, when I went to visit him at Baragwanath Hospital where he lay dying. My sister was one of the nurses in his ward, which made her pain worse in some ways, but gave her more time with him during his last days. I trimmed his fingernails as we chatted. I listened to him as he talked about his disappointment with his eldest son, Mathabatha, the apple of his eye, who had not once come to see him in hospital. But he still managed to retain his dry sense of humour. He listened with interest to my impressions of the University of the North. I also introduced him to my first serious boyfriend, Dick Mmabane, who was later to become my husband.

Dick was a gentle, stockily built man with a keen sense of humour and great generosity of spirit. He could not be described as handsome in the ordinary sense of the word, but his attractive personality made up for what he lacked in physical looks. He had been my classmate at Setotolwane High School, but our relationship had only developed at the tail end of our matric year. He became a great source of support during the difficult months ahead.

The sense of loss I felt when I heard the news of my father's death from Mr Renoster, the Chief Warden of Residences at the University of the North, was immense. The train trip from Pietersburg to Mara later that night, the bus ride to Kranspoort the following day, and the sadness of having to deal with anxious questions about the meaning of death from my nine-year-old brother Thomas, who had been put by my mother in the care of a kind neighbour, all left me drained.

Dick generously sent me money by telegraph which I had to cash at the nearest post office, Mara, some fifteen kilometres away. The only form of transport available at the time was my father's Raleigh bicycle. A young man from the local primary school gave me a ride on its frame to and from Mara. The physical discomfort was nowhere near the emotional pain at the death of my father. If anything, the fact that I had to rely on this primitive means of transport underlined what it meant to lose a provider.

The journey later that week to my father's natal home in Uitkyk, where he was to be buried, was arranged by his old friend Mr Philip Bekker, who gave Thomas and me a lift in his van on Saturday morning – the day of the funeral. The sight of my grieving mother as she sat with other women relatives near my father's coffin was a confirmation of the reality of the loss and the finality of death. My father was unreachable – he lay motionless in the coffin. My mother was also unreachable as a nurturing figure to share my grief – she was nursing her own wound and could not comfort even her own children. We had to deal with our own pain in our own individual ways. Tears were an inadequate answer; one felt numb in between the streams of tears.

My mother had arrived on Friday evening in the hearse accompanied by a busload of relatives from Johannesburg. The evening service had been held in the large family courtyard, and many locals came and held an all-night vigil with singing and preaching. An ox was slaughtered in accordance with custom, to signify the death of a male head of household, as well as to provide meat for the meal after the burial the following day.

The final farewell to my father took place in the local church, where we filed past his open coffin during the funeral service. Dominee Van der Merwe came all the way from Kranspoort to conduct the funeral service – an uncharacteristically generous act much appreciated by my family. My father looked so emaciated from the long-drawn-out illness. His handsome face was but a shadow of its old self. My mother looked frail and was supported by my father's aunt, Rakgadi Maria, and all seven children stood together. Molepo, the last born, then only six years old, was bewildered. He had been travelling with my mother on the many visits to my father in hospital. Morongwa, my sister's two-year-old daughter, whom my mother was looking after at the time, was also confused by the funeral activities around her.

The material deprivation my mother suffered as a result of my father's death greatly increased the sense of loss in our family. Her black mourning clothes, a mark of ritual pollution, signified her vulnerability. Her own mother, *Koko* Mamphela, went to live with her for three months in Kranspoort after the funeral to lend support and companionship. But the gap was too wide to be bridged even by maternal love.

The vulnerability of a widow often takes on concrete forms, which act as further insults to the wounded soul. At the beginning of 1968 my mother had to move out of the comfortable brick house allocated to my father as principal teacher of the local school. She then moved into a mud house on the edge of the village; this served only to increase her sense of marginalisation. She had to cope with not only emotional and material loss, but also the loss of status which she had derived from her spouse. All these she found too much to bear.

In 1969 she decided to return to Uitkyk in search of a better job and greater support from being closer to her family. She took up a teaching post at Ngoanamago School, which offered her a principalship, and thus a slightly higher income. This was the beginning of her wanderings from post to post seeking better prospects. She ended her teaching career at Maupje in February 1979 when she finally retired at the age of sixty.

At the end of 1967, the year of my father's death, I spent the summer vacation in Johannesburg with Dick Mmabane. Here I was rudely interrupted by a telegraphic message from Natal Medical School.

YOU HAVE BEEN ADMITTED STOP PLEASE REPORT TO MRS WHITBY AT THE REGISTRATION OFFICE NOT LATER THAN 11TH JANUARY 1968 STOP

I was dismayed. I could not make head or tail of it. It was my first encounter with a telegram. My anxiety about my admission to the Medical School led me to read the STOPs as directives for me to stop entertaining the hope of being admitted to the School. I burst into tears. Fortunately, the telegram arrived at the house of my mother's elder sister, *Mamogolo* Ramadimetsa, which had been my base during that holiday. She calmed me down and reassured me. It was a rude initiation for a country bumpkin into the world of telegraphic language.

The level of material deprivation which I had to endure in the late 1960s and 1970s seems unbelievable even to me looking back. Train fare for a second-class return ticket was simply beyond the means of my family income at the time. My mother, the only bread-winner, was earning R86 per month as a teacher. I had to appeal to *Mamogolo* Ramadimetsa to lend me R55, which enabled me to buy a ticket from Johannesburg to Durban, shop for some provisions, and have a bit of pocket money over to see me to the Medical School doors. Dick Mmabane gave me some money as well, which helped. I had to take each challenge as it came. I refused to think about where the next block of money would come from.

I sat nervously in the train compartment, before being joined by Khoadi Molaba, from Alexandra Township in Johannesburg, and later by Patrick Jwili and his mother, who joined us at Balfour Station. Mrs Jwili was clearly very proud of her son, who had earned a Masters degree from an American university after having completed his B.Sc. at Fort Hare University in the Cape. She had misgivings about my intention of being in the same class as her son and Khoadi Molaba, who also had a Fort Hare B.Sc. She mercilessly set out to whittle away any remnant of self-confidence I had. How could I, a female and lacking as well the head start of a degree which the other two possessed, hope to make my way at Medical School? Another vote of no confidence.

Patrick Jwili turned out to be a very amusing character who had acquired a fair number of Americanisms and unfortunately did not in the end make a success of his medical studies. He was excluded in third year. As it turned out, Mrs Jwili was partly right. My squeamish nature made my life very difficult. One of the compulsory experiments in Physiology involved pithing a live frog (destroying the spinal cord by inserting a sharp needle into the spinal column), dissecting out its calf muscle, and running a series of tests to measure muscle function under different conditions. There were various stories at Medical School of people whose careers had been frustrated by this particular experiment. One such person, Matsapola, was reported to have stabbed the frog in frustration and left it pinned to the experimental table, walking away never to be

seen again at Medical School. The experiment acquired the nick-
name 'Matsapola' from this unfortunate incident.

Our Physiology teacher tried in vain to desensitise me by encouraging me to play around with my hand in a bucket full of frogs. I
simply could not stand the slimy creatures. In the final exam, by the
time I eventually mustered enough courage to hold on to the frog
(half an hour into experimental time), I was desperate. I squeezed all
life out of the poor devil, and was so confused that I connected gas
for use on the burner, instead of oxygen, to the muscle chamber,
which killed off any prospect of muscle reaction. I was devastated. I
sat down after wiping off tears of frustration and wrote about the
theory behind the experiment in a desperate attempt to redeem
myself. I was relieved to pass Physiology in the end – never mind the
third-class pass obtained.

Anatomy, another major second-year course, was much more
interesting and better taught under the leadership of Professor Keen.
Our first day in the dissecting room was marked by anxiety and fear
of the unknown cadavers. How was one to overcome one's sensibilities, and not only handle dead bodies but dissect them as well?
Necessity triumphs over many barriers. The initial fear of the cadav-
er gradually gave way and with less than reverence some of the students started playing with body parts. It may well be that the unspo-
ken and unacknowledged guilt about breaking an important taboo
compelled one to be outrageous so as to be able to make light of the
moment and live with oneself. We often had to be called to order by
Professor Keen, who insisted on decorum in the dissecting room.

The blind faith of my high-school years, which urged me on to
make the difficult career decision, paid off handsomely. My good
matriculation grades and above-average performance in my pre-
medical courses at the University of the North attracted the attention
of the Medical School administrators. In addition to the full-cost
grant from the Department of Bantu Education worth R450, which
was then available to every African student, I won the 1968 South
African Jewish Women's Association Scholarship worth about R200
and the Sir Ernest Oppenheimer Bursary worth R150 annually for
the rest of my Medical School years.

For the first time in my life I was in the lap of luxury. I could not
bear the thought of spending this considerable sum of money on
myself alone, as many of my contemporaries did. They bought
clothes, music systems, and sometimes even cars. I led a modest life

and sent my mother about R50 every so many months. That support was crucial for my mother to educate my younger brothers.

The rest of my medical student years became less and less interesting as extracurricular activities began to take centre stage. Mediocrity became the hallmark of my performance. I scraped through the remaining years at Medical School, gaining second-class passes as the best grades. So low was my interest in my medical career that I did not even celebrate my final-year success or attend graduation. A career so hard fought for became less and less attractive the closer I came to attaining my goal.

# 3

# Initiation into
# Activism

The company one keeps often shapes one's life in significant ways. My friendship with Vuyelwa Mashalaba, a classmate whom I met in the first few days at Medical School in January 1968, played a major role in shaping my future interests. Vuyelwa was a strikingly beautiful woman with sharp features, a smooth olive complexion, and a strong, well-proportioned body. She exuded self-confidence and spoke with a distinctive, polished English accent. She came from a family of strong, high-achieving sisters, headed by their widowed mother, who lived in Maclear, in the Eastern Cape.

Vuyelwa played tennis and loved classical music. She also had a large record collection of Miriam Makeba's music. She rekindled my love for classical music and tried to teach me tennis. Her enthusiasm failed to compensate for my lack of talent in sports, and we agreed to abandon what was clearly a road to nowhere.

Vuyelwa soon introduced me to her circle of friends, which included Steve Biko, Charles Sibisi, Chapman Palweni and Goolam Abram and, later, to Ben Mgulwa, Aubrey Mokoape, Ben Ngubane and many others who were student leaders at the time. We all attended student body meetings regularly from the middle of 1968. It was a completely new world for me. I listened quietly but with great interest to the debates on student politics of the day, which were dominated by criticism of the white liberal politics of the National Union of South African Students (NUSAS). I had to strain to follow the quick exchanges peppered as they were with acronyms, which were like Greek to me. I also marvelled at the self-confidence of student activists and the facility most of them had in using English to communicate.

Steve Biko was the main critic of white liberal politics, having been active as a NUSAS official and a member of the Students Representative Council (SRC) at Natal. The thrust of his criticism was that white liberals' opposition to racial discrimination was ineffectual and unlikely to lead to any fundamental change in South Africa because it lacked a coherent critique of racism and its socioeconomic manifestations. He contended that few white liberals were themselves committed to non-racialism and social justice to the extent of being prepared to sacrifice their privileged position in society in the quest for greater equity. He cited the ease with which former NUSAS leaders and other activists settled into privileged positions once they graduated from university, as evidence that white liberal politics was viewed as a pastime that one pursued so long as it did not interfere with the 'real' world of white privilege.

Steve also spoke out against the paternalism of white liberals who tended to dominate opposition politics in the 1960s. He felt that their paternalism in part stemmed from their deep-seated feelings of superiority towards black people. He criticised their definition of multi-racialism, which assumed the superiority of Western culture and the automatic assimilation of blacks into its fold. He was critical of the reliance blacks placed on white leadership. He charged blacks with lack of faith in themselves and of having internalised an inferiority complex: such self-inflicted psychological oppression ensured their continued physical and political oppression. He urged black students to see themselves as black first and foremost, and to commit themselves to the total liberation of all black people in South Africa.

Steve's conclusion was that the only way to effect fundamental change in South Africa would be for the oppressed people themselves to take the initiative and to work for their own liberation. He drew on the experiences and the approaches of the Black Power movement in the United States for inspiration, as well as on the Négritude writers such as Frantz Fanon and Aimé Césaire whom he quoted extensively in his speeches and later in his writings.

Ben Ngubane was Steve Biko's main opponent in the debates. Ben's view was that the forces of apartheid were powerful and evil and should be denied the pleasure of seeing disunity among the anti-apartheid ranks. He conceded the points Steve was making in his critique, but disagreed with the suggestion that black politics be consolidated away from the white liberal fold.

Ben defended NUSAS on the Medical School campus to the very last, when the student body finally voted narrowly in favour of Steve's motion of central disaffiliation from NUSAS, thus paving the

way for the black South African Students' Organisation (SASO)* to
operate on a par with NUSAS, using a campus branch affiliation system. Ben argued that NUSAS had stood firm in the face of harassment by the apartheid state and thus deserved the loyalty of all free-
dom-loving students. He was an eloquent speaker, but was no match
for the younger and more passionate Biko. Ben often lost his temper,
and became more cynical and disillusioned, finally fading out of the
political arena, only to re-emerge in the 1980s as an Inkatha official –
a not insignificant political move, crowned with a cabinet post in the
first Government of National Unity in 1994.

The tentacles of apartheid spread everywhere in South Africa in the
1960s. The section of Natal University which catered for black students was known as the University of Natal Non-European Section.
(This became known as the University of Natal Black Section (UNB)
after SASO requested that the name be officially changed in 1970.)
Professor Owen Horwood was principal of the University at the
time. He later became Minister of Finance, and was revealed to have
been party to the Information Scandal which rocked the National
Party government of John Vorster, and finally forced Vorster to
resign. Horwood shamelessly asserted that he had taken particular
care, as Minister of Finance charged with responsibility for government expenditure, not to read the documents he had signed to
authorise the expenditure of vast sums of public money to promote
apartheid. The irony of history lies in the fact that the same man
unknowingly promoted the emergence of radical black student politics in South Africa. For it was Horwood who authorised the financ-
ing of a seminar at Mariannhill which led to the formation of SASO.
Perhaps he would also have pleaded not guilty had he been confronted. How could anyone have expected him to care about black
student politics at the time? After all, he was only a vice-chancellor,
not a keeper of his students.

    Historical accidents do give rise to major tides which sweep the
unwary aside or redirect them into paths that they could not have
anticipated. The formation of SASO and the subsequent maturation
of the Black Consciousness Movement into a political force to be
reckoned with became the main focus of Steve Biko's life. One could
not help admiring this tall, handsome, eloquent and totally dedicated activist.

* SASO was founded in July 1969, with Steve Biko as its first president.

Natal Medical School did not only provide me with medical training, but it offered an environment for the transformation of my life from an innocent rural girl to a person who became alive to the vast possibilities which life has to offer. I took time to absorb the vibrancy around me. I was keenly interested in the discussions, which were a political education for me. I learned about the true history of my country, the struggle to resist conquest, and later the struggle for equal rights with those who had conquered us, the stories of the heroes of the struggle (no women were included in these narratives at the time), and the role students could and should play to take the struggle forward. I began to understand and to interpret my own personal experiences of racism and oppression in the light of the discussions going on around me. Given my rural background and lack of access to news media and political discussions till then, I had not fully grasped the relation between the personal and the political.

The University of the North had not presented me with any opportunities for exposure to student activism during 1967. The University authorities were rigidly part of the apartheid system and ensured that the University fulfilled its mission of training blacks for subservient roles in society, discouraging any public debate on political issues. The then Registrar used to boast, *My vel is my graad* (My skin is my degree), an acknowledgement that he held this senior position simply because of the colour of his skin. The SRC at the University of the North was no more than an efficient organiser of entertainment activities, posing no challenge to authority at the institution. I did not once attend a student meeting or hold a political discussion at the University of the North. Social life revolved around entertainment events such as ballroom dancing, sports, picnics and parties. A fine preparation for life as a petit bourgeois on the margins of society and power.

At the University of Natal the circle of friends centred on Steve Biko coalesced into a tight-knit community as the activism intensified. I was drawn closer into this circle and began to adopt some of the behaviour of the group. I shed the wig I used to wear whenever I felt I needed to look more 'respectable' than my short boyish hair suggested. The 'black is beautiful' slogan of the time had its desired impact on all of us. Some of us switched over to the use of our African names instead of the 'slave names' we had hitherto used. I also became more daring in my outfits, taking advantage of my figure and the fashion trends of the time, which were affordable even to me with my shoestring budget: hotpants became my speciality. Hot pants were exceedingly short pants which fitted snugly around one's body, hovering tantalisingly around the limits of modesty.

Once tested, the boundaries of conventional behaviour began to fall. I started experimenting with smoking cigarettes by offering to light for those needing a smoke. I would comment that it was unlikely I could smoke, but continued to take a puff or two until I got hooked and started buying cigarettes myself. I chose the mild blend Vuyelwa smoked. I also started drinking beer and other alcoholic beverages shared by the group. I slowly but surely embraced the student culture of the 1960s.

We lived at the Alan Taylor Residence, which was a segregated residence for black students at Natal University. An old army barrack situated next to the Mobil Oil Refinery in Austerville, not far from Durban Airport, it had been used during the Second World War to house troops and was then renovated to serve as a student residence when the Medical School was established in 1951. We commuted daily by bus to and from Medical School in Umbilo Road, some five kilometres away, to attend classes and participate in university activities. Only preliminary* and first-year students attended classes at the Alan Taylor premises. The level of pollution from the oil refinery was such that one could see traces of soot when one blew one's nose, and the bed-linen would be covered with a black layer of dust if one left a window open on a windy day. We justified our cigarette smoking by pointing to the inevitability of inhaling carcinogens (cancer-inducing substances) in the environment in which we were forced to live. A lame excuse for engaging in risk-taking behaviour, but it sounded very smart at the time.

We used to have parties on weekends at which we drank beer and sat around in the smoke-filled room of one of the members of the group, talking politics, listening to Malcom X's speeches on tape, as well as those of Martin Luther King, discussing banned books which were secretly circulated amongst friends, sharing jokes, and also singing and dancing. Our weekends were carefree and full of fun. We became welded together into a sharing and caring community. At the beginning of each year younger people who were new stu-

---

* Preliminary year (popularly called Prelim) was used as an academic support year for those students who did not have satisfactory matriculation mathematics and science grades to be admitted directly into first year.

dents joined the community – Malusi Mpumlwana, Keith Mokoape and Seolo Solombela were the most notable additions to our group.

The year 1970 marked the real turning point in the maturation of the Black Consciousness Movement. Steve Biko and Barney Pityana were participants in a seminar of student leaders of all colours and political persuasions, held at the Abe Bailey Institute (now the Centre for Conflict Resolution) at the University of Cape Town during the 1969 December holidays. In the preparation for their presentation a lot of their own thoughts were clarified, and their papers reflected a growing sense of confidence in the importance of their mission as student leaders and the role they were to play as liberators of their own people.*

Maturation brought about a growing sense of the need for self-definition. Common terms of the time such as 'non-white' and 'non-European' exemplified the extent to which both blacks and whites in South Africa had accepted European 'whiteness' as the golden standard against which all else was to be measured. Steve articulated his thoughts on this issue in the regular feature he contributed in the *SASO Newsletter* with the title 'I Write What I Like', under the pseudonym of Frank Talk, both defiant symbolic statements by the author. The term 'black' was adopted and defined as referring to 'those who are politically, socially and economically discriminated against, and identified themselves as such'. It was thus possible for one to remain a 'non-white' by virtue of failure to identify with the struggle for liberation – a rather interesting twist of logic which shows up the ridiculousness of race definitions and exposes their perilous political foundations. But the 1970s was the decade when blacks of necessity had to redefine race politics as a first step away from their entrapment and disempowerment by centuries of racism. The demands of philosophical precision were not allowed to interfere with this self-definition.

I spent many late nights helping Steve meet deadlines for his articles. He was notoriously poor at managing time. I would write down his thoughts as a stream of consciousness which he would dictate to me, and later I would read the text back to him as he typed with two fingers until it was done – not uncommonly in the early hours of the morning of the deadline.

*The conference proceedings were later published by David Philip under the title *Student Perspectives on South Africa* (Cape Town, 1972).

Aubrey Mokoape, Keith's elder brother, used to engage Steve in serious all-night discussions. Aubrey's sympathies lay with the Pan Africanist Congress, with which he had cut his political teeth as a high-school student. Steve enjoyed the debates he held with Aubrey. He found him challenging and intellectually stimulating, forcing him to clarify his own thoughts on a number of questions in his espousal of the Black Consciousness philosophy. Aubrey argued from his Africanist perspective against the inclusion of 'Coloureds' and Indians in the Black Consciousness Movement. As he became more and more liberated by increasing levels of alcohol, he would argue that Indians should be reminded that there was a ship leaving Durban harbour every Thursday for India which they should be encouraged to make use of. And what about the 'Coloureds'? someone would ask good-naturedly. He would respond good-humouredly in the style of some of the 1960s Pan Africanist demagogues: 'The Coloureds - eh - the - eh - Coloureds – underground!'

A number of African students shared this view and expressed their reservations about sharing a political programme with Indians. For example, Klaas Mogotlane summed up his feelings by stating that he would hate to see Steve dying for the liberation of Indians! Langa Duba, a final-year student in 1969, would occasionally stagger into Steve's room after his regular weekend binges, and express his dismay at the company Steve was keeping: 'Biko, you are going down, my friend. Your room is full of curry! You are going down, my friend!'

Goolam Abram (Gees), himself classified Indian, used to laugh at this anti-Indian rhetoric, particularly that coming from the Langa Dubas of those days. He was also Aubrey Mokoape's friend and would listen to the invitation to take the ship to India as an 'honorary African' and be able to laugh off this brand of Africanist fantasy. Gees understood the depth of Africans' anger towards Indians and the reasons for their mistrust. The rise of Idi Amin as the leader of Uganda and his expulsion of Asians simply fuelled the fires of hatred and mistrust. Strini Moodley, the SASO Director of Publications at the time, devoted an entire address to warn Indian students that they would face the same fate unless they dedicated themselves to the struggle for liberation and justice for all.

Barney Pityana became more and more part of the community of activists at UNB from 1970 onwards. He had fallen victim to the mass expulsions from Fort Hare in 1969. He was elected the new Permanent Secretary of SASO after the annual General Student Council in June 1970. Steve managed to negotiate with the Alan Taylor authorities for the use of space at the residence as premises for the national head office of the fledgling organisation. Barney's presence injected a measure of greater discipline into the running of SASO. His methodical approach to tasks and his organisational skills boosted SASO's image considerably and transformed it into a more professional national student organisation. Steve used to concede that Barney was a better organiser and writer because he was more disciplined. Barney and Steve complemented each other's strengths as well as mitigating each other's weaknesses.

The location of the SASO head office at UNB made political sense in the light of the central role played by the Natal Medical School community in the leadership of the nascent Black Consciousness Movement. In the first place, Natal University was the most liberal of campuses with a significant black student population, in stark contrast to the oppressive political climate at the other universities set aside for exclusive use by black students. One could with advantage exploit the professed non-racialism of Natal University. In the second place, medical students had a sense of leadership and mission in relation to their less fortunate counterparts in the so-called Bush Colleges* where political activities were more constrained. SASO was thus able to function in a supportive environment which allowed open access to all.

From 1970 onwards I became increasingly drawn into activism as a friend of Steve and Barney and as a member of the SASO local committee, whose chairperson (or chairman, in the language of the time) I later became. We organised many discussion sessions on campus, canvassed for active membership, and got involved in work camps as part of our commitment to active engagement in the problems which plagued oppressed communities. Medical students ran a clinic at the Alan Taylor Residence for poor people, named Happy Valley Clinic, after the ironic name of the surrounding district where desperately poor communities lived. We participated in the weekend sessions at this clinic. The Happy Valley Clinic was a shoestring affair which was enthusiastically used by the local people – more a commentary on their desperate circumstances than a reflection on

*The university colleges established by the Nationalist government for the exclusive use of black people in line with the policy of separate development.

the quality of the service it offered.

We also established contact with another poor community in New Farm, near the Gandhi Centre in Phoenix. Mewa Ramgobin, then married to Ela Gandhi, a grand-daughter of the Mahatma, was an enthusiastic supporter of the new student politics and assisted our work in the area. We soon opened a clinic at the Gandhi Centre which served the poor people in that area. Our knowledge of community development was dangerous, but our enthusiasm compensated for many potentially devastating errors of judgement in our dealings with the local people.

An added complication to community development at New Farm was the entry of predominantly white students led by Dr Rick Turner, a political science lecturer at the University of Natal known for his socialist views. Rick used to visit the Alan Taylor Residence and became friendly with all of us. He spent long periods of time arguing with Steve about the analytical limitations of Black Consciousness, which a socialist perspective could remedy by adding a class analysis to address some of the complexities of power relations in South Africa. Steve in turn pointed out to Rick that an economic class analysis which ignored the racist nature of capitalist exploitation in South Africa, and in many other parts of the globe, was itself inadequate. White workers identified more with white owners of capital than with black workers, Steve would conclude. The debate would drift into a discussion of the false consciousness of white workers, ending with Steve challenging Rick to go out and conscientise white workers to prove that his approach would work in apartheid South Africa. Steve's often-quoted remark in this regard was: 'Go and talk to Van Tonder [a stereotypical conservative Afrikaner worker] about solidarity with black workers, and see what his response would be.'

Both viewpoints were part of the reality of social relations in our society, but each laid emphasis on one aspect of the South African problematic without due consideration of the complexities of its multi-dimensionality. The further development of Black Consciousness depended at that time on its greater recognition of the importance of divisions within the black community along lines of class, gender, age and geographic location. So, too, Marxists in South Africa, as elsewhere, needed to recognise the importance of racial categories as a determinant of a person's place in a racist society, as well as developing a better-integrated analysis of gender, age and geographic place.*

Few white activists saw the conscientisation of whites as an attractive proposition. It was not surprising that Rick Turner took his disciples to the New Farm area to work in the same community where we had been engaged. It was the height of insensitivity on his part, and engendered a lot of anger from black students, who saw it as a demonstration of white arrogance and a direct challenge. If ever there was a case of Black Consciousness needing to stand up to white people, one couldn't have written a better script than this one. The dispute was finally resolved through discussions in which Steve participated in a mediatory role, but it left a nasty taste in the mouth.

The greatest challenge to my nascent leadership qualities came in December 1971. I was assigned by the SASO head office to lead a student work camp in December 1971 to Winterveld, a huge squatter area near Pretoria, which continues to present a problem to local authorities and development workers. We were accommodated by Sister Doris, who ran her own private clinic in Mabopane, a nearby township, and were co-hosted by the local Catholic church run by two priests, one of whom I still remember, Fr Clement Mokoka. It was not an easy assignment. We were far from prepared for the tasks we were to undertake, namely, assessing the needs of the local community and identifying a project we could undertake effectively in the limited time we had over the December holiday period. Only youthful enthusiasm could explain our courage in tackling such a complex task without the requisite training.

Problems surfaced at a number of levels. Firstly, our hosts were not as supportive as had been expected when we made the original arrangement. The Catholic priests were quarrelling between themselves and wanted us to take sides in their conflicts. Sister Doris was a temperamental woman whose real focus did not seem to have been nursing care. She was often away from her clinic, commuting to her home in the Pretoria township of Mamelodi, leaving us to run the clinic without supervision – a scary experience especially with deliveries of babies, which came unexpectedly.

Then again, communication with the SASO head office and guidance from its staff were not what they should have been. Harry

*A more elaborate critique of this aspect of the Black Consciousness Movement in South Africa is to be found in my contribution to *Bounds of Possibility*, edited by Barney Pityana, Mamphela Ramphele, Malusi Mpumlwana and Lindy Wilson (Cape Town and London, 1991).

Nengwekhulu, the Permanent Organiser, who was directly responsible for project direction, was often not accessible, as he maintained
an extensive travel schedule to keep in touch with all the SASO
branches in the country. Whenever I finally tracked him down, his
attitude was dismissive. He urged us to be patient with the teething
problems we were experiencing. I doubt that he could have offered
more support anyway, given the pioneering nature of the work we
were doing at the time. We operated on a shoestring budget which
left little fat for our basic living needs – a recipe for discontent in the
ranks.

Our group of students consisted of about ten activists from different campuses around the country. Welding such a group into a team
was a task too daunting for an inexperienced twenty-four-year-old
to accomplish without assistance. There was a particularly difficult
woman who became increasingly hostile towards me as her frustration grew along with her disillusionment. She threw tantrums and
made herself thoroughly unpleasant.

We all became increasingly disillusioned when the local population failed to respond to our attempts to conscientise them. Their
sense of powerlessness seemed to be complete. The reality of the
powerlessness of the very poorest of the poor threatened the foundations of our idealism. It became difficult to see how these same
people were ever going to rise up against their oppressors and liberate themselves. Not only were they exploited by their white employers, but they also seemed to offer little resistance to black money-
makers who preyed on them, posing as healers, money-lenders and
landowners. They seemed so resigned to their fate that one questioned the wisdom of our attempts to engage them in trying to
change their circumstances.

I was particularly horrified by the extent to which some medical
professionals were acting as sponsors for quacks who posed as healers. One particular case involved a 'Doctor' Mohlala who ran a private clinic which included a maternity section. A prominent general
practitioner acted as his sponsor, no doubt for a significant consideration. 'Dr' Mohlala claimed to have done his training in Obstetrics at
the University of the North – an impossibility, because that
University had no medical school. The quest for healing often makes
people most vulnerable to exploitation and manipulation by
unscrupulous people. The end of the work camp came not a moment
too soon. I had learned a few lessons about the real world of com-

munity development – the complexities of a culture of survival were to become clearer much later.

My years as a student activist were a time of immense personal growth. As a SASO local chair, I participated in leadership development seminars, which were then referred to as formation schools. I benefited enormously from them. As a result I was able to transcend the naked anger which comes from waking up to the realisation of having been cheated out of a common heritage in one's own society. It was painful to realise how one had been systematically disadvantaged simply because of the colour of one's skin, an irrelevant attribute. But it was essential for one to become much more focused on defeating the ends of the oppressors. It was not an easy transition. To live with the knowledge of having been cheated and yet not to seek personal retribution takes a lot of energy and maturity.

I remember Barney having to use threats of leaving us to our own devices because some of us would not accept that some white people could be part of the resource group at one of the leadership development seminars in the early 1970s. The younger, more radical element felt that there was no scope for collaboration with whites in view of their acquiescent racism. Grudgingly, we had to accept that there were truly good white people who were as passionately committed to liberation as we were. Anne Hope, a member of a lay Catholic sisterhood, was a case in point. She was one of the most important resource people in leadership training seminars for young black activists. She used Paulo Freire's methods to help SASO develop a sound methodology for its conscientisation programme. She trained eight of the top leaders, who later trained us.

The confusion which reigned amongst new converts like me was both a reflection of the proverbial over-eagerness of the converted and an indicator of the danger of political analyses which by their very nature have to operate at the level of generalities to make sense. Distinguishing between white racism as a system to be fought and individual white people who may be innocent bystanders in a racist society was a nuance too complex for many young enthusiasts to grasp. The danger of fundamentalism looms large under such circumstances. Our respect for Barney's integrity and our confidence in his leadership made it possible for us to accept his judgement grudgingly.

I became increasingly self-confident and vocal in student meetings and in national student forums. I had begun to understand the culture of public speaking and the idiom of political discourse. Mastery of the art of using the standing rules of conduct in meetings to neutralise and subdue political opponents in debates was an essential part of the culture. I became quite an aggressive debater and was known for not suffering fools gladly. Moreover, I intimidated men who did not expect aggression from women. Soon a group of similarly inclined women, Vuyelwa Mashalaba, Nomsisi Kraai, Deborah Matshoba and Thenjiwe Mthintso, became a force to be reckoned with at annual SASO meetings. Ours was not a feminist cause at that time – feminism was a later development in my political consciousness – but an insistence on being taken seriously as activists in our own right amongst our peers.

Our political activism stretched beyond campus engagements. Protest meetings against the continuing imprisonment of black political leaders on Robben Island, commemoration services for those killed in detention, and solidarity meetings with struggles elsewhere in the world were part of the menu of political activism. There was not a dull moment. We linked up with off-campus organisations such as the Natal Indian Congress and other cultural groups which used culture as a safe haven for restricted political expression.

Steve's energy became increasingly focused on his political activism at the expense of his medical studies. It became difficult for him to maintain a balance between his personal development and national service – a common problem of many student activists. It came as no surprise that he was finally excluded from Natal Medical School in the middle of 1971, after failing a supplementary examination for his second-year courses which he was repeating. He was naturally disappointed, but he was not given to brooding over a problem for too long. His attention turned to securing a base from which to pursue his activism. SPROCAS 2,* a joint project of the Christian Institute headed by Dr Beyers Naudé and the South African Council of Churches (SACC) headed by Mr John Rees, presented him with an appropriate base. The project had just presented its report of a study coordinated by Rick Turner which challenged the churches to devise an active programme to promote justice and peace.

The outcome of deliberations on the SPROCAS report was a decision to establish the Black Community Programmes (BCP) as a way

* SPROCAS 2, The Special Project for Christian Action in Society.

of responding to the need for development necessitated by decades of injustice. A parallel white consciousness programme was to have been started to create awareness amongst whites of the evil of apartheid and the need for repentance. Bennie Khoapa, a social worker who was then working for the Young Men's Christian Association (YMCA), was chosen as the Director of the Black Community Programmes. Bennie had been a supportive admirer of the young student activists of the day and used to organise an end-of-year party for all of us to sit on the lawn of his house in Umlazi Township sipping beer and enjoying a braai. He was only too pleased to have Steve as his assistant in the new venture. As it turned out, Steve had thought through some of the issues more than Bennie had, and was enormously helpful to Bennie in negotiating with the Christian Institute and the SACC for a proper supportive relationship that would not stifle the new venture.

Steve had identified the need for documenting the lives of black South Africans as vital to encouraging them to become agents of their own liberation. One had to write history to make history. Documentation and research amongst blacks were, and remain, under-developed for a variety of reasons. The oral tradition which is strong amongst Africans did not lay a firm foundation for respect for the written word. Then again, the deliberate under-development of blacks by means of Bantu Education discouraged the emergence of a love for the written word and good record-keeping. Moreover, the instability of the life of the poor and marginal, subject to forced removals and the vicissitudes of inadequate shelter, led to the loss of many important historical and other documents. Finally, the scarcity of black researchers and social scientists made blacks vulnerable to becoming the objects of other people's studies, with all the risks of limited insight inherent in that form of scholarship.

The annual reports of the Institute of Race Relations in the 1960s and early 1970s were a case in point. They were chronicles of the victimisation of blacks at the hands of the apartheid regime. Blacks were denied any active role in the chronicle. Nothing positive about what blacks did was reported with any prominence. It was as if such positive reporting would reduce the impact of the reports on the oppression blacks suffered. Blacks were depicted as the ultimate victims, completely lacking in agency.

Necessity and passion are powerful motivators, overcoming the lack of social science and formal research training. Single-handedly

Steve designed the first edition of the *Black Review*, a comprehensive report of what went on in the black community: the good, the bad and the ugly. The areas covered included political developments, education, housing, worker issues, arts and sports. The data were derived from newspaper cuttings, visits to newspaper libraries, and Hansard reports on parliamentary proceedings. Malusi Mpumlwana (who had also been excluded from Medical School at the end of 1970) and Tomeka Mafole and Welile Nhlapo (both of whom had been expelled from Fort Hare earlier for political reasons) became Steve's temporary assistants in the enormous task of putting together the first edition of *Black Review* during the second half of 1971 and the whole of 1972. Ironically, Steve's pioneering work could not be publicly acknowledged without jeopardising the publication of the report: the banning order which was served on him at the beginning of 1973 prohibited him from participating in any publication – part of the state's attempt to limit the spread of ideas of political activists in apartheid South Africa. To protect the baby he had given birth to, other people had to claim credit for it. The first issue of *Black Review* consequently bore the name of Bennie Khoapa as editor.

The success of new ventures often rests on sound administrative capacity – a factor which many radical movements ignore at their peril. Ms Hester Fortune, a beautiful and self-confident woman who was executive secretary of the Black Community Programmes, was the pivot around which the organisation revolved. She kept a measure of sanity in the office of the Black Community Programmes at 86 Beatrice Street in Durban, which became a hive of activity, attracting welcome and unwelcome visitors who wanted a piece of the action. Hester had the sophistication to keep a necessary balance in the office, avoiding complete openness and lack of discipline, whilst creating a welcoming, supportive environment where serious work was possible.

I spent more time during 1972 at 86 Beatrice Street than I did at Medical School, even though it was my final year of study. I helped Steve with his new tasks and became completely absorbed in them. The pursuit of an academic degree was no match for the excitement of being part of a process that was shaping history. Strong personal bonds with fellow activists contributed to the commitment to the cause and the desire for active participation. Bennie remained a restraining yet supportive influence on youthful over-enthusiasm. He was like a true elderly statesman of the kind of society we were yearning to establish.

Activist life was not without its frustrating moments. The biggest tension arose between the demands of my body for long hours of sleep (eight hours minimum a night) and the culture of late nights which was an integral part of activist life at the time. I could not keep pace with the rest of the activist community. Irritability was an early warning sign for me as the nights became too long for my body to bear. A second problem was my body's need for regular meals. I remember one particularly unpleasant experience of a train journey to Johannesburg with Steve. We had been doing the usual last-minute rushing around when we realised that we had to leave immediately to catch the train, which left Durban at lunch time. We travelled third class, so our carriage stopped quite far from the shops at Pietermaritzburg Station. Steve, who was not particularly agile and was also very tired, could not make it to the café to get us some food before the train pulled out of the station. I felt like screaming from my hunger pangs, which were compounded by the knowledge that the next meal would only be the following day in Johannesburg.

Steve knew what was coming, so he quietly positioned himself on the uncomfortable bunk and fell asleep. I could have killed him! I eventually also fell asleep. We were met at Park Station by Bokwe Mafuna, who took us to his one-roomed house in Alexandra where it took time to prepare brunch. We finally ate at about ten o'clock. My hunger pangs were by then tamed. The frail body had a lot to learn to incorporate the emerging activist in me.

My increasing activism made me more and more defiant towards authority figures at the Medical School. The patronising ways of some of the teachers particularly irked me. The Dean, Professor E. B. Adams, who was also the head of the Department of Medicine, had an unfortunate manner in this regard. He saw no problem in probing the political views of students in his tutorial group. He completely ignored any body language from us indicating our discomfort with his inquisitions. He was particularly preoccupied with developments in what was then Rhodesia, and would open the tutorial discussions with 'Ms Ramphele, what do you think of the situation in Rhodesia?' I would respond by shrugging my shoulders, because I really did not think that I could hold any sensible political discussion with a conservative English-speaking white South African like him.

I was also critical of his bedside manners. He seemed to me patronising in his treatment of African patients, who would be referred to as 'the old boy' or 'old John' or whatever was the first name of the patient. He was undoubtedly a good medical specialist, but my antipathy towards him overshadowed my respect for his professional competence. Our relationship became increasingly difficult. After a while I stopped attending his tutorial sessions.

But he would not let his authority be challenged. He called me to his office in the Dean's suite and demanded an explanation from me. I went over the top in my defiant attitude – I lit a cigarette and refused to put it out when he told me to do so. I told him that when he stopped talking politics in his tutorials he should let me know, so that I could then attend, because we had nothing in common to discuss politically. He was appalled. He reminded me that he had the power to report me to the Medical and Dental Council for my bad behaviour and that my medical career would be at risk. There was no retreat for me – I dared him to act as he pleased. He dismissed me from his office in a rage.

When I completed my final exams at the end of that year, he made it known to his colleagues that he would not have me in his firm in Ward D at King Edward VIII Hospital. Those who knew me assured him that he need not worry about that prospect, as the feeling of antipathy was mutual. I remember seeing him at the international departure hall at Johannesburg Airport a decade later, and not being able to bring myself to go up to him and greet him. Whether he recognised me or not, I shall never know.

The end of final-year medical examinations was a great relief. We had to go up to Howard College, the main University campus, to take the Hippocratic Oath the very next day after the results became known. We were given use of graduation gowns, which we signed for and had to return afterwards. The auspiciousness of the occasion and its symbolic significance escaped me. My mind was on more important things. I had to rush back from the ceremony – I did not even stay for the tea which was part of the celebrations, because I felt I had to get back to Beatrice Street to complete some or other task which was of greater importance to me. Upon my return to Medical School, I simply left the borrowed gown in the office from which I had collected it, though there was no one to receive it at the time.

I was shocked several months later when I received a letter of demand from the University to return the gown or else pay for it. I wrote back to explain what had happened and to assure the University that I had returned the gown but had unfortunately not signed it in. The University was insistent: they had lost too many gowns to irresponsible students. I lost my cool. I wrote a not-so-polite letter back stating that I attached no value to academic dress, as demonstrated by my graduation *in absentia* earlier that year even though I was in Durban at the time. That settled that.

Looking back now, I feel ashamed of my behaviour at the time, but in the circumstances of the period I felt quite good about my defiance. As a woman, an African woman at that, one had to be outrageous to be heard, let alone be taken seriously.

# 4

# Growing Up
# the Hard Way

For most men a choice of career is a separate exercise from the important task of identifying a life partner. Their wives are often people they meet whilst pursuing the career of their choice. Social pressures on most women, however, often make them subordinate their career choices to the need to become desirable as a prospective marriage partner. Young women have almost to position themselves strategically to enter upon the role of a supporting spouse. My own naïveté did not alert me to this, and may partly explain why I seem to have been reasonably successful at making important decisions in many areas of my life and yet made repeated disastrous choices in my personal relationships.

It may well also have to do with the fact that I paid very little attention to friendships in my childhood and teenage years. I was quite happy keeping my own company, particularly with a book in my hand, or simply sleeping. I preferred the company of adults who ignored me and left me alone to my thoughts or day-dreams. My friends were few and far between, and I did not feel the need for friendships to become complete as a person. But my poor choices may also have stemmed from my discomfort with traditional relationships with men which I observed around me, and which I felt did not suit me temperamentally.

I do not recall having any of the teenage anguish of struggling for an identity or being preoccupied with my appearance or my self-image or with the need to be accepted by my peers. I was quite at peace with myself and remained attached to my mother as the most important person in my life. My brothers and sister found me a bit of a pain because of my attachment to my mother and my independence and self-confidence, which they felt went over the top.

Being top of one's class is a decided disadvantage for any girl at school. None of my classmates felt comfortable with me because they thought I did not have any reason to respect them, and I appeared self-contained to the point of being aloof. Dick Mmabane, who was my classmate in Standard 9 and 10 at Setotolwane High School in 1965 and 1966, decided to take a chance after a long period of watching and waiting. His interest in me was indicated in a gradual, tentative way – he later confessed that he had expected me to dismiss him at first base.

Although I was nearly nineteen years old, and in Standard 10, I had not till then really been interested in males. There had been one or two teachers who showed an interest in me, but I was not responsive. On the contrary, I was quite appalled by the advances of an elderly married teacher, which I regarded as an insult. In fact I threatened to report him to the headmaster if he dared to repeat his advances. I lost all respect for him and made a public show of not paying attention to his lessons. I openly read magazines during his periods to indicate my defiance. Mine was a trump card he could ignore only at the risk of losing his job. He was indeed fortunate that this incident happened in the days before sexual harassment was recognised for what it is.

My relationship with Dick started playfully, but became quite intense over the following months. The intoxication of being madly in love is the stuff first encounters are made of. I could not help wondering why I had not been interested in this wonderful experience before. It is such an affirming feeling to be loved and adored so openly. My heart leapt into a happy rhythm each time we went out together.

Dick's mother, Machipi Mmabane, was no ordinary woman. She was a strong, self-reliant person who had had to fend for herself and her seven children, working herself up from her rural background in the Warmbaths area of the Transvaal, through informal trading, to becoming a successful owner of a fish and chips shop in Zone 4, Diepkloof, in Soweto. Dick's father was a shell of a man, who had known better days. I got to know him as a somewhat unstable person who spent his days drinking home-brewed beer at the local beer garden.

Dick's mother provided well for her eldest son; one of seven children, he was the apple of her eye. He dressed well and was well spoken. It is not surprising that he was chosen to speak on behalf of the final-year class at our farewell matric dance at the end of 1966. It was a memorable occasion for me. My sister Mashadi had sent me a fashionable powder-blue short-sleeved crimplene suit, a pair of black patent-leather high-heeled shoes and stockings. It was my first real occasion to dress up. I felt good and Dick looked approvingly at me when I joined him at the party. The evening just melted away. We bade goodbye to our high school days and moved into the world of adulthood.

I had not bargained for the complications of love relationships. We parted after spending a few days together with some friends in the old township in Pietersburg. The December holidays seemed interminably long because I missed Dick so much. It was a relief to catch up with him at the beginning of the 1967 academic year at the University of the North, where we were both new students.

No sooner had I settled in than I began being harassed by his former girlfriend, who was a senior student at the University. She made it clear that she would not let a 'fresher' (a newcomer) win a love tussle with her. Even though I loved Dick, I felt I was not going to get involved in fights over boyfriends and made that known to both Dick and his former girlfriend. Although Dick was unambiguous in declaring where his interests lay and that their relationship was over, it took a while before she stopped bothering me, and her dislike for me was quite visible whenever we met. I did not feel that I was missing anything by not being liked by her.

The social life at the University of the North was rather unimaginative. Social life revolved around a mixture of old-fashioned formalities and some spontaneous activities particularly amongst the younger students. The older and more mature students tended to be rather formal in both dress and manner. One was expected to walk to and from classes with one's friends, to dress up for dinner, and to be walked by one's boyfriend from the dining-room to one's residence, where lovers stood around and chatted until study time at about 7.30 p.m., when all made for the library to settle down for two or three hours of work. It was also customary for the men to accompany their girlfriends back to the residences after the library and to steal a goodnight kiss at the end. Male residences were completely out of bounds for female students, and men students could only get as far as the entrance hall of the women's residences.

I got bored with this routine and preferred the company of my female friends with whom I could be completely uninhibited. We would walk together to the local shopping centre after our practical laboratory work was done, buy ourselves snacks, including hot *vetkoek*, and enjoy ourselves. I did not have many fancy clothes, nor cared to dress up except on special occasions.

The world of science students was a little on the margins of campus social life. The Science Faculty lay at the lower end of the campus, hidden away behind trees. Our laboratory work also entailed a different schedule from social science and humanities students, who were often free in the afternoons. Dick had registered for a law degree, so our worlds grew apart. I got to see Dick less and less during the week. Senior science students play a useful role as laboratory demonstrators and often help new students with their studies. My friends and I got to like one particular senior science student who was a laboratory demonstrator in Botany. He had a great sense of humour, which made our meal-times more pleasant than the monotonous menus would have ordinarily permitted.

I did not realise that Dick was becoming jealous of what he saw as a close relationship until it was almost too late. It was customary for Dick and me to go to Pietersburg together on Saturday mornings, for window-shopping and seeing a movie at the cinema or visiting friends in the township. I waited in vain one weekend for Dick to come and call on me for a walk to town. On Monday afternoon I ran into him and innocently asked where he had been on the weekend. He dismissed my questions lightly without showing his true feelings. I asked him to walk me to the library, and did not detect the irony in the tone of his voice when he suggested that I ask the science student (let's call him Sidney) to accompany me. Unfortunately for me, Sidney was near by and I innocently asked him to walk me to the library. Dick was devastated. I remained blissfully unaware of the depth of his anger. One of Dick's friends had to intervene to make me aware of the pain I had caused him in my innocence. We made up, and I became a little wiser.

My insistence on going to Natal Medical School the following year began to create tensions with Dick. He feared that he might lose me if we parted. In my innocence I saw no reason for his concern. I saw no conflict between my career plans and our continued relationship. In any case I would not have been prepared to change my plans for the sake of our relationship – not because I did not care for him, but because I wasn't prepared to give up my career. I did not share his anxiety about what distance could do to a love relationship between young people like us. I was, after all, still very green.

We spent the December holidays together in Soweto and had a

good time. I was staying with my aunt, *Mamogolo* Ramadimetsa, in Orlando West, and he would come and visit or take me out. We went to visit his many friends together, saw countless movies, ate out and generally had fun. His mother was clearly very proud of her son as a first-generation university student and indulged him a great deal. She even justified buying a house for him in the same area as her own, Zone 4, Diepkloof, in part because he was the eldest son. We had the use of her pick-up truck and never wanted for anything.

It was sad for us to part at the beginning of 1968, but I assured him of my love for him, and promised to remain faithful. We kept in touch by letter and he sent me money to visit him over the Easter holidays. I focused on my studies and ignored many advances from young men at Medical School. I made it known to everyone that I was not available. At the end of 1968 Dick's mother passed away suddenly. I comforted him as best as I could during the December holidays, which we spent together. His sisters urged me to remain faithful to Dick. They reminded me of the pain he would suffer from losing the two most important women in his life – his mother and myself. I took their concerns seriously.

The year 1969 brought many changes in my own life. My increasing activism and my deeper involvement in the circle of activists brought with it a greater openness to others around me. That brought along its own complications for my relationship with Dick. Steve Biko had been pursuing me seriously for a while, but I had kept him at bay by reiterating my commitment to Dick, to whom I considered myself virtually engaged. I was safe behind this armour for a while.

In the second half of 1969 it became increasingly difficult to resist Steve's advances. I fell hopelessly in love with him, but would not even admit this to myself. We conducted a semi-platonic friendship which frequently 'degenerated' into passion. I became increasingly distressed at my dilemma. How could I desert Dick after all these years, particularly after his mother's death? I could not bear the thought of hurting him. But what of my passionate love for Steve? I was faced with a serious dilemma.

There was really no one I felt I could turn to for advice, because in a sense I feared that they would advise me to follow my heart. But I could not live with the implications of such a decision for Dick, who had been so good to me over the years. I lived in a daze and enjoyed each day as it unfolded. A fellow student, Victor Mafungu, a gentle person who was like a brother to me, used to come and study in my room, and would watch with concern as I floated on this enormous love affair, which I was refusing to acknowledge.

Some of my homeboys at Medical School, particularly Joel Matsipa, who knew Dick well, started expressing their concern about my relationship with Steve. I tried to play things down by emphasising its platonic nature as befitted a relationship between activists, but the intoxication of the love affair was self-evident. Both Dick and Steve started putting some pressure on me. Dick urged me to finalise our tentative marriage plans for the summer of 1969/70. Quick action was of the essence to preserve our long-standing relationship. In contrast, the nascent love affair with Steve needed time to unfold. Consequently Steve urged me to take time to make a final decision about marriage. Any delay would work in favour of my relationship with Steve – a fact of which both contenders were acutely aware. I dared not think of even raising the possibility of postponement because it would simply confirm what Dick was beginning to suspect. But a final decision was too frightening to contemplate. I was stuck.

Steve also had poetic talents which he displayed occasionally when moved emotionally. He told me about the poems which he had written as a pupil at Mariannhill High School and had shared with a Catholic nun whom he liked and respected. The intensity of our relationship brought him to write a poem entitled 'A Love Supreme'. I hung on to its every word. I still wonder what became of the poem over the years. It probably got lost in one of the many police raids.

Parting for the summer vacation was not easy. Steve pleaded with me not to make any final decisions about marriage until the following year. He asked for an address at which he could write to me, and I fatefully gave him Dick's home address where I anticipated spending most of my holidays. Steve was going to be attending a student leadership seminar at the Abe Bailey Institute at UCT and promised to keep in touch.

I spent a week or so with Dick. The relationship was quite evidently changed. He disapproved of my smoking, but I refused to give it up. His sisters also disapproved, but I was not prepared to compromise. Perhaps there was some vain hope in me that he would pick a fight over it and put the relationship at risk, thus rescuing me from my dilemma. But he knew the limits beyond which he could not go, so he resigned himself to this new me, and even bought me cartons of cigarettes from his family business. I went home to my own family in Kranspoort for the rest of the holidays.

Unbeknown to me, Steve dutifully wrote to me and repeated his plea that I should postpone any marriage plans until I was clearer in my mind about where my real feelings stood with regard to the two men in my life. Dick must have opened the letter, and decided there and then to expedite our marriage plans. He sent me a telegram announcing his intention to come and visit to finalise arrangements for the wedding. His relatives had been to see my family a few months earlier to ask for my hand in marriage – *go kgopela sego sa meetse* – literally 'to ask for a water container'. My paternal grandfather did not believe in the custom of *lobola* (bride-wealth) and asked the Mmabanes to give whatever token they felt appropriate to mark their appreciation of the gift of a wife. The token given amounted to about R200. This family involvement also made any reversal of commitments difficult.

I resigned myself to my fate, and even allowed myself to get excited. Dick would not hear of leaving me behind. We left together in my cousin Mbatha Ramphele's car after a day or two. I went to stay with my aunt in Orlando West whilst a hasty wedding party was being arranged by Dick's relatives. The only people from my family who could participate in the wedding celebration were my sister Mashadi and my cousin Rosemary Mogomotsi. We signed and sealed our marriage in front of a magistrate, and I vowed to make it work.

When I got back to Medical School in late January 1970, I was a married woman and proudly showed off my wedding rings and photographs to all who would see. To my homeboys there was an underlying message of 'I told you so'. But my response to Steve was more complex. I do not know how I could have been so insensitive in showing off the same items to Steve without any regard to the hurt it would cause him. He was devastated. He could not believe that I could have killed my relationship with him without so much as an explanation or some apology. He assumed I had received his letter and ignored his final plea.

All he said was 'I see' to the display of my new status, and walked away deeply hurt. He nonetheless respected the distance I had placed between us. I steeled myself in the determination to remain a faithful wife. Steve and I met in the context of our student activism, and pursued a platonic relationship. When he visited the University of the North later that year as the first President of SASO, Dick was one of the people who hosted him. Dick lent Steve his pyjamas – an interesting symbolic declaration of triumph.

I paid frequent visits to my husband, even during term-time, to reduce the yawning gap between us. The fourth year of study was not very demanding in view of its focus on practical training in hospitals. I did not enjoy this aspect of my training at all. I did not like the sight of blood – a common companion of medical practitioners. Moreover, I resented the use of helpless patients as 'interesting cases' for teaching purposes. Many patients with painful conditions that evinced classic signs and symptoms had to endure endless queues of eager medical students who all wanted to feel the lump or enlarged organ and to elicit a wince from the hapless patient. Students would talk about 'a liver in ward such-and-such' which was a must for their colleagues to go and feel. I could not associate myself with such depersonalisation of people, and their reduction to the level of inanimate organs of the body.

King Edward VIII Hospital, where I was stationed, was a real hovel of a place – a typical apartheid institution. It was (and, at the time of writing, still is) an old, overcrowded, untidy hospital with a constant shortage of linen and with poor-quality food for patients. Children in the paediatric wards would often be swimming in their own excreta. It was not a pleasant place to work in. I did only the bare minimum to stay in the course and qualify for promotion to the next level of training.

It was inevitable that cracks would appear in our marriage. It was a relationship based on celebrating past ties rather than facing the challenges of the divergences that had grown up between us. However much I remained faithful, Dick would not trust me. The physical distance between us did not help, nor were my frequent visits sufficient compensation. Dick started drinking heavily and neglected his studies. At the end of 1970 he still had not made enough progress to stand a chance of completing his degree within the foreseeable future. His elder sister Ellen, who had taken over the running of the family business after their mother's death, expressed her concern about Dick's increasingly irresponsible behaviour. She found it difficult to accept his poor performance at university as well as the demands he was making on her for material support. I unwisely entered the fray and expressed my own concerns. He resented my own critical comments and flew into an uncharacteristic rage.

Our December 1970 holidays were not pleasant. He drank more and more heavily as if to spite me. He accused me of being unfaithful, which really hurt because I could have chosen to be unfaithful but had been impeccably faithful to my marriage vows. He also became quarrelsome about my smoking and political activism. I went back to Medical School unhappy and worried about the future of our marriage. I buried myself in my activism and took pleasure from my circle of friends.

The crunch came in June 1971 when I got back home from the annual SASO conference at Natal Medical School, which I had attended as the local SASO chair. I found that Dick had turned our house into a shebeen, and that he was in the company of township no-hopers – people who had given up the struggle to make their lives meaningful outside the solace of alcohol. It later turned out that he had dropped out of university and had had an affair with an old girlfriend from his school days whom he was later to marry. He made it clear that he regarded our relationship as dead in view of the priority I seemed to have given political activism, by spending time at the SASO conference instead of coming home directly at the end of term. On top of it all he also claimed I had been unfaithful. I was devastated.

The following morning he arranged for me to be taken to my aunt's home in Orlando West with all my personal belongings. I took all but my mother's cookbook – a treasure which she had reluctantly let me borrow because she appreciated my love of cooking. The loss of that cookbook is one of the regrets I continue to feel about the break-up of my relationship with Dick.

My aunt was saddened by the breakdown of my marriage. Her husband insisted that I had to be taken back to Dick's family home to ensure that they would not be faulted for having failed to follow the custom of first finding out the extent of the breakdown before concluding that there was no chance of a reconciliation. The encounter at the Mmabanes was humiliating, to say the least. At the meeting of the two families, Dick refused to discuss any of the issues which had caused the tensions in our marriage except to say that I had become too much for him to handle as a wife. The message was clear – we had grown apart.

Traditional systems stand powerless in the face of breakdowns which arise out of the kind of tensions that undermined our marriage. There was no real remedy for the insecurity which my husband felt in relation to the 'new me'. He had married an ideal which he hoped he could salvage from the past. I in turn had not been prepared to acknowledge the depth of the fault-lines which had arisen in our relationship. I went back to Medical School at the beginning of the second semester in 1971 emotionally exhausted and bewildered at the turn of events. Marriage breakdowns represent a vote of no confidence in one's own decisions at a very fundamental level. It is not surprising that many people refuse to face up to that reality even when presented with compelling evidence. I was no exception.

Steve had in the interim got himself married to Ntsiki Mashalaba (a cousin of Vuyelwa's), who had fallen pregnant with his child. He explained to me that after the hurt I had inflicted on him he had given up on romantic love and wanted to settle down and concentrate on political activism. When I came back from my disastrous holiday I sought him out and told him all about my marriage which lay in ruins. He listened as a true friend and asked me if I thought I had given it my best, and urged me to find out what could be done to save the marriage. I had my doubts. My letters to Dick remained unanswered, and finally I accepted the obvious.

Steve continued to support me as a friend with great integrity. He did not once say 'I told you so', nor took advantage of my distress to get even with me. It was only a matter of time, however, before the old fire flared up again. The love letter which Steve put into my hand on the way to a party with some members of our activist circle had been long in coming. I knew instinctively what its message would be. I could not wait to confirm this. At the first opportunity I went into the toilet and read it. I came out glowing with utter happiness. But how were we to conduct our love affair in the light of Steve's marriage?

That night was the happiest I had experienced in years. We celebrated our reunion in style. We naïvely vowed not to hurt the innocent party – Steve's wife. Ntsiki was then on maternity leave and later returned to Durban to a post as a nurse at the McCord Hospital. Life became increasingly complex as we tried vainly not to make our relationship a public affair. But it was impossible to stop the tongues wagging. Although our long friendship and common political commitment helped to create some respectable explanation for the inordinate amount of time we spent together, it was not easy.

Over the many years before and after my unsuccessful marriage, I got to know and love Bukelwa Biko, Steve's elder sister, who was a senior nurse at King George V Hospital, a local tuberculosis treatment centre. We became very close. I used to talk to her about the difficulties of our triangular love relationship. Though she was very sympathetic, she made it clear to Steve and me that we had made this bed and had now to lie in it. She could not believe both of us could have been so stupid in making such decisions about our private lives. She would adopt a matronly tone and say, 'You kids are really silly – you must face the consequences of your foolish decisions.' That was easier said than done. She remained an important pillar of support, financially and emotionally.

My divorce was finalised during the course of 1972. I became free again. But tensions over the triad intensified. Some friends started taking sides. Vuyelwa was, understandably, the most vociferous critic of our relationship. She confronted Steve with the hurt that he was causing her cousin through his infidelity, but was told firmly to mind her own business. Others were more diplomatic in their approaches to Steve, but he told them that he was caught on the horns of a dilemma which history had visited on him.

Steve and Barney set up a joint house during 1972 in Umlazi Township. Both their wives, who were nurses at the McCord Hospital, joined them, and later their children, Nkosinathi and Loiso, also came to stay. It was a communal home in every sense of the word. Activists used it as their own home, putting a major strain on limited financial and housekeeping resources. I kept my distance out of respect for Ntsiki, and for fear of causing a scene.

Disaster struck us at the beginning of 1973. I had arranged to do my medical internship at King Edward VIII Hospital in Durban in order to be close to Steve. The Schlebusch Commission, instituted by the government to investigate a number of organisations (including NUSAS and the Christian Institute), reported on its findings and the government promptly slapped banning orders on eight NUSAS student leaders, eight SASO leaders, and a number of people associated with the Black Consciousness Movement.

Steve had been running a leadership training seminar in Port Elizabeth with several Black Consciousness leaders, amongst whom were Barney, Harry Nengwekhulu and Bokwe Mafuna, as part of a national youth leadership development programme sponsored jointly by SASO and the Black Community Programmes. They were detained for a while by the security police before being transported individually to their various places of birth. Steve found himself back in his mother's home in Ginsberg, King Williamstown; Harry was taken to Sibasa, in Venda in the northern Transvaal; whilst Barney was confined to New Brighton Township in Port Elizabeth. Banning orders subtly employed traditional controls to discipline errant black political activists by sending them back to their natal homes. Symbolically they can be said to have invoked parental control over political transgressors. In practice they put parents in a difficult position, making them sometimes try to restrain their children from taking too many political risks.

The news of the banning orders was devastating. The entire top leadership of the Black Consciousness Movement was immobilised at the stroke of a pen. The banning orders varied in their severity, but were issued by the Minister of Justice under the Suppression of Communism Act of 1950, and centred on the following:
– Those affected were prohibited from participating in specified political activity, a list of names of organisations being provided with whose activities they were not allowed to be involved.
– They were prohibited from attending or addressing political gatherings of any sort.
– They were prohibited from publishing or participating in activities which could lead to the dissemination of any sort of publication. Quoting banned people was a criminal offence.
– They were not allowed to enter any educational institution, or participate in teaching.
– They were prevented from attending any social gathering, defined as a meeting of more than one person other than the restricted person. Exceptions were made for bona fide family gatherings or religious services.
– The area of restriction was circumscribed, and most banned people had to report to a local police station weekly and sign a register as proof of compliance with their restrictions.
– They were prohibited from any contact or communication with other banned people.
– The local magistrate was empowered in each case to grant permission to relax restrictions, but in practice he did so only with the approval of the local security police.

It is interesting that the thrust of the Schlebusch Commission report was ambivalent about the Black Consciousness Movement (BCM) itself. The National Party government was still unsure whether the BCM had not perhaps bought into its own ideological programme of separate development. It liked the growing distance of the BCM from white liberals, but was cautious about the direction in which the leaders were taking the movement. It decided to be safe rather than sorry. This ambivalence gave Steve the space to continue to work for BCP by setting up a regional office in an old Anglican Church building at 15 Leopold Street, King Williamstown. He was greatly assisted by Fr David Russell, then ministering to the poor people who had been forcibly removed from different parts of the Eastern Cape and dumped at Dimbaza, a new township near King.*

Steve called me from a public phone at the earliest opportunity after arriving in Ginsberg Township. He sounded very depressed and angry. His main message to me was simple: 'I am not prepared to lose you again; we have to remain closely in touch whatever happens.' That was not a difficult injunction to agree to from my side. Nothing was going to stop our relationship from growing to its full potential. I lived off the warmth of the feelings between us and the wonderful memories of our intimate times together. Calls were few and far between until he installed a phone in his mother's house.

Regular commuting to and from King then started. My first aeroplane trip took place the following weekend, at the end of January 1973. It was a bumpy flight, particularly for those in the tail-end seats, which were customarily reserved for blacks in apartheid days. I was met at East London Airport by Mapetla Mohapi and Malusi Mpumlwana, and taken to Zwelitsha Township to Nohle Haya's† home. There complicated arrangements were made for my accommodation to enable me to spend time with Steve without either falling foul of the law relating to his banning order or offending his wife. This was complex and frustrating. I had to wait till late that evening before setting eyes on Steve, and much later before we had the privacy to be able to unwind. It was the first of many visits.

On my return to King Edward Hospital in Durban I arranged with my fellow interns, Jayshree Moodley and Goolam Abram, for a special dispensation to work irregular hours so that I could accumulate enough credit time for long weekend visits to King. They were very supportive. I also put in an application to transfer my internship in

*King is the popular name for King Williamstown, also referred to by the locals as eQonce, its Xhosa name.
†Nohle subsequently became Steve Biko's secretary and married Mapetla Mohapi

the second half of the year to Livingstone Hospital in Port Elizabeth, to be closer to Steve. I started living from one visit to the next and spent an inordinate amount of money on telephone calls to Steve. Such was the cost of a long-distance triangular relationship.

Conducting a love affair on a migratory basis is difficult at the best of times, but in our case there was more than the physical distance to contend with. Port Elizabeth was an unfamiliar place for me. I had only visited it once for the purpose of attending a conference of ASSECA (the Association for the Educational and Cultural Advancement of Africans), which was modelled on the NAACP amongst African-Americans. ASSECA was run by conservative middle-class Africans led by Mr M. T. Moerane, editor of the *Bantu World*, a Johannesburg paper for the township African market. Our attempts to infiltrate ASSECA and harness it to the cause of black liberation were soundly defeated by a vigilant Mr Moerane, who used the chair effectively to deny our group of delegates a voice. I had no good memories of Port Elizabeth.

Returning to Port Elizabeth as a doctor in training a year later was a different experience. Livingstone Hospital was as unlike King Edward Hospital as chalk from cheese. It was a modern, clean and well-run hospital which was a pleasure to work in. The doctors' quarters where I lived were pleasant and airy, and the food was superior. I was glad about the change from Durban. I also preferred the cooler Port Elizabeth weather to the humid heat of Durban.

My departure from Durban had been hasty. I do not remember any regrets other than that of leaving some of my friends with whom I had shared many happy moments. This was particularly true of fellow interns, who were also former classmates. Xola Pemba, a well-built rugger-bugger of a man, became particularly close and protective of me. We enjoyed many beers together during weekends when we were not on duty. But internship duties were demanding, and the working hours long. The spirit which had been characteristic of Alan Taylor Residence and 86 Beatrice Street had died. Durban had nothing more to offer me.

If I had found the medical internship at King Edward VIII Hospital tough and demanding, worse awaited me during my surgical internship in Port Elizabeth. Weekend duty started at eight in the morning on Friday and went on until four on Monday afternoon. At the end of the month one would be lucky to get more than a wink of sleep on Friday and Saturday night. The casualty department looked like a battlefield – motor-vehicle accidents; stab wounds on chests, abdomens, even on necks (in one case the knife was still *in situ*, the attacker having failed to pull it out of the bone, where it had got stuck); various cases of assault on victims who were invariably drunk. It was a mess.

I had to learn to work fast and to master the technique of inserting intercostal underwater drains into stab chests – on one occasion I counted ten intercostal drains in one night. These drains were inserted under local anaesthetic, and could be difficult with restless drunken patients. I relied on the theatre nurses who were highly skilled, and they taught me a lot.

By any standard 96 hours of duty is too long for anyone to do justice to any job, let alone one which involved life and death decisions. One wonders how many fatal errors were made under such circumstances. I revolted after a few months of this punishing schedule. I refused to wake up for Sunday morning ward rounds and asked the sister in charge of the ward to let my seniors know that I was too tired to join them, and that they should leave all instructions in the patients' folders for my attention later in the day. The head of my firm, Mr McQuaide, a specialist general surgeon, did not seem to mind and did not make an issue of it, although my registrar took a dim view of what he perceived as insubordination. I was pleased years later to see that interns had organised themselves nationally to protest against this inhuman system, which has now been modified, though it is still demanding.

It is also worth recording the conditions of service under which we worked as newly qualified doctors. The remuneration system discriminated between blacks and whites. White people earned significantly more than blacks. There was also different pay for 'Bantus' (as Africans were then called officially), 'Coloureds' and Indians. To add insult to injury, women also earned less than men. As an African woman I was thus at the bottom of the pile in terms of salary. My take-home pay amounted to R240 in 1973. I had to clothe and feed myself, travel and entertain on this amount. In addition, my widowed mother relied on me more and more for support to educate my brothers. She was still earning less than R200 as principal of a lower primary school. It was a tall order.

From Port Elizabeth the commuting to King continued, and in fact intensified. I became quite expert at hitch-hiking after work on a Friday afternoon. Leaving Livingstone at about 4 p.m., I would invariably arrive in King by 7 p.m. The trip back was made on the late-night railway bus, which ran between Umtata and Port Elizabeth via King. Hitch-hiking was then relatively safe.

The few weekends I did not travel to King, I spent with Steve's younger sister, Nobandile (Bandie) Mvovo, who was married to Mxolisi; they lived in Walmer Township. Nobandile had come to Durban in 1971 to do a year's secretarial course, which Steve arranged for her to improve her skills. She came to stay with me in my room at Alan Taylor Residence. Steve and I notified the matron, Nomangesi Radebe, a native of King, who gladly agreed to turn a blind eye to this infringement of residence rules. Bandie was blissfully ignorant of my relationship with Steve. She took me as just a friend. One day she asked me who my boyfriend was. I simply said to her that he lived off campus and that she would meet him one day. That day came when she walked into her brother's room and found me in his bed.

I also saw a lot of Barney and Dimza Pityana who were living under intolerable conditions. The local security police in Port Elizabeth made their lives a misery. No sooner would someone arrive in Barney's mother's house than the security police would be knocking at the door, insisting on taking down the names of those present, questioning the purpose of their visit. It was blatant harassment. The move into their own house in New Brighton Township merely shifted the locus of battle with 'the system'. One could hardly conduct a decent conversation with Barney without the intrusion of these crude men. They were certainly a different breed from most of the King security police.

The migrant love affair bore semi-planned fruit at the end of 1973. I became pregnant, to my great excitement. Towards the close of one of the many weekend visits, I developed an acute abdominal pain. I was distressed. Steve took it lightly as an exaggerated sense of my unhappiness about having to part from him. I became increasingly uncomfortable on the trip back to Port Elizabeth. On arrival at the doctors' quarters I was so ill that I had to be admitted immediately.

The doctor who saw me insisted on an emergency operation. It could have been any number of problems causing an acute abdomen, and he was taking no chances. I was distressed at the thought of losing this love child and at the thought of Steve not being able to be with me in that hour of need. My last plea to the anaesthetist before I went under was for him to spare my baby. It turned out that I had a large degenerating fibroid on the surface of my womb, which had become inflamed. The operation was a success. I was discharged after ten days and had to go home to the Transvaal to await the arrival of my baby at the end of May 1974.

I went home via King, where I spent a week or so with Steve. On my arrival at East London Airport I was searched by security policemen, who probably suspected I was carrying written communications from Barney to Steve. They were disappointed, but had a consolation prize in finding old banned literature from my Natal Medical School days which I forgot that I was keeping safe for Steve. Bandie, who had packed my bags from Port Elizabeth, had simply thrown in all the books she found in my room without checking. I was later to be charged under the Suppression of Communism Act and given a suspended sentence for being in possession of banned literature.

It was not easy to face the prospect of not seeing Steve for the months until the baby was born. We parted on a sad note, but the sense of sharing the creation of a new life made the yawning physical distance ahead of us bearable. As already mentioned, the pregnancy was only partly planned. Steve was clearly ambivalent about having a love child in the circumstances, but I desperately needed to have something more tangible from our complex relationship. I was after all twenty-six years old and rather liked the idea of motherhood. The thought of sharing in the act of creation with Steve was exhilarating.

Passionate as our relationship was, it was fundamentally unsatisfactory for me. The constant awareness of sharing one's loved one with someone else hurts. The head and the heart were pulling in different directions. 'You have brought this misery upon yourself; this man was all yours, but you rejected him,' I would remind myself. But the heart ached.

I went to live in Johannesburg with my sister Mashadi, who was then staying with my mother's younger sister, Mamotšatši Mabaso, in Zola Township in Soweto. It was an overcrowded four-roomed house, which was difficult to keep clean with the ten children my aunt had. I became the housekeeper and spent many frustrating days battling with ill-disciplined children who messed their knickers before their mother came back from work. My aunt is a happy-go-lucky person who just laughed off my concerns about her children's poor toilet habits.

I kept in touch with Steve through regular letters, but it was hard. There were no phones within easy reach. Weeks passed without my hearing his voice. I felt abandoned, and had many tearful days. The situation was exacerbated by a threatened abortion in the seventh month of pregnancy. I had to spend many weeks at Baragwanath Hospital on strict bed-rest to prevent the loss of the baby. I was relieved when I finally gave birth in May 1974 to Lerato (a Sotho word for 'love') – a beautiful girl who looked just like Steve's younger sister, Nobandile Mvovo. After some further neonatal problems, including jaundice, Lerato was strong enough for me to start enjoying her.

I travelled with my sister and Lerato to Pietersburg in June to stay with my mother in Maupje, where she was teaching at the time. It was not easy to adjust to life in a rural area after all the years away, but we managed to make ourselves comfortable with financial support from Mashadi and Steve. But it was an arrangement which could not be sustained. I missed Steve a lot and also yearned to get back to work after all the months of 'idleness'. I decided to leave Lerato with my mother at the beginning of July, when she was barely six weeks, to return to King, and to find employment to support her and my mother. It was a difficult decision, one I was to regret.

Back in King it was wonderful to reconnect with Steve again. I soon found a job as a medical officer at Mt Coke Mission Hospital, a few kilometres from King. It was convenient to be so close to Steve and yet have an independent base so as to avoid stepping on his wife's toes.

Mt Coke Hospital was even then an old facility run largely by Methodist missionaries. There were about six doctors on the staff and a large complement of nurses and general workers. It had about a hundred beds and catered largely for the poor local black population. It had a very busy out-patient section, which provided comprehensive care; a maternity section, which had good antenatal and intranatal care; a paediatric unit; and a medical and surgical section. I was put in charge of the paediatric ward.

I learnt a lot from my colleagues. Medical School does not prepare one adequately for the real world of primary health care. I learned the proper treatment regimens for common paediatric problems, diagnostic skills with minimum technological aid, tooth extraction and so forth. But I failed to learn any surgical operations. There were regular caesarean sections performed for complications of pregnan-

cy or labour, but I just could not bring myself to do the actual operation. Nor could I successfully act as an anaesthetist: there were none
at Mt Coke. The surgeon had to do the operation and at the same
time keep an eye on the nurse who observed the anaesthetised
patient's condition.

I take my hat off to those with the expertise and courage to carry
out operations successfully under such conditions. I lacked both. I
could be used only as an assistant to the surgeon. But the experience
I gained at Mt Coke over the six months I worked there stood me in
good stead later in life.

In August 1974 Lerato suddenly died of pneumonia at the age of two
and a half months, barely a month after my departure. It was a
tremendous blow with which I had difficulty dealing. The loss of
one's child is a loss of part of oneself. It inflicts an intensely intimate
and personal pain, particularly when it happens without warning,
and you are not even there to share the last moments or, indeed, try
to prevent the death. Lerato's death left me feeling cheated, but also
guilty at having left her at such a tender age with my mother.

I remember the telegram which came bearing the news. A colleague at Mt Coke Hospital left it in my room for me to read without
any warning. I could not believe it, and had to be restrained in my
screams of denial. I was taken by Malusi Mpumlwana to Ginsberg to
Steve's home to share my grief with him as the father of my child,
and to make arrangements to go to Pietersburg for the funeral.

I found little comfort in Steve's company, and felt deeply cheated
by fate in losing my first and only child. Although her conception
had only partly been planned, I had welcomed it, and she was a
source of great joy to me as the embodiment of an intense love affair,
as her name indeed signified. My pregnancy had been difficult, and
so the sense of appreciation and thanks for a normal, beautiful baby
had been immense. The disappointment at so brief an encounter
with motherhood was deep.

In my laments I kept repeating to Steve how unbearable and
unfair it was to lose the only person who belonged to me in a complete sense. Steve had to remind me in the end that Lerato was his
child also and that his pain was all the more unbearable because he
had been denied the opportunity to get to see and know her. Steve's
mother offered her comforting words in her own dignified way: 'We
cannot fight against what God has let happen; ours is to accept and

bear the pain.'

The aeroplane trip to Johannesburg in the company of Steve's elder brother Khaya was difficult. I kept hoping for the impossible – that I would discover it was all a mistake. But being met at the airport by some of my relatives put paid to such fantasies. We travelled together in a minibus with close relatives to Uitkyk where the funeral was to be held.

My mother was deeply affected by Lerato's death. She arrived a few hours after us, having been to fetch my daughter's body from the mortuary in Pietersburg. She felt she had failed me, but from all accounts she did what was humanly possible when Lerato developed a respiratory infection, but was limited by the poor state of health-care services in rural South Africa. Lerato died from lack of high-level care, ironically at the same hospital where her mother was born in 1947. There was no doctor available at the time of her admission, and the nurses on duty were not trained to handle emergencies such as those presented by severe respiratory illness in babies.

The tiny white coffin which contained her body looked so pure and innocent, but represented a barrier to my urge to cuddle her. I derived little comfort from suggestions from relatives that she was too pure to settle in this sinful world. Her beautiful face looked peaceful, but distant. Steve, being banned at the time, could not share the funeral rites with me, but his brother Khaya was with me to represent him. The wound of this loss remains to this day. It is covered by a thin scar, given to bleeding at the slightest scratch. And there have been many excruciating scratches.

# 5

# Community Life
# in King

Steve Biko became the central focus of a new community of activists in King which gradually grew stronger from the time of his banning order at the beginning of 1973. The community was a product of his qualities as a leader, and was also an essential survival strategy for him to deal with the potentially devastating impact of the banning order, which was expressly intended to isolate activists and consequently render them impotent.

The quality of life of people under banning orders depended on a number of factors. Firstly, the temperament of the local security police was a crucial determinant of the kind of surveillance under which one was placed. The more vindictive and aggressive they were, the more stringent and unpleasant the surveillance, and consequently the worse life would become for the person and his or her family.

Some areas of the country, notably Port Elizabeth and Johannesburg, were notorious as areas of high surveillance. The security police harassed people and their families in the most outrageous ways. Personal privacy was violated by constant searches often made without search warrants, and general nastiness was the hallmark of these security swoops.

Car registration numbers of visitors were noted down and their owners threatened with arrest if ever seen again visiting the banned person. Telephones were tapped as a matter of routine, and mail was monitored and tampered with, often with serious consequences, as when letter bombs were planted to kill political activists. The Port Elizabeth security police developed the reputation of being the most extreme harassers. They made Barney Pityana's life an absolute misery, and eventually drove him and his family into exile in 1978.

Then again, the more gainfully employed one could be, the less likely one was to be isolated and frustrated by one's banning order.

The space for gainful employment itself depended on one's professional skills, the employment prospects in the area of restriction, and the willingness of employers to resist security police pressure not to employ a banned person. The people worst hit were those whose professions involved teaching or depended on government employment, such as nurses and social workers. Mrs Winnie Mandela, banned for many years during the 1960s, and then banished to Brandfort in 1977, endured frustrations in this regard because she could not practise as a social worker. Many teachers left the country in the sixties and seventies for want of employment.

The support one derived from the local community was also vital for survival. The success of the security police's surveillance depended to a large extent on their ability to engage an army of informers who would keep watch over one's every move. Neighbours were a particularly valuable resource for the police, and many succumbed to enormous pressure to act as informers. When neighbours refused to cooperate, the security policemen had to take turns positioning themselves in the vicinity of the banned person's home, a less effective form of surveillance because of its higher profile.

Without doubt, the personality of the banned person made a lot of difference. The more determined and resourceful the individual, the least likely the security police were to hamper the person from leading a reasonably meaningful life under the circumstances. It was a game of nerves where the will of the banned person was pitted against that of his or her captors. The stress generated by living in a state of low-intensity warfare took its toll on many. From the point of view of the security police the desired outcome was for banned people to become their own gaolers and effectively lead isolated lives for fear of arrest for breaking banning orders. Sadly, many South Africans spent miserable years imprisoned in their own homes.

Steve was fortunate enough to be able to organise his life in King in a manner which permitted him a reasonable quality of life. All the factors I have mentioned worked in his favour, and he progressively neutralised attempts by the local security police to harass him. Charles Sebe, shot to death in 1991 on the orders of Oupa Gqozo, the military ruler of the Ciskei homeland, was a particularly nasty customer in his capacity as security policeman in 1973–4. He was rude and crude, and was used by the local white security policemen as a thorn in Steve's side. Charles Sebe would burst into Steve's mother's house, to which Steve was restricted, at odd hours of the day and night, and search for alleged visitors, even walking into Steve's mother's bedroom, from which he would be forcibly extracted by an angry Steve. On one occasion Sebe drew a firearm in the house and threatened to shoot Steve. In the end Steve warned the local security chief that unless Sebe be withdrawn from these missions, he could not guarantee what would happen under provocation. Fortunately, to everybody's relief, Charles Sebe was withdrawn. But other nasty cops, such as Warrant Officer Hattingh, remained a pain in every way.

As the community at King grew and developed, the transition was made from student activism to professional development work, which proved challenging for both Steve and me. The Black Community Programmes had been set up as the wing of the Black Consciousness Movement to give practical effect to the philosophy of black self-reliance, self-help, and liberation through development of the whole person. Bennie Khoapa, its Director, gave Steve the intellectual space and institutional support to develop programmes to give effect to this thrust. The Eastern Cape Regional Office of BCP as a consequence became a hive of activity.

I was able to keep in touch with developments from my nearby base at Mt Coke Hospital. I arranged to be picked up whenever it was necessary, and Malusi Mpumlwana, who became Steve's general assistant, would drive over to take me to and fro. I would help around the office and participate in all the social activities, which invariably ended late at night.

There was little evidence of a traditional church atmosphere in the disused Anglican Church building at 15 Leopold Street, where an office took shape. Mapetla Mohapi also set up the regional SASO office in the same premises, further expanding the range of activities conducted from the same address, to the great displeasure of the local security police. Student activists from Fort Hare and the Federal Theological Seminary in nearby Alice called regularly to enquire about new developments or to participate in community development projects.

At this address too, an increasing number of international and important national political figures called on Steve. These visits further angered the security police, whom we referred to as 'the system' (because for us they represented the system of oppression and repression). 'The system' tried in vain to catch Steve breaking his banning order. But we had developed an efficient early warning system, which frustrated them. In a desperate attempt to disrupt our work, they once broke into our office premises and destroyed files and damaged equipment. But there was no way of stopping us.

One of the international visitors who became interested in our work was Angela Mai, a German citizen of South African origin, who had inherited some money from her relatives which was frozen in South Africa. Over the years she used it to support good causes. She was alerted to the work of BCP by Dr Beyers Naudé, the Director of the Christian Institute. She became interested in supporting a proposal to set up a community health centre in one of the villages near King, and agreed to give the R20 000 estimated as the cost of setting up the centre.

I was asked to help set up and head this centre, which was to be built in Zinyoka, ten kilometres outside King. I was absolutely thrilled. Here was an opportunity to work formally in an environment where I could live out my commitment to the process of liberation, and also work with Steve. But I did not bargain for the difficulties ahead of me.

None of us had any knowledge about setting up a community health centre. I did not have the slightest idea where one ordered medical supplies, or what quantities would be required, or what the costs would be. So I had to visit medical colleagues who were in private practice in the area to enquire. Some were friendly and helpful, but others possibly saw me as a potential future competitor and were cold.

I became increasingly frustrated by the high expectations my activist colleagues had of me, and their unhelpfulness in crucial areas where I needed assistance, such as having ready transport to important meetings or coping with numerous telephone calls. Steve expressed concern about my growing impatience and urged me to relax a bit more. I did not think that he understood how heavily the responsibility of setting up the centre weighed on me.

My colleagues at Mt Coke also became concerned about my frequent absences from the hospital. I did the barest minimum of work to honour my contractual obligations as a medical officer. I even stopped playing bridge with my colleagues, an activity I had come to enjoy during my employment at Mt Coke. Dr Mzimba, who was the leading light in the bridge club, taught me the game, but in the end I was beating him because of the utter recklessness of my opening bids, which unnerved my opponents. Once I gave up playing I missed the fun, but had greater challenges to attend to.

The security police must have complained to the Mt Coke superintendent, Dr Adendorf, a gentle old man, about my association with 'bad elements' at 15 Leopold Street. Dr Adendorf called me to his office, and adopted a fatherly tone, urging me to be careful about the company I kept. I thanked him for his concern, but indicated that I knew what I was doing.

The changed circumstances in the growing community of activists in King, and the stressful conditions under which I worked to get the health centre up and running by the beginning of 1975, put considerable stress on my relationship with Steve. I became increasingly frustrated by his unavailability, and became demanding and irritable. Steve remained fairly inattentive. It was unbearable.

On one occasion, three weeks after I bought my first car, a maroon VW Beetle, I got so angry at Steve's lack of attention that I decided to drive off from a party in Ginsberg Township to Nohle Mohapi's house in Zwelitsha Township, where I spent the night. After breakfast the following morning, I drove to Mt Coke Hospital. I must have been driving at about 50 km/hour on a gravel road outside Zwelitsha when I heard the sound of a bus behind me. I tried to adjust the mirror to see the traffic behind me, but just at that point the car swerved slightly off the road. I panicked and turned the wheel abruptly whilst slamming on the brakes. That was it. The car overturned, and I found myself having to leave the car through the broken rear windscreen. I could not believe the suddenness of the accident, and the extent of the damage to my new car!

An acquaintance stopped soon after and gave me a lift back to Nohle's and notified Steve. There was no sign of serious injury – I had a few bruises only. After arranging for the car to be towed away I fell asleep. I woke up after an hour or two in absolute agony. I was convinced that I had broken my back and that I was going to be paralysed. I became hysterical. I was then taken to Mt Coke Hospital and admitted. The doctors sedated me, and each time I woke up I would ask about my imminent paralysis.

Steve could not come to visit me because Mt Coke was outside his area of restriction. This increased my distress, particularly as I blamed him for having created in part the circumstances which had led to my accident. I was very angry with him. It took a long discussion afterwards for us to make up. He reassured me of his love for me, but indicated that the triangular relationship and his growing national profile were bound to continue to constrain our ability to give full expression to our relationship. There was a side of me which felt that he was not really trying, and that he might well be enjoying having the best of all worlds.

The pace of preparation for the health centre increased and I became more and more involved. Mr Flask, a local 'Coloured' builder, worked furiously to complete the clinic building before the end of 1974. Malusi suggested the name Zanempilo (Bringer of health) for the centre, a reflection of the idealism behind the project. Mr Flask was a gentle person who was obliging in every sense. He tried his best to satisfy our expectations, and did so at a very reasonable cost. As soon as some rooms became ready for use, we set them up. The stocking of the dispensary was the most demanding. We had to decant liquid medicine from the large containers into 50 ml, 100 ml and 200 ml bottles. We also had to count out tablets into twenties in dispensing envelopes. Without the assistance of the community of activists, we could not have managed.

Zanempilo Community Health Centre opened its doors to patients in January 1975. Staffing the centre was arranged before the end of 1974. I poached two of the best nursing sisters I had got to know from Mt Coke Hospital: Mrs Nontobeko Moletsane and Mrs Beauty Nongauza. They in turn recruited two junior nurses during the first few months in 1975 to make up the full complement of nursing staff. Two local women were also engaged, one as cook and the other as cleaner and washerwoman. Soon another woman was employed to help with the increasing load of cleaning work.

Zanempilo was a comprehensive health-care centre built on land which was owned by the Anglican Church and which it shared with an old parish church building that served the local village community of Zinyoka. The centre had an outpatient section where locals came with minor and major ailments, a maternity section with an antenatal clinic, a labour ward, a nursery, and a lie-in ward for post-delivery care. We also had a panel-van which served as both ambulance and mobile clinic for villages beyond walking distance from Zinyoka. The centre was open for emergencies for 24 hours, 7 days a week and 52 weeks of the year. I was on duty all the time for the first year of operation of Zanempilo: a tall order indeed.

It soon became quite clear that the staffroom which served as my initial accommodation was inadequate for my needs and those of the staff who had to be available for after-hours duty. Mr Flask agreed to build a staff house for an additional R4000. This turned out to be a very comfortable base for me. It had three bedrooms, a bathroom, and two living-rooms – quite a buy at R4000. The kitchen continued to be provided by the clinic building until much later on, when a kitchenette was added to the house. Mziwoxolo Ndzengu, a Ginsberg resident, joined us as an ambulance driver and also came to stay in the staff house. His retiring, reliable and loyal nature made it easy for each of us to maintain our privacy under the same roof. Much later, in 1976, a nurses' home was added to cater for the needs of nurses on overnight duty as well as of an increasing number of nurses coming from outside King who needed accommodation.

It became plain from early on that there had been a serious underestimation of the cost of running such a service, but it was difficult to find willing sponsors. Most of those approached indicated their preference for funding capital and not running costs – a real dilemma for development workers. What is the point of building structures and not supporting their operations? We had to endure many hardships on this score. My salary was about R600 a month, hardly adequate to support myself and to help my mother. But, to add to the hardships, we were also not always paid in time because of the shortage of funds. It was hard for the nurses, who had even fewer resources to fall back on and had more family commitments.

The South African Council of Churches under John Rees became the major channel for development funding. But the Joint Screening Committee of the SACC, established to assess project funding proposals and requests, proved a major stumbling block to new ventures seeking funding. It played the unfortunate role of gatekeeper for international aid. The fact that our project was black-led and black-run did not always sit comfortably with some of the leading figures in the funding world. They expected the project to fail either because of incompetence of the staff or because of repression from 'the system'. But after Bennie Khoapa put pressure on the SACC, Zanempilo secured funding, to the relief of all concerned.

As the work of Zanempilo grew, my incompetence in Xhosa became a major embarrassment. I used to rely on nurses to interpret for me in my consultations. One day after about three months of working in this manner, I decided to take the plunge and launched into the language. It was difficult for me coming from a Sesotho background to master the clicks and nuances of the Xhosa language. But village Xhosa with its *hlonipha* taboo (the respectful language register women use to avoid saying their male in-laws' names or any syllable appearing in those names) added to the challenge. My activist colleagues were not helpful, because we tended to follow the path of least resistance, speaking English as the common language.

I made my intention to learn Xhosa known to some of the influential old women. I pointed out the advantages of direct communication for all of us. They were delighted that their *Mosothokazi* (Sotho woman) was going to learn the local language. The process of becoming pupil to village women was mutually beneficial beyond the level of language. We developed respect for each other as they were put in a position of authority over me, being experts in something in which I was incompetent. The medical expertise I brought into the relationship could then be seen in a less mystified light: doctors do not know everything. I was also drawn into a closer human relationship with the women of Zinyoka. They referred to me as *Iramram* (the delicate one, a reference to my small physical frame).

Zanempilo became the meeting place for activists in the Eastern Cape. It was also a haven for Steve where he could meet visitors away from the vigilant eyes of 'the system'. It took 'the system' a while to overcome their reverence for the medical profession and the respect they had for a place of healing. Once that 'ethical boundary' was overcome they became quite outrageous in walking around the health centre, and had to be physically restrained in some cases from entering the labour ward with a delivery in process. We had fierce arguments about their lack of respect for the dignity of the patients.

One of the early visitors who came to Zanempilo was Donald Woods. Steve's political instincts led him to ask me to go and see Donald, then editor of the East London *Daily Dispatch*, with a view to getting Donald to visit him. Steve had in mind exploring a collaborative relationship for the benefit of the Black Consciousness Movement (BCM). Donald Woods was at that time an honorary president of NUSAS and had publicly declared his opposition to what he saw as the separatist politics of the BCM. I drove to East London, having made an appointment to see him. I was shown into his large office where he was seated behind an impressive desk.

Donald is a big man with a penetrating look and a smile which shines from the heart. He welcomed me and asked in his Transkei Xhosa what he could do for me. I told him that we were concerned about the fact that newspapers such as the *Dispatch* gave enormous publicity to homeland leaders like Buthelezi and Matanzima but none to those opposing the system from a radical perspective. He demanded to know who the leaders of this radical movement were. I then told him about Steve and the philosophical approach of the BCM. He showed genuine interest and I invited him to King to meet Steve. He responded positively and promptly.

Later I was rather taken aback when I read Donald's book *Asking for Trouble* and found his recollection of our first meeting to be radically different from mine. His account is of a petite and cheeky young woman who burst into his office demanding to see him, and firing questions about his neglect of leaders such as Steve in favour of the Buthelezis of the day. I can only surmise that he must have been disorientated by the shock of meeting for the first time an African woman doctor who was young and self-confident. He must have anticipated the worst.

Not only did the meetings Donald subsequently had with Steve lead to greater publicity for the BCM, but Steve also began to write a regular column under Mapetla Mohapi's name, to bypass his restriction orders. These columns explored current affairs and offered a perspective which had been lacking in the media until then. Donald also asked Steve to identify young blacks who could be trained as journalists. Thenjiwe Mthintso became employed by the *Daily Dispatch* under this scheme. Our relationship with both the newspaper and the Woods family grew with time.

Donald Woods apart, the flow of visitors to Zanempilo included people who came to see the novel idea of a comprehensive community centre run by activists. These visits also exposed us to potential funders. The positive aspect of this flow of human traffic for those of us working at Zanempilo was the excitement of sharing ideas away from the demands of attending to the sick and poor. It lifted one's spirit and enabled one to keep the perspective of being part of something larger than the daily chores.

We established the routine of holding monthly regional staff meetings at which all heads of divisions within the Eastern Cape Black Community Programmes reported on their work and received constructive criticism and suggestions. The Eastern Cape region grew rapidly under Steve's leadership. It had a Transkei office in Umtata, headed by Mrs Ndamse, which specialised in the establishment of self-help sewing and knitting groups amongst rural women. Mrs Ndamse's previous involvement with the Young Women's Christian Association (YWCA) and Zenzele put her in a strong position to head this section of the work.

The King activities included Research and Publication, headed by Malusi Mpumlwana, who worked with Thoko Mbanjwa, later to become his wife. It was responsible for the preparation of all BCP publications, and was closely directed by Steve, whose name could not be openly associated with the publications in view of his banning order. Thus Malusi's operation was legally based in Durban under Bennie Khoapa but in practice it was physically and intellectually located in King.

Later Mxolisi Mvovo, Nobandile's husband, came to head the sales division of our rapidly growing home industries. He also took charge of Njwaxa Home Industry, which was started by Fr Timothy Stanton, a Community of the Resurrection priest, who was based in Alice at the Federal Theological Seminary. Fr Stanton had been moved by the extreme poverty of the people in the villages surrounding Alice, and had induced some British parishioners to help finance a home industry producing leather purses and tobacco pouches. This industry grew under the joint direction of Mxolisi and Voti Samela, a qualified leather artisan, producing belts, handbags, horse saddles, nail bags and, later, sandals and shoes. The load of orders became such that some of the women in Zinyoka, whom we had identified as needy on the basis of their children's nutritional status, were organised into a piece-job group as part of Njwaxa Home Industry to do the finishing-up tasks.

In 1977 the thriving Njwaxa Home Industry moved from its humble premises in a mud house to a well-constructed and well-equipped corrugated-iron factory, financed by ICCO, a Dutch church group which funded development work. It supplied small and large clients all over the Eastern Cape and farther afield, even as far as Durban.

Our own work at Zanempilo grew from small numbers to a brisk flow of people from the village of Zinyoka as well as from more distant villages where we offered mobile clinic services. The majority had minor problems, but the few with major problems were referred to local hospitals, especially Mt Coke, from which I continued to receive support from my former colleagues. Our ambulance service also became active in meeting the needs of villagers lacking transport to reach medical help. This service was particularly welcomed by expectant mothers and their families. We did most of the normal deliveries at the clinic and referred difficult cases to hospital.

I remember three particularly traumatic fatalities which resulted from lack of experience and poor judgement on my part. Contrary to conventional views, doctors don't bury their mistakes easily, if at all. They remain with one throughout one's life. The first was a neonatal death after a difficult breech delivery in a teenage mother, Mamoswazi's daughter, who should have been referred to hospital in the first instance before labour advanced. But I was too inexperienced to know better.

The second case was that of a young woman who died of a hypersensitivity reaction to penicillin after receiving oral treatment for tonsillitis. We had omitted to ask her if she was sensitive. There is a risk attached to high-volume primary health work where health workers are under pressure to attend to long queues of people. We learned the hard way not to neglect the basics.

The third was the worst of all. Bukelwa Biko, Steve's elder sister, then a nurse at Fort Beaufort Mental Hospital, came to see me during the course of August 1975 with what she believed was cardiac pain from coronary problems. She had been having chest pains for a few days which had not responded to simple analgesics. I dismissed her concerns. After all she was an African woman, thirty-three years old with no family history of heart disease. How could she think of such a diagnosis? I reassured her, sedated her, and sent her home to rest at her mother's house in Ginsberg. She collapsed and died the following morning. I could not forgive myself. How could I have ignored her long history of cigarette smoking and use of the contraceptive pill after the birth of her only child in 1963? There was no way of explaining away my guilt or of comforting the family in their distress. I felt I had betrayed the trust Bukelwa and her family had placed in me.

But there were also joyous moments. A woman who had failed to conceive after two years of marriage came to seek help. On examination I discovered she was still a virgin. I shyly enquired how she and her husband conducted their intimate relations. She acknowledged she had suspected that all was not well with what they were doing, but feared being critical of her husband. It was thus left to me to discuss the simple solution with the husband. A few months later, the delighted woman came in to show off the evidence of my successful intervention.

We also became popular with local civil servants and other professionals who preferred our care to the impersonal service they received from many of the local hospitals and general practitioners. We charged fees on a progressive scale, and also benefited from the higher rates we could charge the few who had access to medical aid. Thus there was some redistribution of limited resources within the community.

In addition to my medical responsibilities I had to take over the directorship of BCP in the Eastern Cape from Steve when his banning order was further tightened in the first half of 1976. It was a blow which he took in characteristic style. I was simply told by Bennie and Steve that as the second most senior staff member in the Eastern Cape I would have to run the regional office. There was no formal induction – I just had to learn as I went along.

My dual responsibilities increased my burdens, but also accelerated my growth as a person. I had to develop skills managing time to enable me to balance the many and often conflicting demands placed on me. I spent the mornings at Zanempilo attending to patients and other responsibilities. Afternoons were set aside for administrative duties at 15 Leopold Street and attending to staff members who reported to me. I also made time to visit projects in other parts of the Eastern Cape, a responsibility Steve had not been able to discharge because of his restriction orders. A visit to Umtata in March 1977 was the most memorable. Here, in the first 'independent homeland', I had to deal with Mrs Nobantu Ndamse, whose late husband had been a homeland politician; she herself was quite favourably disposed to the benefits of 'independence'. This was to be a source of tension between Mrs Ndamse and me later. But it was interesting to see how the elite in Umtata benefited from 'independence' whilst the lot of the poor at best remained unchanged and in most cases worsened.

As part of my new job I had to set aside time to receive visitors and do some public relations work for BCP. Potential funders had to be entertained, and Steve was enormously supportive in imparting some of the skills of communication appropriate to the task. He sat in on a number of discussions with sponsors and important parties, in spite of the prohibitions of his banning order. He could rely on the elaborate early-warning protective system developed by the community around him.

I was also compelled to be more focused, disciplined and goal-directed in my daily activities in order to accomplish as much as possible in the limited time available – a training which has stood me in good stead since then. I became increasingly adept at scheduling my daily activities and not being distracted until I had completed set tasks. The risk of rigidity and impatience with those otherwise inclined was a constant concern. Malusi, who could never keep time or hurry himself to do anything, was a particularly difficult customer to deal with. He was, and still is, disarmingly charming, and would soothe my ruffled feathers with an engaging smile.

The closely knit community life which emerged over time also provided an outlet and focus for social life. We used to play card games, particularly casino, drink beer, organise braais (barbeques), dance, and engage in ordinary activities which made for a good time. Soon people from the surrounding areas, particularly from Ginsberg Township, started joining in, with mixed outcomes.

The negative outcomes were many. Firstly, the already stretched budget of the clinic took strain from the regular demands of feeding uninvited guests. I used to become upset when some people literally camped out at the centre for an entire weekend, expecting to share breakfast, lunch and supper with those of us living there. Meat and drinks were purchased from people's own pockets, but there were some who were less generous and managed to contribute little. Steve and I used to share our frustrations around this problem, but found no solution except the occasional joking remark. Steve would try to shame non-contributors into mending their ways, though this had limited success.

Steve also had to bear the brunt of the transformation of his mother's house into 'a people's home'. Everybody and anybody felt free to call at Mamcete's* any time of the day, and expect to be fed and, if need be, accommodated. Mamcete used to cook samp and beans in a large pot and prepared enough gravy to feed the multitudes. She was a very good cook, and her bread and scones were legendary. We would descend on them as they came out of the oven until we were stuffed. But that all came at a cost which few visitors bothered about.

Then again, the continual festivities did not make for a healthy

---

* Steve's mother's clan name, by which she is fondly known.

lifestyle. Too many late nights and too much alcohol are not good for anybody, but their impact on those on 24-hour duty like myself was considerable. I used to resent the inconsiderate noise from the late-night parties which disturbed my sleep. In some cases I would simply have to join in because my complaints went unheeded.

Steve also suffered from the late nights, but once he got going it became difficult to get him to stop. And for as long as he kept going, all the admiring activists stayed on. He had difficulty waking up after such punishing partying. I remember many frustrating mornings when I would plead, cajole and sometimes cry from utter frustration, trying to get him up for an important appointment. He would open one eye and disarmingly say, 'Just now, Toto – just now.' ('Toto' was an endearing term he used for those he loved.) 'Just now' often extended to half an hour.

But living in community robs one of the pleasures of privacy. Members of our community and other 'hangers-on' felt free to come and go as they pleased, and to use Zanempilo resources and facilities ad lib. It was most frustrating for me to try and balance my professional responsibilities with the expectations of members of the community. Some of them soon came to regard me as a difficult person who spoiled their fun. I often yearned for the opportunity just to curl up in bed undisturbed for hours on end.

We also hosted many out-of-town activists who came to visit and, occasionally, to relieve me in my onerous tasks. Dr Dubs Msauli, a general practitioner from Mdantsane Township in East London, also a member of our regional BCP board, was a real help to me. He would come on a Saturday afternoon and be on call for the rest of the weekend, thereby enabling me to take a break from the health centre. In 1976, the burden of work became so intolerable for me that Dr Seolo Solombela joined me as an additional medical officer.

Seolo was a lovely person to work with, but it took him time to fit into the community. He was rather traditional in his views about the place of women in society, and had a hard time coming to terms with my position in the community, both as his boss and in terms of my participation in what he regarded as manly activities. For example, he took a dim view of my joining in the eating of the sheep heads after braais. I made it clear he had a choice between sharing with me or distancing himself from this violation of tradition by abstaining and preserving his honour as a man. He followed his best interests. Community life in King grew more complex with the arrival of new members and the intensification of the activism. There are interesting similarities and differences between religious and activist communities such as we established in King. In some ways political activism is a form of religion. For one thing, as in the case of religious conviction, political activists are moved by something larger than themselves – a belief in a future which might be better than the present, a desire to be engaged in the establishment of a better order, and compassion for the underdog. Secondly, they share a sense of fellowship with others who are similarly committed. The need for renewing such fellowship in ritualised meetings – church services or political gatherings of the faithful – is also a common feature. At these ritualised meetings one renews one's commitment to the vows taken earlier. The repetition of political slogans and the singing of liberation songs also serve to cement the bonds of fellowship, much in the same way that the Creed serves to bind together Christians in the re-affirmation of their faith.

Then again, there is a common desire of individual members of such communities to conform to the group. The more fundamentalist the tendency, and the more insecure the community feels, the more likely that conformity will be enforced. The repressive climate created by the security police also put demands on activists to conform to certain behaviour so as to minimise security risks.

One can also say that both religious and political activist communities tend to operate on a model of overt leadership, be it a superior, bishop, guru or political leader. The risk of a personality cult developing is extremely high in both cases. The more insecure and fundamentalist the tendency of the community, the higher this risk becomes.

Finally, the willingness of individuals to sacrifice or subordinate their personal ambitions or goals for the sake of the group is also a notable similarity. This tendency is often closely tied to a willingness to engage in communal sacrificial acts, either symbolic or involving actual physical violence. Such sacrificial violence is sometimes justified as an important and necessary act to contain communal violence by focusing it on a sacrificial victim.* Some of the most gruesome necklace murders[†] committed by political activists in the 1980s involved the sacrificial death of fellow activists suspected of disloyalty. The symbolic purification of the community by fire has signifi-

---

* See René Girard on *Violence and the Sacred*  (Baltimore, 1992).

† Killing a victim by setting alight a motor-car tyre filled with petrol, which is placed around the person's neck.

cant psychosocial implications. Religious fundamentalists are also known to engage in sacrificial violence, both directed at the self, as in the Waco case in Texas in 1993, or directed at others, as in the case of 'holy wars' or crusades aimed at settling political scores.

There are, however, some important differences between the two kinds of community. In the first place, religious communities suffer less from the burden of personal responsibility for their own and other people's redemption. The belief in a force superior to humans helps to keep a measure of humility about personal abilities within religious communities. Activists who are non-believers are entirely on their own on this score – a huge historical burden for anybody to carry.

In the second place, there is a greater recognition in religious communities of the need for renewal and recharging one's batteries than in activist circles. Most, if not all, religious communities prescribe a time for reflection and formal periods of retreat from daily activities. In most cases one also has to have a confessor or counsellor to guide one's spiritual growth. Activist communities, whilst recognising the importance of recharging batteries, often feel that they cannot afford to allow sorely needed individuals time out. Burn-out is a likely and common outcome.

Burn-out becomes an even bigger problem for leaders who often lose perspective on the source and nature of their problems, and become more and more driven to accomplish set goals. It is under such circumstances that tyranny takes root as subordinates are driven beyond the bounds of their human capacities. A vicious cycle set in motion by the self-sacrificial leader's increasing demands for respect and loyalty, and sustained by the fear or unwillingness of subordinates to question the leader's judgements, often lies behind the tragic degeneration of liberation movements into vehicles of human rights abuses. Fundamentalist religious groups are also vulnerable to these abuses.

Our King community had elements of both the good and the bad. Most of us came from Christian homes and had a religious basis for our political commitment. But few, if any, of us were practising Christians; in fact some of us, including myself, actively distanced ourselves from the church, for we saw it as having failed to proclaim the good news to the poor and to fight for the liberation of the oppressed. The church in South Africa was divided into three segments: those supporting apartheid, those passively accepting the established order, and a small segment which opposed apartheid actively. We had to rely mainly on our own resources for personal development.

The best-placed activists in many historical settings seem to be those who combine a spiritual and a political base. They are able to draw on the strengths of the two commitments, which are mutually reinforcing. One could in fact go as far as saying that it is not possible to be truly spiritual if one has no real concern for the oppressed and downtrodden people of the world in which one lives. Thomas Merton, Martin Luther King, Sister Theresa and Desmond Tutu are a few examples of people whose spiritual growth has been related to their personal responses to the circumstances of their time and place.

There was a healthy custom of vigorous debate within our community which worked against the tendency towards conformity. Mapetla Mohapi often had more radical views on many issues, and would engage Steve and Malusi in long discussions. These discussions intensified after his change of jobs towards the end of 1975 from being a SASO regional organiser to becoming the executive director of Zimele Trust, which focused on self-help projects for ex-political prisoners. Mapetla's exposure to the despair of ex-political prisoners, the divisions amongst them, and their inability to work together in groups for the common good, made him less starry-eyed about the notion of black solidarity on which we pinned so much of our hopes for the process of liberation. He also had important points to make about the need for more radical strategies beyond simply conscientising the oppressed to challenge their oppressors. There had to be a more directed programme of resistance which went beyond individual defiance of the 'system'. Even to discuss such directed resistance, a metaphor for the armed struggle, was of course a high risk in view of the vigilance of the 'system'. Mapetla had a sharp wit and nerves of steel underneath his casual exterior.

Contact with those people working for the Border Council of Churches (BCC), a regional body affiliated to the SACC, kept us alive to the importance of valuing different strategies to address the problems of development in our country. Mr Temba Sibeko, then Director of BCC, was an older man with a very different approach to life. He was nonetheless supportive of our work, and resisted security police pressure to inform on us. We often made fun of Mr Sibeko's peculiarities: his driving style (hunched ridiculously right up against the steering wheel), his manner of speaking which would often lead him to laugh at his own jokes though they escaped the rest of us, and his ineffectual leadership. Steve was very sensitive about our mischief-making at Mr Sibeko's expense, and would call us to order.

The openness to internal debates helped to develop leadership amongst younger members of the community. Steve was a very supportive leader. He enabled people to go beyond the limits they placed on their own capacity and agency. In fact, in certain cases one could say that some people were promoted beyond their level of competence, simply because with Steve about they had the self-confidence to do things they could not otherwise do. Some of those unfortunate people could not sustain the momentum of action at the same level once the support system came apart.

The risk of a cult of personality developing around the leader of our community remained high. Steve did not seek it, but it was in fact imposed on him by people who needed the security of a visibly strong leader. It would also have taken a superhuman to remain unaffected by the open admiration of friend and foe for the positive impact of his ideas and their successful implementation in practical terms. The nature and scope of Steve's contribution to liberation politics in South Africa are all the more remarkable given the constraints of the banning orders under which he operated. And Steve was not superhuman.

The increasing local, national and international attention he received put him into an ever-brighter limelight. Local activists became more and more conscious of the privilege of basking in this glory. 'The Son of Man' label which was attached to him, though it started off as a joke, assumed an aura imbued with symbolism. He became over time surrounded by admiring hangers-on, with negative results for his lifestyle. Moreover he became more daring in breaking his banning orders, reassured by a supportive and protective local populace.

Our own personal relationship took a dip and reached an all-time low. I was one of only a few people who challenged him on the recklessness of his lifestyle. He became impatient with my criticism. The stress of the triangular relationship was also taking its toll. I remember one particularly unpleasant confrontation between us in Mdantsane Township where we had gone in my car to visit Dubs Msauli. Steve would not hear of us going back to King, even though it was already past midnight. After failing to convince him to come along, I threatened to leave without him, and he dared me. Something in me snapped. I took my keys from him, asked those ready to leave to come along, got into the car and drove away. I was furious. Steve had to phone Thenjiwe in King to pick him up later that morning.

He could not forgive me for carrying out my threat. For weeks afterwards we suspended our love relationship and came together as fellow activists with a job to do – a capacity we perfected over the years in our difficult relationship. We were able to switch the focus of our relationship between collegiality, friendship and a love affair. Its multi-layered and multi-faceted nature ensured its resilience.

Like many popular idealistic leaders in history, Steve did not escape the folly of admiring available women at every turn. After all, even pastors such as Martin Luther King and presidents such as J. F. Kennedy have fallen prey to the comfort of adoring women, as well as the exhilaration of unlimited access to their attentions. It must be a welcome break from the tough political battles these leaders have to contend with. There must also be some need to make good the self-sacrificial life which comes with political commitment, often early on in one's life, robbing one of the carefree pleasures of youth. Steve had affairs with women on the BCP staff, within the broader community of activists, and outside. Most of these were fleeting affairs with women who enjoyed the reflected glory of an important man.

I remained blissfully unaware of these escapades, and was there-fore saved the added pain. I felt a mixture of revulsion and empathy for Steve when he confessed to me, at the end of 1976, when we both decided to confront the unsatisfactory state of our relationship. My lack of awareness up to that point was in part due to my extraordi-nary work-load and my lack of enthusiasm for the endless parties where these affairs blossomed. It also had to do with my own over-confidence in the indestructibility of our relationship. This had sur-vived many storms, and had so many dimensions that it could grow at the levels of pure friendship or collegiality even during the most difficult emotional periods when intimacy was impossible for weeks on end. But we both knew we were destined to end up together.

For their part the security police were determined to break us up and the King community for good. With the outbreak of the Soweto riots in June 1976 and the increasing restlessness of schoolchildren and

young activists all over the country, the security forces intensified
their repressive measures. Captain Schoeman, a tough vindictive cop
based in East London, virtually moved into the King security police
offices with a mission to discipline us and break our hold on the
region.

Mapetla Mohapi was the first to be detained under Section 6 of the
Terrorism Act in July 1976. He was suspected of involvement in
transporting youngsters across the border to Botswana. We later
came to understand that one of these young people was a security
police plant. Mapetla died in detention, allegedly from hanging himself with his jeans from the grille of the door of his cell in Kei Road
Police Station.

We were devastated. We refused to believe the story of suicide
which was supported by a note on tissue paper written to Captain
Schoeman (of all people). Why would one write a suicide note to
one's torturers and not to one's loved ones? Mapetla had been
resourceful and had only a day or so before his alleged suicide
smuggled a note on a strip of toilet paper to his wife Nohle, reassuring her of his ability to cope. We suspect that in spite of a later
Supreme Court finding, which accepted the suicide story, he was
throttled by his captors and then hung up when they realised they
had gone too far. I was asked to attend his postmortem examination
on behalf of the family. Fortunately, Dr Dubs Msauli also came along
and gave me much-needed moral support. It was one of the most
painful duties I had to carry out as an activist medical practitioner. It
is bad enough losing one's friend and colleague, but to stand by as
his body was being cut up was very traumatic.

To add insult to injury, I was detained on the late afternoon of 6
August 1976 as we were preparing to leave to bury Mapetla in
Sterkspruit, in the Aliwal North district. And so I was prevented
from taking proper leave of Mapetla – a double blow. I was one of
the first activists to be detained under the newly promulgated preventive detention clause of Section 10 of the Terrorism Act. So too
were Malusi and Mxolisi. I remember parting from them in the
reception area of the brand-new King Williamstown prison, convinced that we would be kept in detention until the day of liberation,
which we naïvely imagined as being around the corner. We had a
long way to go to 'around the corner'.

I had fortunately been advised by a visitor to Zanempilo, as I was
being led away by an impatient Captain Schoeman, to take a small

cuddly blanket I had bought to wrap myself with on the trip to Sterkspruit. That blanket became a constant companion during my detention, especially on the first night when I was still unsure about the cleanliness of the prison blankets. I had heard horror stories of lice-infested bedding, but I need not have worried. It was hard sleeping on the thin felt mat on a cold cement floor, but at least the blankets were clean. I remember my fury as I heard the convoy of buses drive past on their way to Sterkspruit. Mapetla was no more.

It was a matter of a day or two before I identified a helpful-looking black woman warder who lived in Ginsberg Township to help me communicate with the outside world. She brought me newspapers, cigarettes and messages from Steve. Steve reassured me that he had briefed a lawyer, Mr Griffiths Mxenge, to look after us in detention. The warder remained a lifeline keeping detainees informed on what was happening outside, until she was trapped by her white colleagues, and later charged and dismissed from her job.

Subsequent police swoops netted Steve and Thenjiwe Mtintso, Seolo Solombela, Thoko Mbanjwa, Pumla Sangotsha, Nobandile Mvovo and many other activists across the country. Replacements had to be found to keep vital services and projects going, and in some cases the very replacements would be detained promptly in a determined effort to bring all our efforts to a standstill. Thenjiwe and Steve were held under the dreaded Section 6 of the Terrorism Act, a clause that licensed torture to extract information. The majority were held in preventive detention. Some were beaten on their way to prison by vindictive policemen bent on getting their own back by assaulting the 'cheeky Bantus' who had outsmarted them at every turn in their surveillance.

Though I had started off alone in the women's section for about ten days, more detainees came in during the following nights. I remember hearing the heavy metal gates open and then becoming aware of voices, which I strained to recognise. After the warders had gone I would shout or make audible noises in an effort to establish contact with the new arrival. After two weeks of this trickle, we requested and were granted permission to share a common cell. We were thrilled.

Our communal cell did not have a toilet but we had access to one during working hours, by attracting the attention of the warders to let us in and out of the cell. We later learned to use this system to discipline the warders if they had been uncooperative. We would take turns – seven of us at one stage – in calling them. As soon as the warder had locked the cumbersome door, we would call her back to let the next person out. In the end they kept the door open throughout the day, locking us in only when they went off duty in the evenings.

The three warders who looked after us were different in both physical stature and personality. The eldest was an old unhappy woman who spoke with such a deep voice one would swear that it was a male voice. She neglected herself and was smelly and unpleasant. She used foul language and always invoked prison rules to turn down reasonable requests from prisoners. The regular prisoners called her 'Hodoshe', a Xhosa word for a large green fly.

The most senior of the three women was a mousy woman who was cold. She played the game by the rules and did not allow any friendliness to develop between herself and prisoners. In contrast, her other colleague was named 'NoNice' by us, because she was such a nice person. She engaged us in conversation whenever she had a chance to do so, and was generally helpful.

We had access to an exercise court yard where we walked around and enjoyed the sunshine for an hour or so each day. We took up yoga, learning from a book which was brought to us from the men's section. It belonged to Gibson Kente, a well-known playwright, who was unfortunate enough to be arrested in the vindictive swoop on anything black that moved in the Eastern Cape. Having brought his show *How Long* on tour to the Eastern Cape, he got caught in the crossfire. We loved yoga and some of us got quite good at it: head and shoulder stands, relaxation postures, and long stretches.

We were also allowed to order our own food on set days; it was bought with the rest of the prison supplies, and delivered to us individually – not a bad service, and a remarkable improvement from the first two weeks of prison food. Prison food has a bad reputation throughout the world, but in South Africa it was worse, because of the racial discrimination involved. Africans got the worst diet:

Breakfast: at about 7.30 a.m., a large tin mug of sweet black coffee and soft porridge with no milk.

Lunch: at 11 a.m., samp with no beans, and tomato-sauce colouring added to it. Sometimes there would be shredded stewed meat or vegetables.

Supper: between 4 and 5 p.m., soft porridge with beetroot, cabbage or a slice of bread swimming in it. It would on some occasions be served with vegetable soup which looked appetising, until one looked at the bottom of the mug and found carrot ends replete with soil.

Nobandile suggested that one should drink the otherwise tasty soup without looking at the contents of the mug, and be prepared to stop when one's tongue felt gravel! As at Bethesda Normal College, I could not bring myself to eat food which was an affront to my dignity. I spent the first ten days of detention living on diluted coffee in the mornings, and whatever I could rescue of the slice of bread before it drowned in the soft maizemeal porridge at supper-time. I lost weight rapidly. When I was released I weighed no more than fifty kilograms. But I was healthy because of the yoga exercises we did and the later dispensation which allowed us to buy our own food.

We soon established a thriving prison community, complete with an efficient system of communication with the men on the other side of the divide. We were allowed many privileges, including weekly visits from friends and family. We were grateful for small mercies and got used to the presence of policemen during visits. Occasionally, we would be fortunate to bump into a visitor as we were being shown to the glass cubicle. The treat of hugging someone from outside would be the talk of the week.

Fr Aelred Stubbs of the Community to the Resurrection, who used to visit us regularly at Zanempilo, was one of my notable visitors in prison. He brought me news of the detention of my youngest brother, Molepo, whom I had brought down to King to stay with me in December 1975. I was incensed! He was only fourteen years old, and had gone to live at Steve's home under Mamcete's care after my detention. How could any adult stoop so low as to detain such a young person? I raised hell with the prison authorities. They initially denied that any minors were being held in prison. I remember one of the better-behaved warders, NoNice, whose husband was deputy chief of the prison, assured me that she had been given his word of honour that they did not have fourteen-year-olds in the prison. She added confidently: 'And I can assure you, Dr Ramphele, my husband never lies to me.' I told her I had news for her, and that she might just as well brace herself for her husband's first lie. Armed with hard facts from our good 'prison telegraph system', I insisted that they produce him.

Molepo appeared at the visitor's window uncombed and

unwashed. He had been brutally assaulted by the security police, who initially held him and his friends, about five of them, in the local police cells. He told me that his legs were so swollen that he could not wear his pants for days. He also complained that they were all infested with lice. I demanded that he be seen by a medical doctor immediately, together with the others, and that they be deloused and given toiletries, for which I provided money from my deposit account at the prison. They were kept for a few more days, to let their injuries heal, before being released. They had been detained by Captain Schoeman in desperation after he had failed to find evidence to nail Steve during his detention. They were released soon after.

My sister Mashadi, then on a course at Baragwanath Hospital, came by train from Johannesburg to visit me in detention at about the time that Molepo was also imprisoned. It must have been a trying time for my family, particularly my mother. So many people were dying in detention that relatives had every reason to fear the worst when they got news of an arrest. Mashadi was relieved to find that our circumstances were relatively comfortable and could take comforting news back to my worried mother.

As detainees we spent hours playing card games and Monopoly to amuse ourselves in prison. We became quite addicted to the games we played, and in some cases people would have serious conflicts over cheating or losing games. It is remarkable how much institutionalised people regress in their behaviour. One easily lost perspective on the importance of things in one's life, and over-reacted to ridicule or teasing – a sign of increased vulnerability and insecurity. The excitement about food and other treats from outside, visitors and letters also reflected the increasing emotional deprivation.

But there were benefits as well from being forced to spend time away from the type of lifestyle we had established before detention. Although those of us who were smokers continued the habit, there was no alcohol for the entire four and a half months that we were out of circulation. Our bodies could be detoxified and regenerated. I had also benefited from the first ten days on my own. I needed time with myself after all the hectic months in the constant company of others. I had the opportunity to take a long hard look at myself in the solitude of my cell. There were some things I liked, but others I didn't.

I had been registered as a part-time student with the University of South Africa, a correspondence university, for a Bachelor of

Commerce degree since the beginning of 1975, but had made little headway because of my work and social circumstances. For the first time since my earlier university days, I enjoyed the time alone with my books, and consequently did extremely well in the final-year exam, which I wrote at a venue arranged by my gaolers. I gained a first-class pass and won a scholarship to continue my studies in 1977. That came in handy in the next few years as I pursued my goal of learning to understand the world of business management and administration.

Two or three weeks before our release in December 1976 a number of significant things happened. Firstly, we received a visit from the International Red Cross. They questioned us on our prison conditions, and must have been appalled to find us sleeping on thin felt mats on the cold concrete floors. A few days after their visit we were pleasantly surprised to get beds and linen, including pillows, which we had not touched for the last few months. There were also improvements in the quality of the food we were served.

In the second place, we got to know through our 'prison telegraph system' that Steve had been released from detention. Thenjiwe, who had received the worst treatment from the bully boys in the security forces, had joined us a week or so earlier. She was traumatised physically and emotionally. She had ended up in the Libode Police Station cells in the Transkei, after the security police were done with her, and was later brought to join us.

I remember my excitement at the thought of seeing Steve again after four months! I could not contain myself before his visit to me in prison. He had lost a considerable amount of weight – almost regaining his slender, youthful body which I associated with the beginning of our relationship. He looked devastatingly handsome and sent my heart into a mad spin. I was also fortunate to bump into him before he was shown into the glass cage, and could get a long-missed embrace.

Our release was swift once the process was initiated. It came as a welcome birthday present on 28 December 1976. We were all reunited at the gate of the prison and Steve organised transport to Zanempilo for a big celebration. Thenjiwe was the only unfortunate exception. She was taken straight to her mother's home in Orlando East Township, Johannesburg, where she was restricted under a banning order. Her absence put a damper on our celebration, but there was still a lot to celebrate: couples were reunited, lovers renewed intimacies suspended over the months, and the joy of just being able to walk about in the open or ride in a car was intoxicating. Two marriages were contracted within a day or so of our release: Malusi married Thoko, whilst Seolo Solombela and Pinkie tied the knot. The township community soon came to join in the festivities.

Steve and I had a long frank discussion at the earliest opportunity. He had also had time for reflection after he had deflected the heat of his interrogation, and had physically stopped Warrant Officer Hattingh from an attempt to assault him. He realised how much he had hurt me in a vain attempt to force me to sever our relationship, which was complicating his life both as a married man and as a national political leader. He was amazed at my lack of awareness of the many affairs he had had, which he claimed had been in part aimed at disgusting me and forcing a show-down. He acknowledged that he found me very challenging as a partner because of my strong personality and my insistence on certain basics, on which nobody else challenged him. He recognised how important this was as a braking mechanism in his life, and knew that uncritical admirers were a danger to him in the long term. He also knew that he could rely on my loyalty whatever happened. We renewed our commitment to each other, and agreed to work gracefully but speedily to resolve the triangular relationship.

He realised that one could not sustain a marriage on the basis of guilt about wrong decisions he had made in the choice of a partner. Attempts to protect his wife from the pain occasioned by his continued love for me had not been successful anyway: all three of us were constantly hurt by the tensions inherent in the triangular relationship. He had been criticised by his political colleagues for his unfaithfulness to his marriage vows, but he had made it clear to them that however much he had tried he could not conceive of a life without me. We shared not only a passionate love affair but also a commitment to the liberation of the oppressed in South Africa. Ours was a complete relationship in which we mutually nurtured our shared values. His dilemma was how to deal with Ntsiki, the mother of his two children without doing violence to her dignity. Solitary confinement gave him ample opportunity to reflect and realise that he could not continue to live a lie – he had to harmonise his life and publicly and formally commit himself to follow his heartfelt desire to share his life with me as his marriage partner. On his release he told me that he planned to institute divorce proceedings as soon as possible so that our relationship could be formalised before the end of 1977.

This was music to my ears. It vindicated my conviction that he and I were destined to share our lives more fully. But the continued hesitation on his part had begun to erode my trust in him. I came out of detention determined to force him to choose between his loyalty to his wife and his love for me. I was not going to perpetuate the untidy mess that our lives had become.

Our relationship reached new heights. The sense of comfort in belonging to each other was all-embracing. The song which had been silenced over the trying past months came alive. My heart danced for joy. This time we were not going to let anything stand in the way of our happiness together. We grew back into each other at all levels. Every day became a treat.

On the political front, however, thunder clouds began gathering. Captain Schoeman intensified his disruptive actions in the Eastern Cape. Surveillance on Steve increased. Schoeman brought many unsuccessful cases against Steve for breaking his banning order. In desperation he also began to add traffic offences to his list of charges, but they were thrown out one by one by the courts.

Schoeman charged youngsters in Ginsberg for arson committed at their school, Forbes Grant, and forced my brother Molepo and his friends to become state witnesses. The only strategy that would protect Molepo from perjuring himself by contradicting his confession obtained during detention was to invoke language as a delaying tactic. Molepo was too young to defy the courts and refuse to testify without risking imprisonment, a fate which befell one of his friends. I advised him to insist on a North Sotho interpreter before he would agree to testify in the Grahamstown Supreme Court. It was a tall order in a Xhosa-speaking area to find a suitable person. I was in fact the only one within the jurisdiction of the Grahamstown Supreme Court with the competence to assist the court, but I was not going to volunteer. In the end the frustrated security police had to ask for Molepo to be released, but not before threatening him. He was resolute, and I attended the hearing throughout to support him. The police were furious but powerless.

The security surveillance continued. The final blow came for me in April. I had received an uncharacteristic call from the security police offices in King asking me to present myself that afternoon. I smelled a rat. I phoned Steve and asked that we meet at 15 Leopold Street. No sooner had we arrived than Captain Schoeman came in with my banning order, which he suggested was as good as a warrant of arrest. He commanded me to follow him to his office. I refused. He then tried physically to force me, but Steve intervened and warned him to keep his hands off me.

Undaunted, Captain Schoeman radioed the regular South African Police, who were often in awe of the security police. South African policemen above a certain rank had the legal authority to arrest citizens without a warrant: they only needed to assert that they had reason to believe they were acting in the public interest. They wasted no time in dragging me out of my office and throwing me into the back of the police van, which they drove around at a hellish speed, intending to create maximum discomfort for me. I was thrown from one end of the van to the other until the sudden stop at the police station. My angry but feeble attempts to lay a charge of wrongful arrest and assault were laughed at by the policemen in the charge office.

A very satisfied Captain Schoeman came in a few minutes later and curtly ordered me to his office upstairs. He triumphantly read out the banning order he was serving on me. I was stunned! I was being restricted to the Naphuno district of Tzaneen in the northern Transvaal, an area I had never heard of before. I thought that there was an error somewhere. Indeed there was. My name had not been spelt correctly – a common occurrence. But I pinned my hopes on the identity number, which was clearly not mine. I was convinced that they must have confused me with someone else, whose home was in Naphuno. I pointed this out to Captain Schoeman; he simply asked me to indicate the corrections to him, and proceeded to alter the document accordingly, making a mockery of the legal requirement that the banning orders be given 'under the hand of the Minister', as the document piously proclaimed. He was to pay for this indiscretion.

As a desperate last-ditch measure I asked what was to happen to my responsibilities at the health centre and to my possessions? After all, I had a younger brother to make arrangements for, personal effects to pack, and patients and colleagues to take leave of. Schoeman would not hear of any such things. He said the police would take care of the packing and removal of my possessions. All I needed to do was to give them a list of the clothing I would require on the trip to Tzaneen, which was to start in an hour or so. I was outraged. How dare he imagine that I would let them get their paws on my personal effects! Schoeman replied that in that case I would have to leave as I was. His parting shot was: 'Well, Dr Ramphele, good-bye, you bitch!'

I sat in his office numbed by the events of the past few minutes. How could they send me to Naphuno? Where was I to stay there? How was I to manage without clothing on this long trip into the unknown? It is remarkable how much residual reasonableness one expects even from the worst of torturers and repressive regimes. I had not imagined that their desire to control and isolate would extend so far.

I was dressed in a full-length sleeveless cotton dress and a jersey which I had bought from our home industry in Umtata earlier that year; it had been caught in a nail at the door of our offices in Leopold Street as I was being dragged out that afternoon. I was also at the tail end of a menstrual period, and dreaded the prospect. I had a hand-bag in which I must have had less than five rand. Warrant Officer Hattingh, who was put in charge of my removal from King, also rel-ished what he saw as the final triumph over me. He implored me to accept their offer of packing some things for me from Zanempilo, but I held to my earlier view, hoping that they would relent and take me there. Indeed, Steve had driven to Zanempilo expecting that they would at least let me collect a few things, but it was not to be. Hattingh, whom we nicknamed Maxolo, a Xhosa reference to the scaly appearance of his neck, assured me that they would buy me cigarettes and food all the way. We finally left King at 4 p.m. Another policeman and his wife had been asked to accompany Hattingh and assist him in driving and policing.

The trip turned out to be one of longest in my life, both physical-ly and emotionally. The policemen engaged in light talk and tried to be as friendly as possible, but I was too preoccupied with my own thoughts to respond. We stopped overnight at Zastron, in the north-eastern Cape. It was bitterly cold. They put me in a police cell in the town, and went to a local hotel for the night. The policeman who was put in charge of me was appalled to learn that I had committed no crime, and was a medical doctor, and yet had been made to sleep on a concrete floor in a police cell. He promised to give me a liberal supply of new blankets, which he did, and to make me as comfort-able as I could be under the circumstances.

The rest of the trip the following morning was exhausting. Hattingh got lost and ended up on an even longer route than intended. Schoeman, who originally came from the northern Transvaal, had directed him to take the back route along the eastern part of the country, perhaps to avoid the main cities, where I could possibly be spotted by someone who knew me. If that had been the intention, then it was an impeccable route – completely unfamiliar to me. We arrived at Tzaneen Police Station around 10 p.m. I was smelly and exhausted from lack of washing and proper sleep.

Hattingh was about to repeat the previous night's performance of signing me into a police cell overnight. I flew into a rage, which was not difficult at that point, as I was at the end of my tether. I demanded to be taken where they had planned to take me. There was no way I was to sleep without a bath for one more night. Hattingh contacted the local security police, who came and formally took charge of me as a restricted person in their area of jurisdiction. I only then learnt that I was to be taken to Meetse-a-Bophelo (literally, Water of life) Hospital – an ironical name for a person in my circumstances and, as I was to learn later, also for the locals, who had been forcibly removed from the fertile Makgoba's Kloof area and brought to this arid land.

I was relieved to be finally delivered by the two black security policemen, after an hour-long bumpy ride on a gravel road, to Sister Thubakgale, who happened to have been a schoolmate of mine at Bethesda Normal College. She was shocked to see me there at that time, and under escort by security police. She was very helpful in promptly showing me to what was intended as my new home – a small flat in the nurses' home. She also got a former neighbour from Kranspoort Mission Station, where I grew up, to come to my new room to see me. Matsela Seko was very helpful; she lent me toiletries, nighties and, the following day, a dress to wear. After a long-awaited bath, I fell asleep.

# 6

# Surviving in
# a Wilderness

People often ask me how I could have survived under the conditions I had been subjected to in my life. The short answer is that if you are faced with adversity, you have no choice but to strive for survival. It is amazing what internal reserves come to the fore under stressful conditions – mostly reserves you did not even know you possessed until they are needed.

In his moving book *Man's Search for Meaning*, in which he shares his experiences of a Nazi concentration camp, Viktor Frankl eloquently discusses those things that make for survival on one hand, and those that condemn victims of abuse to an 'existential vacuum', a feeling of emptiness and meaninglessness, on the other. He points out that the most important survival strategy is to turn personal tragedy into triumph: 'even a helpless victim of a hopeless situation, facing a fate he cannot change, may rise above himself, may grow beyond himself, and by so doing, change himself. He may turn a personal tragedy into a triumph.'* I was to learn this the hard way.

My first thought when I woke up the morning after my arrival at Meetse-a-Bophelo Hospital was to make contact with Steve. I was quite sure that none of my colleagues knew where I had been taken to: Captain Schoeman would have made sure about that. I also needed clothing, toiletries and money whilst I sorted out what my next move would be. Above all I longed for the comfort of friends in my predicament.

I decided that my best bet would be to get to a church establishment, Anglican or Catholic, the two most likely in my view to be sympathetic to my plight. On asking, I was told that there was a community of the Sacred Heart Mission in Ofcolaco, near Trichardtsdal, some five kilometres away. I had no money, but armed with my only possessions, a banning order and my empty handbag, I set

* V. Frankl, *Man's Search for Meaning* (London, 1984), p. 147.

off in a taxi to Ofcolaco, promising the driver that I would ask the priests there to pay him the fare.

The first people I met at the mission were two African nuns, Sisters Mary-Theresa and Emily. Sister Mary-Theresa was the more forthcoming of the two. She knew what it meant to have been banned and understood my plight. Sister Mary-Theresa was a vivacious woman who had a gentle matronly manner. Sister Emily, the more retiring of the two, was less self-confident and tended to let Sister Mary-Theresa take the lead. Both wore traditional habits which revealed little of their physical attributes, but one could see that they were on the large side and had strong legs which carried them around the difficult terrain they worked in.

The nuns quickly responded when I asked to have the taxi man paid, even before they had heard my full story. I was then shown into the sitting-room where I proceeded to tell them how I had landed there. I showed them the banning order as evidence of my plight. For the first time since this ordeal had started, I permitted myself to cry. For a while I could not stop. They were tears of anger and self-pity.

Sister Mary-Theresa then went to call Fr Mooney, the priest-in-charge at the time. He listened sympathetically and agreed to put me up and allowed me to use the phone. When Steve's voice came on the line, I burst into tears, but calmed down after a while to give him the details of where I was. I also told him about the errors in the information on my banning order and how Schoeman had treated them. He promised to arrange for the things I needed to be brought to me as soon as possible, and to get a lawyer to come and assist me. He also gave me news of others who had been banned in the last few days, among them Mxolisi, his brother-in-law. Steve reassured me and asked me to remain calm.

A sense of relief descended on me after this call. I could now face the reality of my circumstances. At least people who mattered to me knew where I was. There is something frightening about being in 'non-space' – unknown and amongst people with whom one has no real contact. I experienced the frightening emptiness of it all during the two days whilst being transported to my place of banishment. Many narratives of ex-detainees and ex-prisoners attest to the same overwhelming sense of not feeling like a complete human being until one has made some contact with those to whom one is connected, those who in a sense define one's humanity. It is not surprising that solitary confinement is used as a mainstay of torture.

The ease with which Fr Mooney accepted me caused some of his colleagues a great deal of anxiety. How did he know that I was not a security police plant? They found my story an improbable one. How could I have been dumped in an unknown place? Even allowing for the cruelty of security police, banishment to unknown lands was not their usual weapon. They also were concerned that I looked too sophisticated to fit the bill of a desperate person. The borrowed dress I wore was a pretty, full-length floral outfit which more suited someone attending a dinner party than one stranded in the outback. It was also too much of a coincidence that I should make my appearance on the very day they were discussing how to respond as a community of priests to the growing political tension in the country.

Of the priests Fr Thomas Duane was the most vociferous in cautioning against my acceptance. Ironically Fr Duane later became my greatest friend and supporter. Fr Mooney's final position was that he was going to accept me at face value and would not turn a deaf ear to my plea for help. Should I turn out to be a fraud, that would be on my own conscience. Fr Mooney informed me that he would arrange for me to go and live with the two African nuns at Tickeyline Village, closer to Meetse-a-Bophelo Hospital where I had spent the previous night. He drove me in his open van to Meetse-a-Bophelo to fetch my only dress, which I had washed and left to dry at the hospital, and return Matsela Seko's borrowed dress. Matsela kindly gave me the set of toiletries she had lent me earlier, and we headed for Tickeyline.

Tickeyline is a poor village, hence the name derived from the 'tickey' coin (three pennies in the old South African coinage), which reflected the residents' sense that their lives were regarded as cheap. The houses were mainly thatch-roofed rondavels which were built by the locals according to their means. There was no electricity or piped water, and there was no proper road system. A primary school and the chapel, which formed part of the nuns' mission base, were the only public facilities for this village. I would guess that there were about a hundred households in the village at the time.

The nuns' residence was a humble one. It merged into the surrounding homesteads in its simplicity. It was a two-bedroom house with a kitchen-cum-dining and living area. They used a primus stove for cooking or else made a fire outside in an open hearth. Simple as it was, I was relieved to have such a supportive place to stay. For Sisters Mary-Theresa and Emily were very kind. They made me feel welcome, and could understand my predicament more than the priests could, because of their own backgrounds and their contact with activist priests such as Fr Smangaliso Mkhatshwa. They generously let me have the use of one of the bedrooms for myself. They also promised to pray for me and with me.

Naturally the local security police were disappointed by my decision to leave Meetse-a-Bophelo Hospital, but I told them that they could not expect me to cooperate in my own imprisonment. After all, if they had been so keen to get me to work with patients at the hospital, they should have had more compassion for the patients from whom they had taken me away so unceremoniously. They were a tame lot and no match for an activist steeled by the thugs in King Williamstown.

I spent the next few days hitching lifts to and from Ofcolaco, a distance of a few kilometres, to make phone calls and to send messages to my family. On some occasions I had to walk the last kilometre or so. This was most unpleasant. The weather was very hot in typical Lowveld fashion, and reached 40°C on some days. The grass on both sides of the path was high, and on more than one occasion a big snake would slither across the path, leaving me utterly beside myself with fear. Once I was so scared that I ran all the way to the mission house. Not that I could be described as a sprinter, but fear gave me wings.

Three days after my arrival I was thrilled to see Mziwoxolo Ndzengu, the ambulance driver at Zanempilo, arrive bringing me a suitcase full of clothing and some money. He had flown to Johannesburg, and then hired a car to Tzaneen. It was good to be with someone who was part of my broken community. Mziwoxolo was never very social or known for many words. He gave me a sketch of the events since my departure from King, in headline fashion. In this way I got to know who had been detained or banned, what the latest developments were at Zanempilo, the response of the security police to the anger generated by my banishment, and other essential news. I was grateful for his loyalty. He left the same day.

A day or so later none other than Thenjiwe Mthintso, herself restricted to Johannesburg, arrived at Tickeyline late in the evening. I was overjoyed. With Baba Jordan she brought me a VW Beetle to help me become mobile again. That was Thenji at her best, in one of the many daring missions in her life as an activist. We had a wonderful time catching up on the state of the nation. Thenji and Baba

Jordan brought me news of the intensifying repression which had claimed many more people. Yet despite the bannings and detentions there was no sign of the political struggle letting up. The activism of the urban youth was increasing, many were leaving the country for military training, and boycotts of schools showed no sign of abating. We all felt that 'the system' was on its last legs – we just had to hang in there for the last push. It was after midnight when Thenjiwe and Baba finally tore themselves away.

The following day Mr Raymond Tucker, an attorney from Johannesburg, then popular in activist circles, called on me at Steve's request. After carefully reading my banning order, he told me that it was in fact a banishment order, restricting me to a foreign part of the country – a treatment which had up to that point been reserved for troublesome chiefs who refused to cooperate with the white authorities in imposing controls over their people. Banishment in this new sense was a distinction I was to share with Winnie Mandela, who was banished later in 1977 to Brandfort, a small Free State town.

Raymond Tucker became visibly excited when he heard about the way in which Captain Schoeman had handled the errors in my banning order. His conclusion was that I was not banned legally, and could go wherever I chose. He also felt that there was a case to be made for wrongful arrest, and he was accordingly instructed to institute legal proceedings against the Minister of Justice and Police, Mr Jimmy Kruger. I was thrilled. My first thought was naturally to go back to King Williamstown. I decided to make contact with Fr Stubbs at the Community of the Resurrection Priory in Rosettenville, for he was in my view the best person to help me return home. But I first had to get directions from him about how to drive to the Priory, without giving away too much on the telephone, for it was known to be tapped by the police.

When I called Fr Stubbs I pretended to need the directions for Raymond Tucker, who I claimed wanted to visit him that evening to report on his discussions with me. Fr Stubbs was very vague. He could not understand why Raymond Tucker needed directions to the Priory, where he had been a visitor many times before. In the end I had to make do with what he finally gave me. I confided in Fr Mooney about my intention to leave under cover of darkness that night. He was concerned about my safety, but blessed me and let me go.

When I got back to Tickeyline I fortunately found my younger

brother, Thomas, who had been asked by my concerned mother to
come and see me. He was then a twenty-year-old student, and was
visibly shaken not only by my new place of abode, but more so by
my plans to leave that very night for Johannesburg. In fact I told him
that he would have to drive me out of Tzaneen: it was unusual then
for a black woman to be seen driving a car, and I did not want to
arouse suspicions or draw attention to myself. This was a case of
naked bullying by an older sister, but it was not the time for gentle
negotiations.

We left Tickeyline after dusk. Unfortunately, a typical Lowveld
thunderstorm descended on us as we entered Tzaneen. Thomas's
considerable driving skills were severely tested on the sharp curves
of the Makgoba's Kloof area. As soon as we emerged on the straight
towards Pietersburg, he stopped on the side of the road, visibly
shaken by the stress of events. We had passed through the danger
zone, both physical and political, so I drove for the rest of the way.
The trip was uneventful but for our getting lost around Rosettenville
and having to be directed by a national serviceman. He was blissfully unaware that I was the embodiment of the very threat to national
security which he was supposed to counter.

When we arrived at the Priory, Fr Stubbs was caught completely
off guard. He could not believe his keen political antennae had
missed the hint I was trying to give him earlier that day. In his typi-
cally methodical way he set about making us comfortable for the
night, especially my poor brother Thomas, who was still overwhelmed by the day's events. Thomas had not even begun to understand what being banned and banished meant when he was pressed
into service to break the orders of those restrictions. For a young man
with no political education it was too much, but necessity is the best
teacher, and he rose to the occasion. Fr Stubbs arranged with Fr Leo
Rakgale, one of his brethren, to drive Thomas to the Johannesburg
railway station to catch the train back to Pietersburg the following
day. He also arranged for our trip to King, which was to start very
early the next morning.

The journey offered us time together. We had a long, frank discussion about our individual backgrounds, our fears and personality traits, which drew us closer together than would have been possible otherwise. Fr Stubbs stopped being just another priest to me; he
became a human being, friend and counsellor. When we arrived at
Zanempilo, Fr Stubbs called the staff to see who his companion was

on this unexpected visit. They could not believe their eyes. There
was joy and celebration as people came in to embrace me and welcome me back to the fold. Steve, who was called urgently by phone
without much explanation, was absolutely astounded. 'Fr Stubbs, I
thought I told you to keep her where she was!' But the joy of reunion
was everywhere in evidence. We flew into each other's arms and forgot the nightmare we had lived through over the past few days. The
comfort of familiar surroundings and faces had the desired effect
and the tension which had settled into my frail body began to ease.

After a discussion on the best way to extract maximum political
benefit out of this security police blunder, Steve and I sat back and
enjoyed our reunion. Many of our colleagues and friends in the
region got to know about my return. Yet the vigilant security police
remained blissfully unaware for the entire four days I spent in the
King Williamstown area. They were embarrassed to read about my
presence for the first time in the Monday morning edition of the
*Daily Dispatch*. Donald Woods, the editor, had been one of the first
people we alerted. He came to Zanempilo for a breakfast meeting on
the Sunday. Thrilled to get the scoop, he announced it with a
vengeance. The red-faced security police came to Zanempilo that
Monday morning to find me revelling in my new-found freedom
and acting in my usual capacity.

It was a short respite, but a crucial one on two counts. Firstly, I
settled the score with Captain Schoeman: 6–0, game, set, but not yet
match! Secondly, I received a gift I was not to know about until a
month later – the conception of my beautiful son, Hlumelo, who
became the embodiment of all the happy memories of 'A Love
Supreme', the poem Steve had written for me during our student
days to capture the essence of our relationship. The rude interruption of our lives had upset our plans not to have another love child
until our triangular relationship had been resolved, but my contraceptive pills had been left behind in King together with my other
essential items. Abstinence was not a proposition. Passion took its
course.

With Captain Schoeman nowhere in sight, the police apologised
for the manner in which I had been treated earlier, but made it clear
that I was going to have to be taken back to Naphuno in the end.
They made elaborate efforts to get everything right the second time:
spelling of names; identity number; adequate preparation, by mutual consent, for transporting my personal effects. I was also allowed

to wind down my responsibilities in King Williamstown, which included securing my brother Molepo's release from another spell of detention. Captain Schoeman had been trying to put pressure on him to turn state witness in yet another of his crazy cases against Steve and other activists.

I even had time to take proper leave of the people of the village, whom I had got to love so much. The staff organised a party for me, and Mamoswazi led the women in singing and dancing. Lein van den Bergh, an official of the Dutch development agency ICCO, was one of the guests who shared this bitter-sweet farewell with me. He was to become a lifelong friend. There was a sense in which the sadness of my departure was tempered by the hope of my return sooner rather than later. It was farewell, but not goodbye. I was convinced that I would be back in King before the year was ended. At least that was how it looked from Steve's point of view and mine after a discussion of our future plans. However, history had other things in store for us.

I finally drove back to Tzaneen in my own Peugeot sedan with Mziwoxolo at my side to help with the driving. We followed the security police car to Pretoria, where we spent the night sleeping in my car parked in the basement of the Compol Police Station. Here we were given access to staff bathrooms in the morning and prepared ourselves for the remaining drive to Tzaneen.

There was a sad reunion with Fr Mooney and Sisters Mary-Theresa and Emily at Ofcolaco. They were happy to have me come and stay in Tickeyline while I sorted myself out, but my return signalled the permanence of my restrictions. The Tzaneen security police were thoroughly ashamed of their ineptitude in not having kept me in check. They had only learnt from their King colleagues on the Monday morning with the publication of the news that I was out of their area of jurisdiction. What a disgrace! But it suited me fine: I was one up on them.

I found setting up house in Lenyenye Township, which I had made an absolute condition of my return to the area, an interesting exercise, for it gave me insights into the people I was to deal with for the next few years of my life. The security policemen, having made such fools of themselves, fell over themselves to keep me under constant surveillance. But they were so inexperienced that I would vanish in front of their eyes, and they would later catch up with me with desperation written on their faces. They were also confused by my friendliness. I treated them with courtesy and made a point of greeting them, even when they did not notice me, at the supermarket or other public places.

Nor did the local Township Superintendent, Mr Letsoalo, know how to deal with me. He had never seen an African woman medical doctor, let alone one who was said to be a danger to the security of the state. His dealings with me were also bedevilled by the open involvement of the security police in the administration of the township, and he did not know the boundaries of his limited authority. He was as helpful as he could be under the circumstances. I was given a house on the edge of the township, with two bedrooms, a living-room, a kitchen, and inside toilet and shower.

The local magistrate, from whom I had to obtain permission to go outside my area to shop or attend Sunday church, also found it difficult to deal with me. Later he became quite friendly and would share his ambivalences with me. He was very helpful in seeing that my requests were met. He was also instrumental in my move to a better house in a newly developed area, which was to be my home for almost eight years. He had come on an inspection visit to my first house and was visibly shocked at its inadequacy. I was sad when he was transferred out of the area during 1978; perhaps he was seen as too friendly. I shall never know.

The people in the area were amazing. Sister Mary-Theresa in her own way arranged with a local parishioner in Tickeyline, Mrs Mangena, to let me have one of her daughters, Makgatla, then about sixteen years old, come and stay with me in Lenyenye. The trust accorded me as a stranger has never stopped to amaze me. Makgatla Mangena stayed with me and my family until the end of 1994, almost seventeen years after our first contact.

My neighbours in Lenyenye, all policemen in the regular service, were very curious about me. I have no doubt that they had been warned about me, and that some of them informed on me to the security police, whom they saw as their superiors. I nonetheless decided to behave as normally to them as one does to any neighbour, which added to their confusion. Why was I not spitting flames of rage, as they may have been made to expect? I had decided on a deliberate strategy of vigilant self-preservation with the least expense of energy unless matters of principle were at stake.

Gradually individual members of the Lenyenye Township community started warming to me. They would stop and greet me less nervously than in the first few weeks. I became particularly friendly with some families. Most important amongst them was a young couple, the Mokgashis – Mapula was a teacher, whilst her husband, Matthews, was a local catechist in the Roman Catholic Church. I had been introduced to them by Fr Mooney, who kept contact with me. Our ties were later cemented by the friendship which developed between my mother, who later came to stay, and Mapula's mother, Nkabati Mamorobela, who also lived in Lenyenye. We visited each other's homes, and shared many meals together. Mapula introduced me to the delicacies of the area, particularly pumpkin leaves prepared with tomatoes and a liberal amount of freshly ground peanut meal. Delicious!

In addition to friends, there was the support of my family. My mother had come to see me soon after I got back to Tickeyline. She was saddened by the thought of her daughter being a virtual prisoner in a foreign district. She hated the idea of the constant surveillance by security police, and feared for my safety. Later the ambivalences she experienced would surface: she was grateful that at least I was now more accessible to her than I had been for the previous ten years. Soon she acquired a reputation amongst the local security policemen of a tough, uncompromising woman. She could not hide her loathing of them and their work; she reacted negatively even to their greetings, which I had got them used to making, and would fly into a rage if she detected any rudeness on the part of a policeman towards me.

Repeatedly she reminded them that they were uneducated in comparison with her daughter: 'You are as good as Sub A's.* Are you not ashamed of your behaviour towards this doctor?' I was at times embarrassed by my mother's outbursts, but she left the security policemen in no doubt about where they stood with her. One rude security policeman, Warrant Officer Ehlers, got a fair share of this treatment. On one occasion he ended a verbal confrontation with my mother by remarking that it was not surprising I was so stubborn; I came from tough stock. My mother retorted, 'What did you expect? She comes from here' (pointing to her abdominal area). That sealed it.

During the first few weeks of my stay in Lenyenye, I relied heav-

---

* My mother spent most of her professional life teaching Sub A (Grade 1). Thus for her this was a convenient metaphor for the lowest educational level.

ily on an old-fashioned public telephone, located in a bus depot, to communicate with the world beyond Naphuno district – 'the back of beyond', as Donald Woods so aptly commented in the *Daily Dispatch*. I talked to Steve every three days or so, in violation of our banning orders, which prohibited communication between banned people. I can't imagine that the police were unaware, but what could they have done about it? They would have had to use tapes from the telephone service, but that alone could not secure a conviction even in repressive South Africa. I also spoke to other activists whenever possible after making prior arrangements. But I had to rely more and more on my own personal resources for spiritual sustenance and sanity.

One of the most important ways of maintaining sanity in life is having some real work to do, as many unemployed people so painfully know. The network of support that developed around me in the first few months could not provide the intellectual stimulation and meaning in my life which were essential to survival. I had spent too many years leading a very full life to tolerate endless days of doing nothing. I could not continue to sit and wait for my return to life with Steve.

I was to have another opportunity of seeing Steve in June 1977, when I gave evidence in his defence in a case brought against him for defeating the ends of justice. Such opportunities for meeting were used to the full by political activists across the country, to the great annoyance of the security police, who were powerless to stop us. After all, one was entitled to a proper defence, even under the draconian legal system of apartheid South Africa. I flew to East London, using a small plane from Tzaneen, and connecting with South African Airways in Johannesburg.

It was good to be back in Mamcete's house. We were soon joined by Thenjiwe, who also arrived ostensibly to give evidence. The expected police swoop came earlier than we had bargained for, but they failed to nail us in one another's company – a trophy they coveted. They nonetheless spoilt our fun. We were temporarily detained and released only on the promise that we would be staying in different places. I was by then expecting Hlumelo, and had the opportunity to share this happy event with Steve without the awful distance between us. We also discussed my intention to start a small local health project to keep myself busy whilst awaiting new developments.

We had a huge party in Ginsberg in a house near Steve's home, in celebration of old times. It was attended by all the old party faithfuls, banned or unbanned, who were within twenty-five kilometres of Ginsberg. It was a nostalgic occasion which invoked a past we could not recreate, but it was an important symbolic statement about the bonds which tied us together in spite of the distances imposed upon us. At the end of the hearing it was sad to have to leave King and all the friends. I had to tear myself from Steve, who was, as usual, quite reassuring and urging patience.

Upon my return to Lenyenye, I decided to occupy my time with something creative. So I started a clinic at the back of the local Roman Catholic church, in one of the general offices, in July 1977. Ironically, Fr Thomas Duane, initially a sceptic, had become most supportive of me and had negotiated with the priest-in-charge of the parish for the space. The Black Community Programmes, through its banned Director, Bennie Khoapa, generously made money available to me to purchase modest medical supplies in keeping with the temporary nature of the enterprise. The supportive network of political activists continued to operate against all the odds. I was able to start with the help of a local nurse aide, Morongwa Puka, who had been unemployed for some time.

To remain on the safe side I relied on Morongwa to interpret patients' symptoms. Many people stayed away from the service, in spite of their needs, which became clear later on when I got to know the area better. They could not risk the displeasure of the security police, who were clearly trying to discourage this development. It sounded too familiar, and smelled to them like trouble. They were right. But they need not have worried – not yet, in any case.

It is difficult to explain the series of coincidences which began to happen after my return to Lenyenye, other than in terms of what I believe must be telepathy. I started experiencing discomfort around my lower abdomen towards the end of August. I went to see a Swiss missionary doctor who was the superintendent of Shiluvane Hospital, a local hospital near by. He reassured me about my pregnancy, and advised bed-rest. My attempts to contact Steve over the next week or so drew a blank. I became concerned when he did not return my calls. (I had by then installed a telephone in my house.) A few days later I learned that he had been detained en route to King from Cape Town. I was not overly concerned. He had, after all, survived many brushes with the security police and could take care of himself. It would just be a matter of time before they charged or released him.

My admission to Shiluvane Hospital with a threatened abortion coincided with the beginning of Steve's brutal interrogation, which was to lead to his death on 12 September 1977. I was then sixteen weeks pregnant. His death coincided with the intensification of the threat to the life of my expected baby. With much reluctance, and after threats from me, the security police agreed to my transfer on the same fateful day to Pietersburg Hospital, a relatively better-equipped institution with specialist services. I remember weeping on the way to the hospital in the ambulance, which left Shiluvane at 4 a.m. on 12 September 1977. I ascribed my weepiness to anxiety about the safety of my pregnancy.

Dr Van den Ende, the obstetrician, was the doctor assigned to look after me. He was a well-built, kindly man who had soft eyes and spoke with a strong Afrikaans accent. He explained to me after a thorough history and examination that I had an irritable uterus which was reacting to both the growing baby and the multiple fibroids (benign tumours) in its wall. He cautioned me about the chances of success in maintaining the pregnancy to term, but promised to do his best. I was put on treatment to suppress the contractions, and confined to bed. The nurses were wonderful. I relaxed towards the end of the day, permitting myself to regard this as time to be nurtured.

The following morning I was taken aback when the nursing sister in charge of my care insisted that I breach the order of strict bed-rest and go and speak to my sister on the phone. She had a major family problem to share with me. I told the nurse that that was precisely the reason why I should not go to the phone: my family had to learn to solve their problems without me. I had enough of my own, I said. But she persisted.

Eventually I was wheeled to the phone. It was Thenjiwe on the line. I thought that she had succeeded again in fooling 'the system' and settled down for an update on the state of affairs. After impatient niceties, she asked me if I was sitting down, and then she said the impossible: 'Steve is dead.' It was as if someone had put a high voltage current through me. A searing fire burned inside me. 'No, it can't be true' was all I remember saying.

I went into a state of profound emotional shock. 'It can't be true' was my refrain. Dr Van den Ende had to sedate me. I fell in and out of a state of nightmarish sleep and wished that I could die. But death does not come to those who need it most. There was no escape from the reality of loss.

I owe the survival of my son to many people, above all to the undying loyalty and love of Thenjiwe. She had correctly anticipated that I might learn about Steve's death when I opened the newspapers on the morning of the 13th. The paper, with bold headlines, was indeed lying on my bed when I returned from the fateful phone call. Thenjiwe followed up her call with a visit a day or so later, to share the grief with me. The risks she took were enormous, but characteristic of this very fine South African.

I also owe a debt to the skill and patience of Dr Van den Ende. He constantly reminded me over the next few days to pray to God for 'Serenity to accept the things I cannot change, Courage to change those I can, and Wisdom to know the difference'. This prayer remains my constant companion. I owe much as well to the support and good care of the nurses at the hospital, who went beyond the call of duty, and to Fr Duane, who came to sit at my bedside day in and day out for two weeks after this tragedy. He just sat there, ready for a smile or tears on my part. I felt utterly lost. My world had collapsed around me. Gone were the anchor in my life and the security I had become so accustomed to.

The seismic event which shattered me on that fateful morning had many after-shocks. It was not just the end of the vibrant life of a gifted person with a sense of destiny, but it was the death of a dream. The dream which was killed had both personal and national dimensions. But it was the personal anguish which preoccupied me in my lonely hospital bed. I had none of the traditional support which one gets from family and friends. My sister's visit, though brief, helped. But the worst aspect of the loss was not being able to bury Steve. I remember being even more distraught the day after his funeral on seeing newspaper reports and photographs of the ceremony. There was a finality about the pictures of the proceedings. But my exclusion from the rituals made acceptance of this finality difficult. I kept hoping for a miracle to restore him to life.

There were other aspects to the exclusion. Not only was I banned and thus unable to travel to King Williamstown, but I would have been too ill to travel. I had to refrain from burying him in order to protect the life of his unborn son. What is more, I was not his widow.

How would I have fitted into the rituals, given this fact? It was a bewildering time for me.

The Biko family were also bewildered not only by Steve's death but by the fact that he and his wife had already separated as part of the divorce proceedings which Steve had instituted a few weeks earlier. In fact they reversed his own decision to end his marriage, by fetching his wife to come and take part in the mourning ritual as his widow. This reversal of Steve's own wishes has run like a thread through the continuing confusion about his life. His widow was put in the uncomfortable position of mourning as a wife someone who had taken steps to end the marriage in real life. It is not surprising that tensions often surface within the Biko family around the ambiguous position they made her occupy.

The film *Cry Freedom* was in one respect an inaccurate portrayal of Steve's political life, which Donald Woods had not understood in the relatively short time in which he had come to know Steve. It also misrepresented his personal relationships. The peripheral role in which I was cast belied the centrality of my relationship, both personal and political, with Steve. What the film did was to perpetuate the lie of Steve as a Gandhi-type person respectably married to a dedicated wife who shared his life and his political commitment. When I tried to stop the filming of this movie in Zimbabwe, my attempts were sabotaged by the eagerness of a number of people in the liberation movement, including senior ANC leaders, who were only concerned about the anti-apartheid statement it was making. It all added to the pain of loss by inventing memories which were not in concert with the reality of his life.

But life had to go on, and would go on, with or without my co-operation. I had to spend the rest of my pregnancy on strict bed-rest, nursed by my caring family and Makgatla Mangena. My sister Mashadi took leave for the whole of October to come and take care of me in Lenyenye after my discharge from hospital. My mother also came to see me over weekends, when freed from her teaching duties. Brothers came to stay at various points, and Molepo finally came back from King to stay permanently with me in Lenyenye from the end of 1977.

The Nationalist government was not satisfied with having killed Steve; they also sought to kill his ideas. All the Black Consciousness organisations were banned on 19 October 1977, together with many other organs of civil society such as the *World* newspaper. Organisations like the Christian Institute were also banned. The CI had previously been declared 'affected' and thus could no longer receive foreign funding. Major political actors were detained and banned. The season of repression intensified.

I endured the worst summer of my life in 1977/8. The emotional distress was matched by the harsh physical conditions of my new home. Temperatures hovered around 40°C on most days, relieved only by occasional violent thunderstorms. I had to remain indoors in a house with no ceiling to protect me from the low asbestos roof. I relied on an electric fan, which I kept on for almost twenty-four hours, for some comfort. There was no garden to take refuge in, or trees to shade one from the relentless heat. I also had to contend with the constant screeching of crickets at night. I thought that I would lose my sanity at some point. Captain Schoeman had clearly chosen the worst place for me, as part of his extended torture.

Hlumelo, the shoot that grew from a dead tree trunk, was born on 19 January 1978. It was a long and difficult labour. In the end Dr Van den Ende had to use a pair of forceps to aid the delivery of the head, which was in a posterior position and would not come. I was overjoyed when I saw him – a true shoot from that indomitable tree trunk, an exact physical replica of his father, right down to the fingernails. Malusi prophetically gave Hlumelo his name soon after Steve's death. He said that it was suitable for the baby, be it boy or girl. I forgot the immediate pain of delivery and savoured the bundle of life next to me.

I was fortunate to have my mother with me to help with the care of my son. Hlumelo was a difficult child who cried incessantly. The old women of the village ascribed it to my having cried too much during pregnancy. They were convinced that foetuses pick up the mother's unhappiness and become tense and irritable. It was exhausting coping with my son, but I was so grateful to have him that I could put up with anything. Nobandile Mvovo, who came to see him soon after birth, tried to talk to him: *Xhamela intoni uzo sih-laza kude kangaga? Ba za kuthi singabantu abanjanina xa be kujongile? Ilali yonke imamele isikhalo sakho. Thula mtana ka Dadebawo. Thula Mgcina.* (Xhamela [the Biko clan name], why are you disgracing us so much amongst these strange people? What will they think of us? The whole village is listening to your cry. Please quieten down, my child.) Hlumelo remained unimpressed.

The period of forced inaction gave me the opportunity to mourn and yet to see my plight in a broader perspective. Many other people had lost sons, husbands and loved ones to the repressive system. I was at least in a better position to take care of myself than most other victims of this wanton destruction. The poverty of the people around me and their generosity filled me with humility. I had to stop feeling sorry for myself and get up and walk.

I started planning my life anew soon after my son was born. I arranged for my furniture from King to be transported to Lenyenye. It had been left there in anticipation of my return to join Steve after we had resolved the triangular relationship. That dream lay in ruins. I had to scratch around for the relics of the past and piece my life together somehow.

Fortunately we moved house into a better area in Lenyenye at the beginning of 1978. The house had three bedrooms, a living-room, a kitchen and proper bathroom. We soon established a garden with flowers and lawn in front and fruit trees on the rest of the property. Fr Duane brought me a number of rose plants which flowered throughout the year, providing a delightful array of colours and beautiful aromas for the brutalised senses. My house became liveable space, and I could call it home.

Before long I realised I had to set up a longer-term project in the area. I soon found a base in an old shopping centre and started work in April 1978 with the support of the Roman Catholic Church and Fr Stubbs, then a prohibited immigrant, who arranged for financial support from British Christian Aid and Oxfam. Many other previous supporters of ours re-established contact, notably Mr Lein van den Bergh from ICCO.

Morongwa Puka, the energetic nursing aide who had worked with me before, was happy to join me again but soon more hands were needed. Leah Mafuna, a slightly built woman previously from Kranspoort Mission, my childhood village, also joined us as a nurse aide. Mankuba Ramalepe, a large woman whose heart matches her size, and a qualified nursing sister, completed the complement for a while. Mankuba was later to become my brother Sethiba's sister-in-law. Mmaisaka, a woman whose malnourished child drew our attention to her, became a vital member of the team as a cleaner.

Lenyenye is situated in a basin surrounded by hills, which were dotted with small village settlements both here and beyond.

Outstation services were virtually demanded by the villagers in out-lying areas of the district of Naphuno, which was about 150 square kilometres in size. People also came on foot from Tsonga-speaking areas of the Tzaneen district and in buses and hired open vans. They braved the dusty heat and occasional thunderstorms to reach the clinic and outstation points. We bought a van with a canopy for the clinic activities, and for fetching and carrying supplies from the local railway depot. We soon outgrew both our premises and our energy.

There was real hunger amongst the impoverished locals for a car-ing primary health service. They loved the personal, dignified care they received, and enjoyed my attempts at speaking the local lingo. When the old ladies came to tell me how much better their arthritis had become with my treatment, I would challenge them to demon-strate how they would be able to participate in the local dances – and would join in myself.

I learned a great deal about local beliefs, explanations of the caus-es of disease, indigenous healing methods, and many other things which helped me to understand the people I was to live and work with for many years. I also built on their own knowledge to intro-duce new concepts and healing strategies. For example, a child with diarrhoea would be brought to the clinic with incisions made around the fontanelle and a black substance smeared over it. This local heal-ing method is based on a recognition of the effect that loss of fluids has on the fontanelle of the baby, which becomes sunken. Their rem-edy, although ineffectual, at least provided a basis for introducing the more effective Oral Rehydration Treatment (ORT). I expressed my respect for their diagnostic skills before suggesting a change in the method of treatment. In this way, the old women healers respon-sible for the traditional treatment were not made to feel stupid, but affirmed in their astuteness at having made the correct observations – which was a sound basis for introducing innovations.

The local population was typical of the impoverished rural areas in apartheid South Africa: predominantly women and children, older or disabled men, a few professionals – nurses, teachers, police-men – and a growing breed of civil servants in the 'homeland' gov-ernment services. Old women played an important role as heads of families in the absence of their sons, who were migrant workers. I had to learn to work with them, because they made all the important decisions, including those about health care. It was not difficult to establish a rapport with them. I had been popular with old women in King and became quite good at knowing how to relate to them, affirming them, yet slowly moving them from their tendency to rigidity.

I also learned how to forge better relations between older women and their daughters-in-law, which empowered the younger women without making the older ones feel that they had lost control. I helped the younger ones to understand the game of power between the generations, and to appreciate the real fear older women had of being abandoned by their sons. There were far too many unhappy cases in the area for the older women not to feel vulnerable. I showed their daughters-in-law how little it costs to smooth ruffled feathers by providing inexpensive treats for the older women, such as preparing a warm bath or a favourite dish or even dancing around and making them laugh. But it was not always easy.

The popularity of my work did not please the security police. They intensified their surveillance and introduced further restrictions. In 1979 my area of restriction was reduced from the Naphuno district to Lenyenye Township, which had no more than 850 houses on a dusty piece of land. The captain of the security police who came to serve the order on me found me having breakfast before leaving for one of the outstations. He refused to sit down or to accept the cup of tea I offered him. He stood near the front door, literally shaking in his shoes, as he read out the offending additional clause to my banning order. I continued my breakfast, whilst listening and watching him. He could not believe my cool reaction, and thought that I had not understood the order was to have immediate effect. I assured him that I understood, and he left. The security police were used to dealing with anger, but found civility confusing.

Their attempts to limit my influence met with little success. People made simple calculations about what was in their best interest, and decided to continue to visit our clinic in even larger numbers. The initial hesitancy was soon replaced by greater boldness. Even local chiefs in the area – paid functionaries of the state – defied the authorities in the matter of development projects in the villages under their jurisdiction and listened to us when we came to talk to them. Chief Maake, who was also my patient, went as far as writing a blanket permit for Ithuseng Community Health Programme to undertake any project it thought fit to promote the health of her subjects. This was a blow for the system from the least-expected quarter.

In desperation, the security police tried to encourage me to go into exile. They sent Lisa Williamson, sister of Craig Williamson, the notorious security police captain who infiltrated the international student movement in the 1970s, and later worked for the International University Exchange Fund (IUEF), which he was to destroy. Lisa, unbeknown to me at the time, was also a police officer. She came to the clinic unannounced one morning, wearing a woollen hat to cover her white hair, and accompanied by a young black man, whom she referred to as 'a comrade' from a neighbouring township. She brought me much-needed support from IUEF: a thousand Swiss francs. Over lunch at my house later that day, she suggested that should I want to 'skip' the country illegally, she would be more than happy to assist. My first reaction was anger at her impertinence as a young liberal white woman to assume that if I really wanted to go into exile I would need her assistance. But I also felt that I needed to make one point very clear. I was going to be a pain in the neck of the security police and their masters, and was not going anywhere. This was my country and I was going to help liberate it. Little did I realise that the intended audience was indeed receiving the message.

The pressure of popular demand on our premises led to the building of the Ithuseng Community Health Centre, a scaled-down but much better planned version of Zanempilo. It was not an easy task, given the scarcity of financial resources for large development projects. A combination of dogged determination, supportive friends inside and outside the country, and sheer luck made it possible. Desmond Tutu, then General Secretary of the SACC, rescued me from serious contractual problems when the World University Service (WUS) reneged on a promise to fund the building costs. If it had not been for his help I would have landed in legal hot water.

I had happily signed a contract for R78,000 on the basis of the WUS's promise of support made in 1979. I was later to learn that WUS had been put under pressure by some ANC exiles not to support any activity in South Africa unless requests for such support came through the ANC. I was then, and am still now, opposed to development being held hostage to party politics, and would not have agreed anyway, even if I had been given the opportunity. But the pressure may well have been part of Craig Williamson's plan of sabotage to prevent the emergence of another major community development project. History will have to judge this one.

It was fitting that Bishop Tutu came to open Ithuseng Community Health Centre in September 1981. I was granted permission to attend the festivities. It was a marvellous occasion. Friends came from far and wide to celebrate the resilience of the human spirit. Members of the old King community were represented by Nohle Mohapi and Nobandile Mvovo. Francis and Tim Wilson, as well as the President of the Carnegie Corporation, were also present. It was a bitter-sweet occasion for me. Bishop Tutu had to remind me several times to relax and celebrate, but I remained tense. There were too many mixed emotions about this sphinx that was rising from the ashes.

That weekend the conservative Anglican parishioners of Tzaneen created a scene which left a bitter taste in the mouth. One of the guests at the opening festivities was Mr Venables, a fellow Anglican parishioner. He suggested that Bishop Tutu should come and worship at the local parish on the Sunday morning. He offered to arrange it with the parish. We were appalled when we heard that the parish council refused to have Bishop Tutu worship with them. Some went as far as saying that Bishop Tutu would enter their church over their dead bodies. I was furious and vowed never to set my foot in that church again. The arrogance of the parishioners in debarring a bishop of their church from worshipping with them was unprecedented in my view. I had up to then received little support from the priest-in-charge, who bore me as a cross. He had turned down the invitation to the opening festivities – he had prior arrangements, he said. Bishop Tutu was hurt but took it in his stride.

Putting down roots in Lenyenye was a matter of survival. I had no other option. So Lenyenye became home in every respect. There were three taproots: work, social relationships and intimacy. As regards the first of these, I consolidated my primary health care project. Even though I could not go and work amongst the people in the surrounding villages, I learnt to work through, and with, other people on the basis of trust and faith in their abilities. Mr Lazarus Lekgolo Ramalepe, husband of Mankuba, who was then, and still is, nursing sister-in-charge, came to join us as Programme Officer and Administrator. He has enormous energy, initiative and courage. He started focusing more on the nascent income-generating projects we were struggling to put on their feet, to strengthen and expand them. The brickmaking cooperative was the biggest challenge. It was built on existing capacities and skills within the community. Women who were working in local commercial brickyards at slave wages were brought together to create their own wealth. It took some learning on our part to understand the complexity of communal ownership, particularly by people who had never wielded power or controlled much in their own lives.

Development activists like myself had to learn the hard way that the capacity of poor people to own both the successes and failures of projects they are engaged in is severely limited. One needs self-confidence and self-esteem to be able to acknowledge one's failures and weaknesses. The humiliation of conquest, racism and poverty has undermined many people's self-esteem by labelling them as mistakes of God's creation. How can we expect them to own mistakes? But development work entails a trust in systems, and consequently a move away from personal politics, which is the hallmark of survival strategies for the poor. Poor people's experiences of systems, both official ones and those run by people fighting for freedom, have not inspired them with trust. They have been let down too often, and have too often seen corruption operate in the name of regulations and procedures, to believe that there is reason to trust systems.

But there were many successes. Vegetable gardens began to blossom everywhere. Child care as a social responsibility was explored and finally accepted by a community used to viewing child care as women's responsibility and 'granny' as the only support for over-extended mothers. Many child-care centres have since been built with community participation and support, and are being run by representative village committees.

Projects aimed at the empowerment of women also took root. Many women suffer from the burden of the endless search for firewood in areas that are becoming more and more denuded of vegetation. The building of mud-stoves, making wonder-boxes* and the improvement of housing, all help to conserve fuel and develop a better self-image amongst poor rural women.

Preventive health-care strategies took many forms: literacy classes and Oral Rehydration Treatment (ORT) for diarrhoea became popularised; immunisation and 'Road to Health' cards became a status symbol of good parenthood. Women learnt to work together and to shed their powerlessness at many levels. There were also many

---

* Mud-stoves are cleverly designed mud hearths which provide for the making of fire in enclosed space, complete with a chimney, just as in a metal stove. A wonder-box is constructed out of a cardboard box with a tight-fitting lid, which is lined inside with cushions made from insulating material. One need only get food to a brisk boil for a few minutes, then leave it to cook in the box. Wonder-boxes are particularly good for slow-cooking foods such as samp and beans, which are popular amongst the poor.

opportunities for fun: Christmas parties for the elderly, and outings for younger women, some of whom had never been outside their immediate surroundings.

In Lenyenye I also put down roots in social relationships. I had up to then survived by losing myself in work. In fact I worked myself to a standstill on many occasions. This worried my mother, who was then staying permanently with me. I would be so tired by the end of the day – having seen on some occasions eighty patients and also attended to other project needs – that I would barely have the energy to eat and bath after getting home. As soon as my head touched the pillow I would be asleep. Such a lifestyle protected me from facing the pain of loss, but I could clearly not sustain it.

Fr Thomas Duane was a lifesaver. He was the only person in the area with whom I could have serious intellectual discussions. His regular visits were crucial. In 1979 I started visiting the Ofcolaco Mission, where he was then based, under cover of darkness. I got to know and like the other priests, and enjoyed their Irish sense of humour. With increasing confidence, Fr Duane started taking me out on day-long trips to see the beauty of the Transvaal Lowveld. We drove through Strijdom Tunnel and ventured further east towards God's Window – a true window into a valley of beauty surrounded by rolling hills covered with lush vegetation. The Drie Rondavels, three near-identical round hills set apart in the eastern Transvaal landscape, are also spectacular. We would sit facing them and surveying the horizon beyond for hours on end. Echo Caves, with their tall, flowing rock formations and many recesses, were also a favourite visiting place. We mixed with the predominantly white tourists without a hint of the illegality of our action. On these trips I would ride with Fr Duane in his pick-up truck. His view was that he had nothing to lose if we were caught. He would never give evidence against me or any politically persecuted person. We took the necessary precautions to avoid detection without becoming neurotic about security.

Later I took the staff at the Ithuseng Community Centre, my family and other friends to these scenic areas, and I would then ride on the back of Ramalepe's powerful Ford truck wearing jeans and a cap. We used to be amused that the security police, whom we would come across on rare occasions, did not recognise me, because they did not expect me to defy my orders so openly in broad daylight. They also would not have expected a medical doctor to ride on the back of a truck like a labourer, as was the practice in this farming area. It is interesting how easy it is to fool people who operate on the basis of rigid stereotypes.

A protective community developed and consolidated around me. They came from all walks of life: my family, their friends, fellow workers at Ithuseng, local residents and patients. The security police could not penetrate this protective wall around me, and, when they did, they had no chance of securing a charge for my breaking my banning order. On one occasion we had such a rowdy party that my neighbour, who was the sole known informer amongst my other police neighbours, called his masters. They burst into the house, but in the nick of time I was pushed into my bedroom by my younger brother, Molepo. I quickly got into bed, shoes and all, and was found by the security police only a few seconds later, reading a book. They were frustrated, but knew that they could not get any of my guests to give evidence against me.

There was also an increasing flow of outsiders who came to visit me in Lenyenye: journalists, national and foreign politicians, diplomats, fellow activists and friends. It was fairly easy for them to find me. Many used to come without any prior arrangement. In fact, sometimes prior arrangements by telephone simply alerted the sleepy security police.

Helen Suzman, then MP for Lower Houghton for the Progressive Party, was the only South African parliamentarian who took an active interest in the plight of political prisoners, detainees, banned people and their families. She came to visit me and we had a good laugh about her failed attempts in parliament in mid-1977 to receive an explanation as to why the Minister of Justice, Jimmy Kruger, had served a banning order on me. What security threat did I pose to the state? Kruger simply said, as was the practice, that it was not in the interest of state security to disclose the information, even when he was pressed by Helen to inform me privately by letter. Well, it was impossible to beat that. Such was the importance of state security that citizens had no right to know why their rights were being violated by the state.

The legal suit instituted by my lawyer, Raymond Tucker, against the Minister of Justice for wrongful arrest failed on a technicality. My lawyer had lodged the papers with the Johannesburg Supreme Court instead of the Pretoria Supreme Court. The former had no jurisdiction in the matter because the route of the first journey into exile with the security police from King Williamstown had gone through the back roads of the eastern Transvaal, and had not traversed the Johannesburg Supreme Court's area of jurisdiction. Such is the luck of evil ones.

Helen Suzman remained a tower of strength for me through all the years. She was particularly helpful after my banning order was lifted, and I needed to secure a South African passport to travel abroad. A passport was treated by the National Party government as a privilege, not a right, for black South Africans. One's access to a passport was treated as a reward for good behaviour, and of this the security police were the sole judges. I would phone Helen frantically a week or two before departure on an overseas trip after having waited in vain for an answer to my application. A phone call from Helen to the Minister's office never failed to secure an assurance that my passport was waiting for collection at the local office of the Ministry. What power 'the system' had, but also how fortunate I was to have had the leverage provided by Helen Suzman. Many people were frustrated in their efforts without this assistance. She will certainly go down in history as someone who did not shy away from helping ordinary South Africans in times of great need.

Fr Timothy Stanton's regular visits were also an important source of strength. The coldness of the local Anglican parish priest in Tzaneen between 1977 and 1982 stood in sharp relief to the caring ministry of Fr Stanton. He drove all the way from the Community of the Resurrection Priory in Rosettenville, to pay me visits. My family grew to appreciate his quiet presence and the Eucharist he celebrated with us. My mother would remark that we were lucky to be visited by one so close to the Lord – she referred to him as 'the Visiting Christ'.

Bruce Haigh, the Second Secretary at the Australian Embassy, was also a great supporter and regular visitor. He was a handsome man in his early thirties, always dressed in jeans and Australian boots, with compassion and a commitment to supporting those fighting against the system of apartheid. He would come over for a weekend and participate in parties and picnic outings. We got to be very close over the years.

Bruce once took me on a daring mission at Easter 1979 to visit Steve Biko's grave in Ginsberg. It was a vain attempt on my part to complete ritually the unfinished business between Steve and me. The mission was not successful on two scores. Firstly, there were people digging a grave just near Steve's, most of whom I could recognise from where we had stopped the car near the fence. I could not take the risk of my presence becoming known. I had to be content with a distant view of the grave which had swallowed Steve. Then again, the return to the Eastern Cape exacerbated the pain. King Williamstown looked so desolate and defeated. Any romantic notion I had of returning, even without Steve, died at that point. I knew it was no more my place. I had to add it to my list of losses.

The trip did, however, offer me an opportunity to see Malusi and Thoko, with whom we stayed. Malusi was then restricted to Zwelitsha Township and was going through a difficult transition from political activist to religious convert. His last detention in the middle of 1977, during which he was tortured, had precipitated his conversion. He rejoined the Order of Ethiopia, in which church his late father had been a leading priest. Malusi has continued to grow in his religious commitment, and is currently running a successful grassroots Pastoral Institute in Grahamstown, which trains lay people in leadership for the development of themselves and their communities.

I tried to fill the intellectual wilderness in Lenyenye with structured studies. In 1983 I completed my Bachelor of Commerce degree, which I had first registered for in 1975 with Unisa. I also studied part-time with the University of the Witwatersrand for a postgraduate Diploma in Tropical Hygiene in 1981, and a Diploma in Public Health in 1982. These studies were made possible by a special dispensation for which I had applied, and which was granted. Conditions of my banning order were varied to allow me to travel to Johannesburg for one week four times a year for classes, and one week at the end of the year for examinations. I had to report to the Tzaneen Police Station on departure, and at John Vorster Square Police Station on arrival in Johannesburg, reversing the order on the trip back to Lenyenye.

Re-establishing intimate relationships whilst nursing my wounds was the most difficult process of my time at Lenyenye. I spent the years between 1977 and 1981 without daring to explore close relationships. Everything had died inside me, including dreams. There is not a single dream I can recall from this period except for the first few weeks after Steve's death, during which I had dreams of denial of his death. I would have vivid conversations with him telling him that people were claiming he had died. He would laughingly say in his usual manner, 'You know, Toto, that I cannot die', and I would peacefully continue my sleep, only to wake up to the harsh reality. My system shut out all dreams after that.

It took Sister Liz Elberts, a caring Dominican nun based at Villa Maria, in Johannesburg, to help me come to terms with Steve's death during 1987, ten years after the event. I was introduced to her by Fr Duane. We immediately clicked spiritually and were able to communicate in ways which words were inadequate to express. That she was close to her father and yet had had to give up close family ties as part of her religious journey enabled her to recognise the depth of my pain.

The frenetic pace of work which had helped me channel my anger into creative work had only been successful in dulling the pain. But the ease with which the wound bled was an indicator of how raw it still was. I used to become physically ill from the tension and pain of re-living Steve's death every September. I would go over the circumstances of his death in my mind's eye. I would imagine the pain he must have suffered whilst being tortured. I would see his attractive physique reduced to an inert confused pile by the brain damage he had suffered. I wept for him. But I wept more for myself, and the sense of loss of what could have been.

Moreover, I used to get upset each time some distortion of Steve's role or political philosophy appeared in the media. It was as if I had to protect him personally from defilement. I was not yet ready to let go of the unfinished business between him and myself. But I had to learn to say goodbye to him finally. Sister Liz helped me to let down the protective armour I had developed around myself, and to force open the door I had closed shut to keep Steve's place in my heart sacrosanct. I remained in love with him and was determined to remain faithful to him. She assured me that Steve would not like me to remain trapped in a love affair with a corpse. He was big enough to share me with others.

The process of saying goodbye involves an acceptance of the pain of loss, its incorporation into one's psyche, and an ability to integrate the pain with the memories of shared joys with the departed person. It involves making peace with the unfinished business instead of dwelling on what could have been. It is a difficult process, which I accomplished only with the skilful assistance of Sister Liz over a number of months. I can never thank her enough for this.

I had to accept my loss and stop clinging to what was no more and would never be again. But there are no easy answers to this greatest human problem – the reality of death, which is a companion of all life. Ultimately, one is left with no option but to wait in the hope that everything one has lost will come flooding back again out of the darkness of one's grief, and that one's relationships with the departed loved ones will be transformed into new, non-clinging relationships. I knew that mine was to be a long process of healing.

To tell or not to tell my son, Hlumelo, about the fate that had befallen his father? This question was an additional source of pain and anxiety for me for four years after he was born. His physical and personality likeness to his father added to the burden. How was I to tell him that the person from whom he draws his very being was no more and would never become known to him? Of course if he had understood the meaning of his own Xhosa name he would have known that the passing away of his father was incorporated in his name – shoot from a fallen branch – and thus marked him as a son who was never to meet his own father.

His own instincts must have told him that something was wrong. He took advantage of the preparations for his annual visit to his grandmother in King Williamstown in 1982 to announce to his uncles (my brothers) that he was at last going to meet his father. My brothers reported this to me and insisted that I talk to Hlumelo about his father.

I set the scene in my bedroom with an album on my bed and behind a closed door we sat on the bed in a tender embrace. I showed him a series of photographs of his father, and commented how much they looked alike and told him what kind of person his father was. I then said that his father had been banned just as I was, and that he had been killed by the police after being arrested outside his area of restriction. Hlumelo just turned, looked at me directly and said: 'Ag shame, Mama.' Then after hugging me tightly he said: 'Just be careful not to leave your area without permission.' Having secured my promise to be careful, he jumped off the bed and announced that he was going out to play. It was as if he was relieved that the big question has been answered for him.

I lay down and cried softly – both out of relief and in awe at the ability of one so young to absorb so deep a pain.

During the course of 1981, a group of old friends from the University of the North started visiting Lenyenye on weekends. They were a rowdy lot who added to the raucous parties we had. Sipo Magele, a tall, well-built, handsome man in his early thirties, who lectured in Pharmacy, was one of the regular visitors. We developed a relationship, which issued in a marriage in 1982, and a son, Malusi Magele, on 16 March 1983. I had no illusions about my relationship with Sipo. On the contrary, I probably had too low an expectation of what was possible. I was unashamedly seeking a companion with whom I could possibly grow old. The door to the special place in my heart was still shut – I was not yet ready to share Steve's place with anyone else at that stage.

Malusi's conception also served to reduce my hyper-anxiety about losing Hlumelo, my only connection with my past. I used to be neurotic about Hlumelo's safety. I would jump out of the bathroom semi-clad at the sound of a car starting in the driveway – I could not trust that others would take sufficient care to ensure that he was not standing behind a moving vehicle. My family would laugh, but understood my neurosis. I had, after all, lost my first child, Lerato, and was not going to let this one slip. I had in a sense made too much of an emotional investment in one child: this could not be good for either of us.

My third pregnancy was even more difficult than the first two. Malusi was born prematurely after eight months' pregnancy, when Dr Van den Ende decided to save me from internal bleeding. Malusi was a mere 1,7 kilograms at birth, he hardly moved after delivery, and was disposed of by my doctor as non-viable. Unbeknown to me, he was rescued by the nursing sister in attendance at the time.

I mourned Malusi for twelve hours before I knew that he was alive. Surprised nursing staff found me crying the following morning. I had to be wheeled to the nursery with my blood transfusion drip to see with my own eyes that he was alive. There he was – a tiny soul with an obvious bruise on one of the ankles. I cried more now because I thought that his legs were damaged. My medical knowledge escaped me at that point – babies born legs-first (in the bridge position) have blood stasis signs afterwards, which clear after some days. Dr Van den Ende had used Malusi's head as a device to apply pressure to my bleeding placental site, to stop me from bleeding to death.

Hlumelo's comment on first seeing Malusi in an incubator two days after his birth was that he was no larger than a Niknak. But

Malusi is a survivor. He survived neonatal diarrhoea in the over-crowded Pietersburg Hospital nursery which was crawling with cockroaches, and a period of underweight as a toddler because of chronic tonsillitis and enlarged adenoids which made eating almost impossible for him, and has grown into a thriving boy who is doing very well at school.

After this brush with maternal death Dr Van den Ende would not countenance anything but a hysterectomy post delivery. He told me what I already knew: I was a bad incubator – I had to lie virtually over my foetuses to ensure their survival, like a brooding hen, and even then I had been barely successful. The physical pain of a large abdominal operation wound was compounded by the need to keep Malusi alive by feeding him myself.

The paediatrician in charge of Malusi was brutally frank with me: 'You can lie there and nurse your pain, but then your son will sure-ly die – I cannot control his diarrhoea.' There were no second thoughts. Dragging a drip two days after the operation, I had to stand in a hot nursery, every three hours, expressing my breasts, and feed Malusi through a slow nasal drip. I would go back to my pri-vate ward, drenched in sweat from heat and pain. I would demand pethidine, an injectable pain-killer, which had been ordered for my post-operative needs. When I used up the usual number of permit-ted dosages, I demanded more, and offered to sign for them myself – the alternative was too ghastly to contemplate.

I fortunately had Dr Lelau Mohuba to take care of the clinic dur-ing my pregnancy, and could afford the luxury of a few months off work. Sipo had in the meanwhile had an unsuccessful time as a Pharmacy Master's student in the United States. He was too embar-rassed to go back to his previous job, and ended up as a pharmacist at Livingstone Hospital in Port Elizabeth, his home town. Cracks began to appear everywhere in our relationship, but I put them down to physical distance.

I decided to leave Lenyenye in 1984, and join my husband in Port Elizabeth in a vain attempt to strengthen the relationship. My ban-ning order had been lifted in 1983 in the first wave of attempts to reform apartheid. I had stayed on because of the need to strengthen the Ithuseng project and ensure its long-term survival financially. Yet I had no anxiety about the abilities of my colleagues to continue the work without me. After all, my entire leadership style at Ithuseng was to work myself out of a job. I worked each day as if it would be the last, and made sure that my colleagues could pick up from where I left off if anything happened to me.

The community of Lenyenye organised a big farewell. A reception was held in the local Lutheran church where many speeches were made and presents heaped upon me. The most notable were two wooden carvings from my colleagues at Ithuseng Community Centre, the products of a self-taught local artist, Mr Makwela. One is a traditional healer with his divining bones; he is in a squatting position focusing on the messages given by the tools of his trade. The other is an old woman walking with a straw dish on her head, deep in thought and leaning on a walking-stick. These two figures were to stand guard over me – the diviner to let the community know if things went wrong, the old woman to walk me back to Lenyenye if need be. It was a measure of the ambivalence of the community about letting me go. I was sad too.

My own family were bitterly disappointed. My mother had tried desperately to burn the bridges behind me in a vain attempt to stop me from ever going back to the Cape. I discovered the extent to which she had gone, during the last few days of my stay in Lenyenye. I had entrusted a box with valuable historical documents spanning my activist years in Natal and the Eastern Cape to an illiterate woman in the village, knowing that she was unlikely to be a target of security police searches. She had, unbeknown to me, disclosed this to my mother, with whom she had become friends over time. I do not know when and how they destroyed the documents. I was shocked to discover that they were nowhere to be found when I went to fetch them from her as I prepared for my departure. After an uncomfortable silence and exchanges of shifty gazes, she confessed that they had been destroyed at my mother's suggestion. I was furious. But what could I do? A mother's love is both life-giving and destructive. In her eagerness to protect me from danger as her child, she had destroyed valuable links with the past.

I finally left Lenyenye for Port Elizabeth in May 1984. It was a sad occasion. My family was distraught. They mourned the end of my easy accessibility to them. The community in the area could not understand why I had to leave. How could I walk away from my beautiful house, thriving project (which they referred to as Mamphela's Clinic) and such love and popularity? But it was time to move on.

# 7

# Forging an Independent Lifestyle

Being black, woman, mother and professional places one in a challenging position anywhere in the world, but more particularly so in South Africa. The boundaries between the various spaces which one has to traverse, and within which one has to negotiate complex relationships, impose constraints on one's approach to life. To stretch across the boundaries of race, class and gender, whilst remaining creatively engaged in relationships across the generations, is a monumental task. 'Stretching' has the potential for creative expansion, but also of rupture, and yet it is the ultimate, inescapable challenge facing every citizen in changing South Africa.

When I became freer to make decisions about my future role, I had to take stock of the skills and capabilities which I had developed over the years of student activism, professional activism and life in the wilderness as a banished person. Some of the survival strategies developed in the furnace of activism have steeled and strengthened me as a person, affording me skills to deal with new and difficult environments with greater confidence. Others were more appropriate to the demands of the hostile contexts I had found myself in, but were inappropriate for the changing world I met with after my departure from Lenyenye. They could become liabilities if not judiciously harnessed.

I had not bargained for what it would take to be a wife after living independently for so long as an adult. Negotiating this role was complicated for a number of reasons. Firstly, Sipo Magele, my husband, had not arranged proper accommodation for us in Port Elizabeth. I realised at the last moment just before leaving Lenyenye in June 1984 that he had not, as promised, got a house for us to live in. So I had to make arrangements with Livingstone Hospital, where I had been offered a job as a medical officer, to obtain a staff house.

The authorities could only provide what was then available – a flat in the doctors' quarters with two bedrooms, a kitchenette and living area. It was hard to adjust to this small space with two children who were used to a bigger house and a supportive neighbourhood. I was back living in almost the same space I had occupied as an intern ten years earlier at the same hospital. We even ate in the same dining-room where I had eaten as an intern. Something was not right, but I hoped that it would be a temporary inconvenience until my husband got his act together.

Then again, I had up to that point always been surrounded by supportive helpers. Makgatla Mangena, my housekeeper and child-minder for both my children, who had become a true companion, had to stay on in Lenyenye to complete her schooling for the year. My mother, too, with her indomitable spirit and maternal love, had to move to stay with my brother Sethiba in Pietersburg. I suddenly found myself having to cope with all the demands of housekeeping, child care, professional work, and being a wife and partner to some-one. It was strenuous.

What is more, like so many women who are my contemporaries, I did not negotiate our respective roles as man and wife with my husband before our marriage. My feminist consciousness was still fairly under-developed. I had not yet acquired the sophistication which would have enabled me to negotiate an equitable partnership. I had been content to play the traditional woman's role in the domes-tic arena, provided it did not clash with my public role, and did not involve abuse and disrespect. Even during my King Williamstown days, my approach to gender roles in the domestic arena had large-ly been traditional.

Two events stand out in my memory in this regard. Firstly, I remember being quite uncomfortable with Fr Stubbs's offer to wash up after sharing a meal with me. I did not mind younger people who were my colleagues pitching in to help with domestic chores, but a priest was another matter, particularly one who was clearly my senior in age and a guest. Secondly, Desmond Tutu, on a visit to Zanempilo in 1976, tried unsuccessfully to get the chauvinists amongst my male colleagues to regard domestic chores as part of the responsibilities of being adult. He told them about the joy of wash-ing his own children's nappies whilst his family was living in England in the 1960s. That shocked me too, but I hoped in vain that my colleagues would at least consider dishwashing acceptable.

Sipo's expectations of the role of a wife were traditional, in keeping with the norm in South Africa. We would both come back from work at 4.30 p.m., sometimes fetch the children together, or else he would do that whilst I was busy with some household chores. Although I employed a part-time cleaner and washerwoman, I still had to do some tidying up and all the cooking because we did not like the food in the communal dining-room. It never seemed to occur to Sipo that I was just as tired as he was after work. I remember one particularly frustrating evening when I was busy cooking in the kitchenette, and Malusi, then a tiny one-and-a-half-year-old, crying next to Sipo, who was blissfully asleep in an easy chair. He could not understand why I was making such a fuss about his lack of attention to his own son, who was right beside him.

The pleasurable moments we spent together – and they were not insignificant – were not enough to stop the nagging feeling that I had made yet another monumental error in choosing a partner. The differences between us became more stark over the few weeks following our arrival in Port Elizabeth. There was no sign of a house materialising in the foreseeable future, and Sipo appeared not to regard this as an urgent problem. For as long as we did not have better accommodation, I could not arrange the household properly, and that was intolerable for me. Sipo had a casual approach to many other things. I was used to organising my life in a manner that tried to anticipate problems as much as was humanly possible. To live with someone who could see nothing wrong with running out of petrol in a car that had a working gauge was too much for me. We had incompatible approaches to life.

My stay in Port Elizabeth was not all bad news. My job as a medical officer was very enjoyable and rewarding both intellectually and financially. For the first time in my working life I was paid an adequate salary, which was augmented by overtime pay for call duty once a week. I also did not have to worry about where the money would come from to run the hospital – a welcome relief after almost ten years of struggling to balance the budgets of institutions in which I had worked. I benefited, too, from being in a more intellectually challenging environment after a life of isolation in the wilderness. I learnt a lot from my colleagues, some of whom had been my juniors at Natal Medical School. They had specialised during the years when I pursued my professional activism, and it was a pleasure to be guided by them. There was mutual respect between us.

During the course of August 1984, after about only two months in the role of working wife, I decided that such a life was not for me. I made plans to leave. I made contact with Francis Wilson, a Professor of Economics at the University of Cape Town (UCT), who was then directing the Second Carnegie Inquiry into Poverty and Development in Southern Africa, and he promised to help me obtain an appointment at UCT to work with him on the study. Francis had been one of the friends who kept in touch with me during my years in Lenyenye. He came several times to discuss the poverty study with me, and had kept me abreast of developments in the wider society. He is an attractive, energetic, creative thinker, who always seems to manage to find a way out of tricky corners. He assured me that he would do his best to help me.

My departure from Port Elizabeth and the end of my marriage were sad affairs. Sipo was distraught. He could not believe that I would take such drastic action without giving him a second chance. Although I did not like seeing him hurt, I had to tell him that there was no hope of either of us changing our very different personalities or of us ever developing an acceptable *modus vivendi*. We had to accept the painful fact of our incompatibility. I had lived for too long as an independent person to play the traditional role of a wife.

I have difficulties living with unresolved problems. As far as I was concerned, our relationship did not have a chance of being set on a new footing. Neither of us, I felt, was ready for the major commitment that would be necessary to renegotiate the marriage contract, and face up to the personal compromises that would inevitably follow if we were to give our relationship a chance to grow. Although my career was not negotiable, I could have been quite content with a slower pace of change, provided there was a willingness on my husband's side to face the risks of ridicule from his peers, most of whom were childhood friends and would have had difficulty supporting his break with the traditional macho habits of Port Elizabeth men.

Most young men in Port Elizabeth townships at the time, and probably in most other townships as well, spent their free time in shebeens or each other's homes drinking and boasting about their achievements, their women and their cars. The fact that in the status-conscious and hierarchical society in which we live my profession is ranked higher than pharmacy, also complicated the prospects for a changed lifestyle for us as a couple. My high national profile as a political activist was another 'liability' in this regard. The chances were too great that Sipo's friends would misinterpret any change in his behaviour as bowing to the demands of a dominant woman. It would have taken a much stronger and more secure person to resist such peer pressure.

Bruce Haigh, my Australian friend, once observed that the very characteristics which men find attractive in strong women are ironically the ones most threatening to men. Non-traditional marriage relationships with set gender roles are difficult to negotiate under these circumstances. Women all over the world are often compelled either to play down 'the threatening aspects' of their personalities to preserve their marriages, or to negotiate terms which suit both parties even if these may put the marriage at risk. Most women, given the limitations of their circumstances, opt for the former. But I chose differently.

My brother Sethiba, then a teacher in Pietersburg, flew to Port Elizabeth to help me with the physical move to Cape Town, and to provide support in the event of Sipo attempting to obstruct my planned move. The drive to Cape Town on the last weekend in September 1984 was tiring, but I was relieved that I had made the decision to move, and followed through with it.

My attraction to Cape Town had been kindled by previous visits. The first was at the beginning of 1976, in my capacity as the Eastern Cape Regional Director of the Black Community Programmes. There are not many cities set against a magnificent mountain and caressed by two oceans, as one finds here. I was struck by the beauty of Cape Town.

The second visit was during 1982 whilst I was still banned and expecting Malusi. I had been encouraged by my lawyer, Kathy Satchwell, who was then working in Raymond Tucker's law firm, to apply for permission to go on holiday, a possibility I had not entertained before. She told me that other banned people such as Beyers Naudé had already taken advantage of this privilege – another example of how one could use biases within the system to one's advantage. I had never heard of a black banned person ever applying for a holiday, let alone being granted permission. But I did not wait for a second prompting. I grabbed the opportunity to get out of Lenyenye. Sipo and I drove to Cape Town on what I hoped would be an opportunity for us to be alone together as man and wife for the first time in our married life. It was an interesting trip which partly fulfilled my expectations. I was again deeply impressed by the wonderful setting of Cape Town with its striking combination of sea and mountain.

On this trip the limitations of my husband became more obvious to me, and our different expectations of what being together meant came to the fore. I had hoped that we would use the time to explore the beautiful environment together and get to know each other better without the distractions of family and friends. His idea of fun was sitting with friends over drinks. There was nothing I could do to create a better balance. I spent the time with friends or resting and reading.

The conference of the Second Carnegie Inquiry into Poverty, held in April 1984, provided the third occasion for me to visit Cape Town. I was then also able to experience a little of the physical beauty of the University of Cape Town, where the conference was held. The campus setting on the side of Devil's Peak, part of the Table Mountain complex, lends a majestic aura to the University. I liked what I saw and enjoyed the intellectual energy which I sensed flowed through the institution. After years in an intellectual wilderness, I became quite attracted to the possibility of being part of an academic community.

During the first three months in Cape Town, from October to December 1984, my sons and I stayed with the Moletsanes, Thami and Nontobeko, at the Anglican rectory in Langa where they lived with their four children. They are a generous couple who are always ready to open their home to many people. It was also a joyous reunion. Nontobeko had been the first sister-in-charge of Zanempilo until their departure in 1976 with Thami's transfer to this parish.

We had an easy relationship as a compound family. Hlumelo found play-mates in two of the Moletsane sons who were the same age. He also joined them at the local school. Malusi enjoyed the pampering of the many people who came through the household. One could not ask for more from friends in time of need.

Langa Township is the oldest of Cape Town's African 'locations'. It is a mixed bag. Family houses of all types stand alongside derelict migrant-labour hostels. The educated and uneducated share community life together. There is stability and order in the midst of apparent chaos. The filthy streets contrast with the meticulous cleanliness of the interiors of individual homes. Appearances are very deceptive in this setting. Services at the local St Cyprian's Church run by Thami Moletsane were joyous occasions in which to experience fellowship with other Christians. The music was glorious. One had a sense of security in Langa.

I spent two months bargaining hard with Lester Peteni, an acquaintance from my Eastern Cape days, who had become the local manager of the Urban Foundation's Housing Division in Guguletu, to secure a house which we could lease. We moved to Guguletu Township at the beginning of December 1984 into a comfortable three-bedroomed house which Lester had been using as a staff house. It was a relief to be in our own home as a family again.

We lived on the main road in Guguletu, NY 108 (Native Yard 108, the nomenclature deriving from colonial days). The township has a mixture of housing types. Firstly, there are old-style houses like long train carriages, subdivided into two- or one-bedroom family units with living-room and kitchen space. These are by far the most numerous of the family housing units. Secondly, after the 1976 Soweto riots, free-standing houses were constructed by the Urban Foundation to ease the pressing housing problems in the townships. These were few, given the limited land available and affordability problems faced by prospective owners. Thirdly, there were the single-sex migrant-labour hostels where men supposedly lived on their own, though more and more women and children began at great risk to join them in the squalid, domitory-like accommodation.

Guguletu, like many similar townships, has poor social services. The few, overcrowded schools were hardly functional during the 1980s, an era of school boycotts and work stayaways. Hlumelo, who attended a primary school not far from our house, would often be dismissed early when trouble was expected, and so he had little effective education in 1985. On one occasion he was nearly run over by a taxi, which came speeding down NY 108, as was commonly the case. I was horrified by the lack of safety for children in the area. I lived in fear.

Guguletu became caught in the vicious cycle of political violence – a common experience of most townships in the mid-1980s which persisted until the 1994 non-racial elections. It also had the dubious distinction of having the highest per capita murder rate in the world, higher than that of Chicago's ghettos. Political violence simply fuelled the existing fires of criminal violence. Some criminals assumed the political metaphors of the time, and became known as *com-tsotsis*, from their adoption of the term 'comrade', popular amongst political activists, whilst pursuing their *tsotsi* (criminal) behaviour. Living in Guguletu in the mid-eighties was not easy.

Our problems were compounded by the fact that our house fronted on NY 108, which was the funeral route. During the many mass funeral processions of the 1980s, which often turned into running battles between the police and mourners, we would be caught in the crossfire. On one occasion, a hole of about three inches in diameter was made in our roof by a burst of buckshot from police firing at fleeing youths. The intrusion of teargas fumes into our house was also a regular occurrence. A military vehicle used to park in front of our house. Though we welcomed it privately when buses with ordinary commuters would come under attack from township youth without any provocation, we hated the security forces' bullying of ordinary people and the ease with which they used live ammunition.

Encounters with the 'comrades' were not pleasant either. One Sunday lunch-time we were sitting in the dining-room and having a family meal when a young man burst into the house. He did not respond when I asked how I could help him. He simply vanished into one of the children's bedrooms. Hot on his heels were vicious-looking policemen who demanded to know where he had gone. We could genuinely say that we did not know.

For the next hour or so – it felt like a whole day – the police searched through the property, in and around the house, and eventually settled on the only bedroom which was locked. They demanded the key from me and I told them truthfully that I did not have it. They then threatened to use teargas to flush out the fugitive. I pleaded with them and pointed out that it would be unfair for my family to be subjected to such unpleasantness simply because someone had run into our house.

The police sought authority from the local Police Commissioner to force their way into the bedroom. They kicked the door in and found a frightened young man in one of the cupboards. He was arrested for allegedly having thrown stones at the police. The police promised to come back and have the door repaired but they never did. The young comrade was later to claim that I had betrayed him – a dangerous statement in the days of the 'necklace' in the township. Fortunately there had been enough witnesses for the claim to be seen for what it was.

Malusi, then only two years old and very tiny for his age, became so insecure in this war zone that he lost faith in my capacity as his mother to protect him. Whenever he heard the sound of gunfire he would slide under a bed and refuse to come out for a while. He also began to bite his nails. Such was the terror of living on the frontline.

My work environment was, in contrast, calm and peaceful. It is amazing how successful the apartheid cities have been in separating the lives and problems of black township residents from those of whites in the suburbs. It was hard to believe that one was living in the same city. This effective separation in part explains the ease with which most white South Africans could pretend to themselves that there was nothing much wrong with the society in which they lived.

SALDRU, the Southern Africa Labour and Development Research Unit, started and run by Francis Wilson, provided a warm, supportive base for my re-entry into the academic world in October 1984. I was given a cubicle, for which I was grateful, in view of the pressure on space in SALDRU. I also had access to Francis Wilson's office whenever he was out of town, a not uncommon occurrence. I spent the first three months of my life at UCT reading all 310 papers presented at the Carnegie conference earlier that year, in preparation for my co-authorship of the report. It was wonderful having all the time to myself in a stimulating intellectual environment.

The year 1985 was one of real growth for me and crucial for the development of my academic skills. My initial intention was simply to sit back and take in what I could from the richness around me whilst regenerating my energy. Years of activism had left me drained in ways which are difficult to describe to anyone who has not had the experience. It was not simple burn-out; rather it was being programmed for action to such a degree that total relaxation became a rare and strange phenomenon for the body and mind – almost painful. One had to learn anew how to relax – just to stop and smell the flowers.

Moreover, I felt a deep need to reflect on what I had been involved in over the previous decade or so. Developing critical thinking, reading and writing skills became urgent. Writing the report on poverty with Francis provided an excellent training for me in this area. We spent most of the first half of 1986 working on the structure of the book: tracing the central themes, deciding on the level of detail we wanted to include, the audience we were targeting and the lay-out, particularly the boxes in the text, which became effective in highlighting case histories and quotations. The title was the most difficult: it was decided upon just before publication at the end of 1988. One gets to know when a title sounds right, and *Uprooting Poverty** did just that.

The collaboration with Francis during the writing of the book bound us together and strengthened our friendship. He helped me to discipline my stream of consciousness and transform it into meaningful phrases, sentences, paragraphs, and eventually themes which hung together logically. I learnt a lot about the English language, the difference between the written and spoken word, and the added care one has to exercise with the former. Split infinitives, a common problem for non-English mother-tongue speakers, especially those from an African language background like myself, were a constant theme which Francis harped on. My admiration for the convenience of computers was kindled over the months while I sat next to Francis as he punched in our thoughts, to have them emerge at the end of four years in book form.

I brought to the project my insights into the reality of poverty and the survival mechanisms which people develop to cope with their difficulties. I was able to inject a less romantic notion of the poor than one which would have flowed from the pen of a male, liberal English-speaking South African. We were also able to present an integrated analysis of race, class, gender, age and geographic location which went beyond what was politically correct in the mid-1980s. In this way we could present a sympathetic case study of a poor, unemployed, rural African man and his misery without denying his own role in the oppression of his wife and children as part of the patriarchal system. Francis's economics background was crucial to the quantitative analytical enterprise. We complemented each other's strengths and weaknesses well.

In 1987 we produced *Children on the Frontline: A Report for Unicef on the Status of Children in South Africa.*† In so doing we stepped on many sensitive political toes. The report gave both statistical and case-study data on the plight of South African children caught in the double jeopardy of structural violence, created by a racist political and socio-economic order, and physical violence, which scarred not only their bodies but their psyches as well.

* Francis Wilson and Mamphela Ramphele, *Uprooting Poverty: The South African Challenge* (Cape Town and New York, 1988).
† Francis Wilson and Mamphela Ramphele, *Children on the Frontline: A Report for Unicef on the Status of Children in South Africa* (New York, 1987).

In the 1980s many children as young as seven were caught in the frenzy of political activism. Stompie Seipei was a case in point. His kidnapping and murder had a sequel in the widely publicised case involving Winnie Mandela. He was one of the many children in the 1980s who were involved in violence as political activists, innocent passers-by, detainees or victims of indescribable police brutality. But we also dared to suggest that children, particularly black children, were also victims of political movements which took advantage of their enthusiasm and dare-devil mentality to fight battles that adults were too scared to pursue. White children too were fighting in the apartheid war as conscripts, pitted against black children in the townships.

We cautioned against the brutalising impact of violence on the children of South Africa, both as its victims and as its perpetrators. We cited Archbishop Tutu's prophetic stance and his outright condemnation of both police brutality and the 'necklace' murders of suspected police informers as equally dehumanising.

There was outrage amongst political activists. How could we criticise the self-defence of powerless oppressed people? Were we not aware of the danger of blaming the victim and thus strengthening the hand of the victimiser? Some critics went as far as suggesting that we were allowing ourselves to be used as agents of American imperialism. How else could we explain our acceptance of the Carnegie Corporation's funding without prior consultation with 'the people'? The fact that Francis Wilson had indeed consulted widely before accepting the sponsorship was a factual inconvenience which was dispensed with lightly. We were both quite satisfied that we had presented an intellectually honest case of the impact of oppression on children, and the dangers of liberation strategies which further dehumanise those caught up in a repressive system.

Our collaborative work brought our different personalities into sharp relief. I had difficulty living with an unfinished product for four years, whereas Francis was quite relaxed, and would quote his mother, Monica Wilson, as an authority who believed that writing up research should take as long as its collection does. I was frustrated by this, but could do little to change the pace of work. It was fortuitous that I could channel my energy into other things between our writing appointments.

I did some session work at the Guguletu Day Hospital, which gave me an opportunity to practise my medical skills and to learn to know the local primary health-care system. It was depressing. On any one day 600 patients would be crowded into the inadequate waiting-room. Some had arrived at the gate as early as 6 a.m., only to be seen for about five minutes by caring but overwhelmed medical doctors after five hours or so of waiting. It was a typical apartheid health facility. I struggled to cope with being part of such an inadequate system, but stayed on because it was important for me to keep in touch with the realities of poor South Africans. Not only did my conscience as a political activist dictate this, but it also made academic sense to maintain a research base.

At about this time I entered the world of Anthropology, through a back door. After working for some time I found my cubicle in SALDRU had become too small for me. It is interesting how one outgrows physical spaces. What once looked perfectly adequate becomes intolerable later under changing circumstances. Francis used a combination of his old boy network and ancestral ties with the Department of Social Anthropology at UCT to secure me an office in the Department at the beginning of the 1986 academic year.

My new colleagues in Anthropology were very supportive. It was a well-run department under Professor Martin West, with well-established rituals. There were regular morning and afternoon teas, a bequest of good English upbringing which Professor Monica Wilson, Francis's mother, passed on during her term as head of department from 1955 to 1973. The Department also had a well-run weekly seminar programme at which staff and graduate students had the opportunity of presenting their work. These seminars provide a collegial, yet critical, environment for personal academic development. But like many academic settings, critical comment can, and does, run the risk of destroying an argument without due regard for a vulnerable person's self-confidence. There were rare occasions when stinging attacks on students' work only succeeded in demoralising them. On one occasion I felt strongly enough about the attack to intervene – to the embarrassment of my colleagues, who felt that I had broken ranks.

During the course of 1986, I took an interest in the plight of people living in migrant-labour hostels in the townships of Cape Town. David Russell, who was then the Anglican priest assigned by the Cape Town diocese to minister to the needs of migrant workers, introduced me to hostel dwellers. They were at the bottom rung of the socio-economic ladder of South African society, and viewed as temporary sojourners in Cape Town, in keeping with the dictates of apartheid, which tolerated Africans in the white urban areas, only so long as they were usefully employed.

Africans in the Western Cape also faced additional problems from the constraints placed on job prospects and social services by the Coloured Labour Preference Policy, which sought to make the Western Cape the preserve of white and 'Coloured' people. African townships such as Langa, Guguletu and Nyanga were deliberately neglected and under-developed so as to discourage family settlement. Large hostel compounds were built to house single African men, and vicious policing of the pass laws was used to criminalise attempts by African men and women to lead normal family lives.

I decided to start a project with the newly established Western Cape Men's Hostel Dwellers' Association (HDA) with a view to strengthening their own efforts to secure their rights to family life and better living conditions. The men in the leadership of the HDA were courageous people with interesting names reflecting their unsophisticated backgrounds: Johnson Mpukumpa, Welcome Zenzile, Super Nkathazo, and so on. I did not anticipate the challenges that lay ahead. With Francis Wilson's help I obtained financial support from the Ford Foundation to fund my own research post until I was given tenure by UCT later in 1986.

The Anglo American Corporation and De Beers Chairman's Fund funded the research costs of my project. It is symbolically appropriate that this mining giant, which organised and benefited from migrant labour, should make some contribution to the study, and hopefully to the elimination of the vicious system they helped create in South Africa. It is a battle which I am still fighting.

Learning to do research in a methodical way was taxing for one more accustomed to the world of activism. It took time for me to come to terms with the demands of scholarly rigour. There was a big psychological hurdle for me to cross regarding the importance of academic work in the wider scheme of things. I had joined the ranks of arm-chair intellectuals who occupied the ivory tower of academic life, the very people we as activists used to view with scorn. How could I justify my presence at UCT and claim it would make a difference?

There is a sense in which intellectual work is not regarded within activist circles as *real* work. Activist intellectuals often have to engage in other activities to justify their credibility within these circles. It is a difficult problem to tackle in a country where the majority of people have been denied educational opportunities to develop the skills to engage in intellectual work. A deep sense of guilt on the part of the survivors of a discriminatory system drives these people to overextend themselves in an attempt to respond to the expectations of their fellow oppressed people, whilst also trying to meet academic demands. Political activists often exploit this guilt to extract the maximum out of them, sometimes with devastating consequences for all.

My choice of a research area and the use of a participatory research methodology were in part aimed at reducing the level of discomfort I felt in my new position – my guilt as a survivor. In this way I could convince myself more easily that my academic work was a continuation of my previous work and did not subtract from my political commitment. It was much more difficult to convince former co-activists and others who feared that my energies would be sapped by the demands of academic life, and that I would be neutralised as an agent of change. Many regarded my entry into the academic world as a loss to the struggle.

What is more, the association of Anthropology with colonialism, a charge political activists often made, did not sit comfortably with me. I could, however, take comfort from the fact that I was not out to become an anthropologist, but was merely using the Department of Anthropology as a convenient base from which to do work which needed to be done. But it became clear as I learned more of the discipline of Anthropology, that it was much more than the 'handmaiden of colonialism'. I learned to distinguish between the prostitution of Anthropology by racists and colonialists to serve their own ends, and Anthropology as a social science. Although a particularly vicious form of Anthropology operated in some Afrikaans-speaking universities, which provided ethnological justification for segregation, there was also another tradition which had earned South African Anthropology a place of honour internationally. Radcliffe-Brown, Monica Wilson, the Mayers and many others had done valuable work which had led to a greater and more sophisticated understanding of South African society.

I also noticed that the method of Anthropology – participant observation – was not very different from what I had used as an activist in community development work. I had to live among the people I worked with, observe what they did, why certain things made sense to them, and what motivated them. Participant observation is a prerequisite of any action which would try to change people's life circumstances. I could build on the skills I had developed earlier to sharpen my research work: communication in the people's own language, empathy and the ability to win the trust of others.

But I was still not ready to become an anthropologist. In one of my first presentations to the departmental seminar in 1987, I drew on my reading of feminist literature from the United States to try to understand the dynamics of gender which I had observed in the migrant-labour hostels of Cape Town. One of my colleagues objected to my use of the term 'patriarchy' to refer to the system of male-dominated power relations I saw in operation. Patriarchy was not a widely used term in South Africa at the time. He told me that anthropologists did not like using such terms, whereupon I reminded him that I was not there to become an anthropologist, and that I would continue to use the term anyway.

Anthropology in South Africa had until the mid-1980s not embraced gender as an important construct in social analysis. Many ethnographic texts had indeed documented the inequalities of power between men and women in the communities they studied, but little theoretical discussion had developed around gender politics, nor was there any serious discussion of feminist literature. The exchange between my colleague and myself was indicative of the tensions which existed between traditional and non-traditional approaches to social science in our discipline. As a newcomer to academic life, I could go where angels feared to tread.

Among many other political activists, Thabo Mbeki, then foreign relations spokesman for the African National Congress (ANC), also questioned my choice of academic base, when we met at a conference at Duke University in 1989 to launch *Uprooting Poverty*. He asked, 'Et tu Mamphela?', to which I replied confidently that he needed to distinguish between good and bad Anthropology. I was becoming more comfortable with the nature of my new academic base.

As my academic work progressed, the migrant-worker research project proved much larger and more demanding than I had anticipated. Not only did I have to cope with the demands of fieldwork for data collection, but I also ran into serious conflict with the authoritarian tendencies in the Western Cape Men's Hostel Dwellers'

Association. The demands of fieldwork were exacerbated by the horrible conditions in which people lived. I became physically ill at the end of 1987 from sheer exhaustion and anger at the dehumanising conditions of the hostels where I spent about three months observing the daily lives of hostel dwellers. As in the case of Una Wikan, who worked in a Cairo slum, one's psyche takes punishment under such conditions.*

But the conflict with the leaders of the HDA was more exhausting. It challenged all the romantic notions I had about the capacity of poor, oppressed people to organise themselves out of their position of powerlessness and become part of the process shaping a more egalitarian society. In the first place, the assumption that all poor, oppressed people would keenly embrace any well-thought-out participatory programme to change their lives underestimated the power of years of oppression in conditioning subordinates to accept their fate as unalterable.

What is more, the leaders of the HDA displayed a style which reflected, reinforced and replicated existing power relations in our society. Older men who were more articulate saw it as their destiny to lead, and their right to be listened to with little or no questioning. And there was in fact little evidence of questioning from the ranks of hostel dwellers. Yet the commitment of the leaders to changing the conditions of life for their fellow hostel dwellers could not be faulted. They took enormous risks at a time when state repression of any movement for change was vicious. Some of them, such as Super Nkathazo, have paid with their lives in the violence of the 1990s. Their followers granted them the reverence they felt they deserved.

It seems to me that the high risks involved in political leadership in an authoritarian system have the potential to breed authoritarianism. Such authoritarianism is not only tolerated by the oppressed, but expected. The feeling of insecurity and the danger of infiltrators lead to demands for strong leadership, even if it comes at a cost. The need for leaders who will not look back when danger looms is a major concern of powerless people.

But I could not come to terms with these realities. Having worked myself into the position of adviser to, and fundraiser and advocate for, the HDA, I experienced a deep crisis when I realised I had to withdraw from this role. I could not continue to be associated with something which was likely to perpetuate inequalities between men

*Life among the Poor in Cairo* (London, 1980).

and women, old and young, and had demonstrated its potential for ruthless suppression of dissent. But withdrawal would put at risk the possibility of the physical upgrading of the hostels into family units which was being negotiated at the time. Who was I to put my moral stance between poor people and the social services they had waited for so long?

It was only after reflecting on the distinction between my role as a facilitator for change in social relations, and that of local authorities as providers of social services, that I was able to free myself from the guilt trap in which I found myself. My conscience was clear. I withdrew from the HDA at the beginning of 1988. That withdrawal had some positive effect on the leadership style of the HDA. I had called their bluff. I felt that their victim status was no excuse for undemocratic behaviour. We resumed our relationship on a much healthier basis; but I was left drained.

At this time I also had to make important decisions about finally leaving township life behind me. We were already living in a University staff house in Lovers Walk in Rondebosch, having had to flee Guguletu in June 1986, when the violent repression of the local population by the security forces took on the proportions of open warfare. This included the burning of shacks in squatter areas in a vain attempt by the police to flush out political activists.

One day in June 1986 I got a call from Nomvume Sotomela, my housekeeper at the time, that there was a rumour of a threat to burn the Uluntu Community Centre, which was situated on the property adjacent to our house. In my view there was just one appropriate response. I drove straight to Guguletu, terrified by the thought of impending danger, but determined to get my son Malusi and Nomvume out of harm's way. We thrust a few personal belongings in the back of the car and dashed to Francis and Lindy Wilson's house in Rondebosch, where we remained as refugees until UCT allocated the staff house in Lovers Walk.

At the beginning of 1987, after many battles with the racist housing system in Cape Town and the UCT bureaucracy, I finally purchased my own house in Mowbray. It had to be registered in the name of the University to circumvent the legal barriers to black ownership of property in white suburbs. Many other black South Africans had to have 'fronts' to acquire property in the land of their birth. My white neighbours, after initially protesting against our presence to the local police, relaxed when they realised that the heavens were not going to fall in. One of them said to the local police that they had not realised I was a medical doctor! How my profession made me less black only white racists can explain.

Early in 1988 Margaret Touborg, then Personal Aide to Dr Martina Horner, President of Radcliffe College at Harvard, came to South Africa to identify potential applicants for the newly established Carnegie Distinguished International Fellowship for the 1988/89 academic year. The thought that I could be chosen did not even occur to me. I did not see myself as an academic, but as someone who had come to seek refuge in the academic world to reflect on a new path for the life ahead of me, and therefore I did not imagine myself qualifying.

However, Margaret not only convinced me that I was the person Radcliffe College were looking for, but made arrangements for my eventual arrival at the Bunting Institute in September 1988, where we were to remain until April 1989. We lived in a two-bedroom flat in one of the Harvard University housing complexes. It was three minutes' walk to the Bunting Institute in Concord Avenue, and five minutes' walk to Buckingham Browne and Nichols Lower School where both my sons went. They were 'latch-key children' but would often call at my office on their way home.

I was able to call upon a stipend and research money to employ a student assistant and regular baby-sitting services. Tracy Walton became our baby-sitter and a valuable support for all of us. She generously used her own car, a station wagon, to drive my sons around to movies or to places of interest. Such luxury I had never known before. I sat back and immersed myself in the community of women scholars and the wealth of Harvard University's library resources. I had the opportunity to engage in discussions with powerful women of all ages who were making a name for themselves in their careers: poets, painters, sculptors, astrophysicists, mathematicians, political scientists, anthropologists, and many more. It was an intellectual feast.

The idea of creating a safe, supportive space for women in academic life has long been recognised by feminists, but it is fair to say that the generosity of the Bunting Fellowship is in a class of its own globally. Men have always created such spaces for themselves, even though they do not generally have to deal with the competing demands of a career and raising a family. Think of all the major fellowships and scholarships that were exclusively reserved for men until a few decades ago. It is a measure of the low value placed on women's contribution to high-level jobs in society that these spaces are such a rarity for women throughout the world.

One of the books which I had the good fortune to read on the rec-ommendation of Jane Cooper, a poet and Bunting Fellow, was by Gaston Bachelard, a philosopher and poet, entitled *The Poetics of Space*.* Jane later gave me an autographed copy when she realised how much it meant to me. Bachelard combined his philosophical and poetic skills to produce an eloquent exploration of space and its symbolic impact on people's lives. It suddenly dawned on me that space had many dimensions: psychological, intellectual, political, social and economic. What the Bunting Institute provided was this multi-dimensional space for women to develop their skills.

Not only did that realisation infuse a new meaning into my own life, but it provided a thematic tool for the collation and analysis of my migrant hostel data. It helped me understand that hostel dwellers' capacity to act as active agents of history was constrained by their limited political, social, economic, intellectual and psycho-logical space. But I also recognised the way in which those same con-straints, as they had done in my own life, also enable people to develop important survival strategies that ensure their ability not only to live within the constraints, but to transcend them as well. I realised that the various constraints work together to set off a vicious cycle, but once such a cycle is broken at a critical point, the transfor-mative capacity of human beings can come to the fore.

Risk-taking is an important element and a necessary condition for people to break the cycle of powerlessness and submission. Making choices in our lives is one of the characteristics which make us human beings, and choice remains with us even as we face death at the hands of torturers – the choice to submit or to die in dignity. I have had to learn that the courage to take risks is not given to all of us. This realisation has enabled me to develop a better approach to the process of empowerment, and also encouraged me to have more compassion for those who are unable to become transformative agents.

One outcome of the space the Bunting Institute gave me was a decision to write up my research data as a Ph.D. thesis entitled 'Empowerment and the Politics of Space', which was accepted at

*G. Bachelard, *The Poetics of Space* (New York, 1964).

UCT in 1991. A book of the thesis, *A Bed Called Home*, was published in 1993.* I had become an anthropologist after all.

For women in my position the 'superwoman syndrome' is an ever-present danger. Terri Apter, amongst others, has explored this syndrome at length. Women trying to juggle the multiple roles they have to play in life – as partner, mother, career woman – face enormous challenges to remain human. 'The trap that the superwoman falls into is the belief that she can have everything because she can do as much as two or three people.'†

There is an assumption in this statement of Apter's which resonates with what many of my sympathetic critics sometimes say to me, that women in this position *elect* not to exercise the choice they have between the various contending demands, and thus avoid the trap. How does one who is a single woman like me with two sons choose between a career and motherhood? Moreover, as a South African in a country where blacks have limited skills, how does one exercise this choice when faced with the relentless pressure to engage in many national and community activities? Lastly, as a black woman in changing South Africa where even fewer black women can participate meaningfully in shaping future social policies to ensure greater equity, how does one make the choice between engagement and non-engagement?

From my own experience, 'superwomen' do not necessarily believe that they can have everything because they can do as much as two or three people. It is a condition of being black and woman in South Africa that one *has* to be a 'superwoman'. My mother did not choose to remain a primary schoolteacher whilst bringing up seven children with little help from her traditional husband. She had to do both *and* thus had to learn to do as much as three people. The doing of what two or three people can do becomes a survival strategy, not the reason for taking on multiple roles. Many ordinary poor women in South Africa are presented with the 'superwoman' title by the historical accident of their birth, not because they seek it.

As a mother, however, I have a very different set of attitudes from those of my own mother. It has struck me that my biological incompetence to carry my pregnancies to term without assistance may be an important factor in my attitude to motherhood. I do not have the

* Mamphela Ramphele, *A Bed Called Home: Life in the Migrant Labour Hostels of Cape Town* (Cape Town, Edinburgh and Athens, Ohio, 1993).
†T. Apter, *Why Women Don't Have Wives* (Basingstoke, 1985), p. 118.

illusion of having been programmed for the nurturing role; if I had been, then something went horribly wrong with the programme. The discomforts and frustrations I experienced in having to lie on my bed with its foot elevated at an angle for months on end did not leave me with too many romantic ideas about pregnancy. Then again, even allowing for my particular problems, there is something truly invasive about pregnancy. Its invasiveness is particularly pronounced as the baby grows, shaping and dictating the mother's every movement.

The birth process is a major challenge to one's body. Whatever form the delivery takes, there is the ever-present danger of death lurking behind the exhilarating prospect of a new life beginning. There is a saying in Sesotho that *tswala e bolaile tsie* (birth has killed a locust), which refers to the fact that once a female locust is fertilised it is destined to die as soon as it completes the process of laying its eggs. In spite of that knowledge, many other female locusts will still engage in the process of giving their lives so that new life can be brought forth.

This locust metaphor has more than a physical aspect to it. There is also the invisible (sometimes not-so-invisible) death of aspects of women's lives as they engage in the necessary sacrificial action to give birth to children and to raise them. The indignity of the birth pains, for those of us who gave birth to our children before epidurals were considered safe and generally accessible, I found humiliating. As Francis Wilson has told me, his mother Monica once commented that the whole engineering and plumbing job around the birth canal leaves much to be desired. I passionately believe that the designer would have been failed if this had been an engineering graduate project.

The compensation of seeing a bundle of life next to one immediately after birth makes up for the mess one is in after delivery. But I had bitter-sweet experiences around the birth of all three of my children. In none of the cases could their fathers be there with me.

Nor does nursing young babies fill me with a glowing feeling. I enjoyed watching them tucking into my breast and relishing the flow of milk. But breast-feeding beyond six months is not for me. I also resented the interruption to my sleep, which one had to endure for the first six to twelve months, depending on the child's temperament. Both my first two babies were screamers, and gave me little time for rest. I was glad to have the family support I had, and eventually come out of that baby period.

I have no fears of the empty nest syndrome. On the contrary, I have developed a relationship with my sons, now both in their teens, which is nurturing but encouraging of independence and negotiation for individual space within the communal space we share. From very early on, I made my children know that much as I loved them dearly, I was but a normal human being who gets tired and irritable and makes mistakes. I have encouraged them to appreciate how important my own personal space is to me, and how vital it was for my best functioning. It is hard for children to understand that, but it is the only way I can retain my sanity as a parent. Once my bedroom door is closed, my room becomes out of bounds for them, unless there is an urgent problem.

My own parenting style attempts to take the best from my childhood experiences whilst shunning the self-sacrificial aspects which made my mother's life a misery. I learned from her how to be a good cook, keep the house tidy, including kitchen corners, and still have quality time. The importance of discipline and getting children to take responsibility she perfected to an art form. I do not have to go as far as she did, because I am not as desperate for quick action as she was with the seven of us. She also could not afford the luxury of negotiation, which I have used to great benefit with my sons. My mother's use of physical punishment was a reflection of both its acceptance in her own environment and time, and the pressure under which she was operating that made tolerance of mistakes difficult. She had to run a tight ship to keep us all afloat. I have watched myself slipping into impatience under pressure, and know just how easy it is for parents to be intolerant.

I still make sure that I have the time to prepare occasionally the apple-pies, pancakes and waffles which my sons love. But I have learnt, and can afford something which my mother could have done with – having wives! I have accepted that I cannot fulfil all the expectations of motherhood and parenting, nor do I wish to do so. I do not enjoy some of the chores essential for a normal well-functioning family, but make sure they are done to perfection by those capable of doing so.

Unlike a lot of other women in my position, I have no guilt feelings about my domestic arrangements. I believe that I compensate adequately those who make my life comfortable, within my limited means. I am indebted to all those women who have played this effective wife role in my life. It is not an accident that men have over the years protected their privileged access to the services of their wives. Wives have throughout history freed men to succeed outside the domestic arena. Until society is better organised, I see no end in sight for the essential role of the 'wife', male or female.

Widowed well-to-do African matriarchs in the Pietersburg region, where my parents came from, used to marry wives late in their lives to secure essential support in their old age. This applied in particular to childless women. The marriage involved customary bride-wealth and all the other traditional rights and obligations. The young married woman was free to have male friends and bear children, but the children belonged to her 'husband', the older woman. It may not be an egalitarian model to follow, but it illustrates the complexities inherent in dealing with the problem of adequate domestic support.

Balancing my role as mother and professional has become more of a challenge over the years. Whilst I was still a professional activist in a supportive domestic scene with extended family members around, it was not a major problem. It became a problem in Port Elizabeth. My move to Cape Town did not initially present major problems. But as my work became more demanding, the balancing act grew more taxing. It is, however, perhaps fair to say that the biggest problem for me in my mature years is not presented by being a working woman, but by the competing demands of national agendas, which impinge on the delicate balance between mothering and work-time achieved through trial and error over the years.

The spectre of the role of honorary male looms large for women in my position. It is a role in which many women in my position find themselves. How does one function in roles which were previously the preserve of males? There is a variety of responses. Some women have chosen to operate in such roles as though they were men. Their focus is to 'fit in' and show their male colleagues that they have what it takes to succeed in these roles and, as with Margaret Thatcher, to beat men at their own games, including the making and winning of wars. They see their success as proof that they are able to transcend the stereotypical female inadequacies. At one time some of these women went as far as wearing pin-striped dark suits, just like their male counterparts. Some of them became aggressive and more thoroughly unpleasant in wielding power than their male colleagues. A few even joined in the bashing of women who failed to 'make it'.

A second category of women finding themselves in male preserves try to do the best they can in an environment they find alienating. They often have to manage without the support of role models and mentors, because they are trailblazers. They sometimes suffer self-doubt because they are outside networks of affirmation and encouragement. They also have to contend with the stresses brought by the pressures of work on their personal lives. Their families and friends are often not well placed to support them; on the contrary, their long absences from home generate tensions, because their families feel neglected and subordinated to the ever-encroaching world of work. Unless some network of support emerges or a mentor takes them in hand, these women are likely to crumble or to switch tactics and develop survival strategies similar to those of the first group.

The third category comprises women who somehow manage to negotiate a role which draws on the best in their femininity, whilst not shying away from the strengths which they derive from the masculine aspects in their personality. Such women bring the integrative strengths of the female personality to boost their capacity to tackle multiple roles simultaneously – an essential ingredient of success in executive positions. But the importance of being able to focus on specifics in a goal-directed way is often lost to women. Women who have the potential to succeed but who fear success and consequently fail to thrive, often experience discomfort in the process of focusing on goals and temporarily shutting off the world around them. I have benefited enormously from learning this skill from my male colleagues.

Success in negotiating the world dominated by males also depends on the extent to which one succeeds in changing the way the system works. The work schedules of many institutions assume the presence of wives to enable executives to survive the punishment of long hours. Gentle reminders that women executives do not have wives not only help create space for these women, but enable men to laugh at themselves and the assumptions with which they often operate. The closing time of Pick 'n Pay, our local supermarket, serves as a useful metaphor to remind my colleagues that 5.30 p.m. is my cut-off time for work, unless there is an emergency. I have to buy fresh bread, milk and fruit daily for my family – a chore some of them don't have to think about.

The critical factor of success for women seems to be the ability to recognise the danger signals, and seek out mentors to assist them in working towards a healthier balance between the feminine and masculine tendencies in our personalities. These mentors need not be people who share one's plight. If anything, there is suggestive evidence that successful mature males may be in the best position to fill such a role. Mature men who are successful or retired from successful positions are likely to find bright, goal-directed younger women unthreatening. Their own personal security also allows for a relationship of equality to evolve in which differences of opinion and standpoints are not seen as a threat but are fully explored and an agreement to differ may be reached. They also are in a position to let their protégés gain insight into the workings of the systems they are trying to negotiate, thus saving the young executive a lot of pain from expending energy in wrong directions. Mature male mentors are also likely to help young executives identify both their strengths and vulnerabilities without being constrained by what is 'politically correct'. Too much attention to ideologically correct positions can be imprisoning for someone charting foreign waters.

I do not intend to suggest that all women executives fit neatly into these three types. In the real world, women, like men, experiment with different strategies before settling for the combination which works best for them. My own life has moved through elements of all three approaches. It could in fact be argued that one needs to go through the aggressive phase to assert oneself in a world where sexism has conditioned both men and women to dismiss women in positions of power. It is only when you realise that you do not need to shout that you tend to calm down and speak in more measured tones. True, sometimes you fail to realise that you have the audience's attention, and continue to shout. The greater sensitivity which develops as you mellow brings with it the crises I have already described under the second category of response to the honorary male role.

The complexities of negotiating the role of a woman executive are, however, dwarfed by those facing black women executives. These women share the frustrations of their black male colleagues, having to survive in a cultural environment which is alienating in its arrogance. If you are successful, it is because you are an exceptional black, and your individuality is then celebrated in a way that excludes any examination of the context that makes success so difficult. Then again, you have to deal with the amazing tendency for white colleagues to expect you to be an expert on all aspects of black social life simply because you are black. You are expected to explain why people of Soweto do this or that even if you have never been to Soweto at all. In other societies one has to be a social scientist and acquire that particular focus as an area of study, before one is expected to give authoritative running commentaries. It is a pain.

Black executives also share the burden of deflecting the unrealistic expectations of other blacks, who often expect them to provide easier access to the resources hitherto denied by an uncaring system. It is difficult to get people who have been excluded from positions of power to trust systems and not to resort to personalities as a link into resources. The anger generated by perceived reluctance to be helpful is an added burden on black executives.

A conversation around my dinner table on this issue triggered an interesting response from one of my guests. She asserted that there is a fundamental difference between Africans and Jews in their responses to the success of one of their own. She used the metaphor of a step-ladder to illustrate the point. Jews hold up the ladder when they see one of their own making his or her way up, knowing that individual success is good for group success. Africans, in contrast, may initially hold up the ladder, but as soon as they perceive too rapid a movement upwards, they fear that the individual, if too highly elevated above the rest, would forget the group who provided the support. Initial support turns to sabotage – they pull down the ladder, with devastating consequences. The message of the dinner party conversation hit home. But I quipped that some of us have proactively devised alternative ladders.

Unlike their male counterparts, black women executives have to fight cultural stereotypes held by many people in society, including their own colleagues, about the place and role of black women. Black women executives fit the role of the witch perfectly: they are the ultimate transgressors. One way in which people attempt to deal with the transgression is to find a male connection with whom to identify the woman executive. The male connection resolves the enigma of a successful woman – she is seen as acting because of, or on behalf of, him. Her own discomforting agency is thus denied. In my case I am often amazed at how Steve Biko gets dragged into whatever is being reported on me – seventeen years after his death. Would the same happen if our genders were switched?

A most effective way of establishing this male connection is through the status of widowhood. A widow's status cannot be seen independently from that of the man to whom she is connected. In my particular case, the fact that I am not Steve Biko's widow is treated as a minor inconvenience which is brushed aside. I have over the years acquired the dubious status of 'a political widow who could never be'.

Political widows who do not qualify to be widows in the ordinary sense find themselves in a curious social space, and are faced with a particular set of problems. In fact the eagerness to label a woman who was linked to, but not married to, a deceased political personality signals society's anxiety to re-establish its own equilibrium by symbolically removing her from the liminal unknown to the liminal known where social tools exist to deal with her.

References to me in the media, even as recently as early 1994, illustrate some of these issues. I quote from a *Boston Globe* article, which appeared on 20 April 1994, with subtitle, 'Biko's Lover: Banished and Pregnant'.

Ramphele was prohibited from leaving the remote village of Lenyenye, a thousand miles from her lover. Lenyenye was sweltering, desolate, and pointedly impoverished, a dumping ground for 'surplus' unemployed black South Africans who were no longer viable members of the country's labour pool. And she was pregnant with Steve Biko's child.

Her tenuous emotional and physical state almost resulted in a miscarriage. It was during that ordeal that Ramphele, struggling to keep her child alive in a neighbouring hospital, heard the news of Steve Biko's death.

This material was extracted by the *Boston Globe* from a book by the South African journalist, Allister Sparks, called *The Mind of South Africa*, published in 1990. On my arrival at the Kennedy School of Government in January 1994, where I took my position as a visiting scholar, I had to force the Publications Section of the School to retract a similarly worded introduction. My professional interests and achievements had received no mention in the article proposed by this academic institution.

Similarly, in 1991, when I was appointed to my current position as Deputy Vice-Chancellor at the University of Cape Town, one of the country's leading glossy magazines, *The Executive*, introduced me as 'The mother of Steve Biko's son becomes UCT executive'. I asked them if they would have introduced any male executive with a comparable reference, and forced them to publish an apology. I also object to the extreme insensitivity to my son. Little thought seems to go into how a teenager would feel about being described in the public media as a 'near miscarriage'.

, I can only infer that my public persona is an uncomfortable one for patriarchal society to deal with, and has to be given 'respectability' by summoning Steve from the grave to accompany me and clothe my nakedness. In summoning him to my side, society chooses to forget the multi-dimensionality of the relationship I had with him as colleague and fellow activist, and only dwells on the aspect which presents me as an instrument of his nurture and a bearer of his son. My comments are not intended to deny the important role Steve played in my personal life, but to pose the question about the extent to which that relationship has become a marker on my body to enable society to relate to me.

There are, however, other inferences which one can draw from this eagerness to bestow the label of widow on me. The public role of the political widow derives from her relationship with her husband, and thus she is there not as a woman, but as someone standing in for a fallen man. She becomes the ultimate honorary man. Her relationships are supposed to be shaped by, and flow along the contours of, her late husband's relationships. His friends and comrades become her friends. So too his enemies become hers. Her agency is not completely eliminated, but constrained. It is an effective form of social control of women who may be too independent for the comfort of existing social structures.

The agency of the political widow is by definition constrained by those sponsoring her role. To the extent that their goals, strategies and tactics and her own converge, a political widow continues to enjoy the patronage which comes with the role. Any major divergence, particularly if it takes on a public nature, poses major threats not only to the continuing relationships, but to her very public status. In so far as she can re-negotiate the terms of her engagement with public affairs, she is able to enlarge her socio-political space as a public figure in her own right. It is a tough balancing act fraught with risks and danger. The support society offers to one comes at a price. I have had to take risks in losing social support, which tends to come at a cost to my independence as an individual.

There is a final difficulty which many black executives, male and female, often face when they find themselves in the public limelight. It is not difficult to be a celebrity in a situation in which others sharing a similar history have been prevented from succeeding by a vicious discriminatory system. Being the first this, that or the other, though reflecting personal accomplishment, should also be seen as an indictment of a society which has denied many more black people the opportunity to excel. The double jeopardy of being black and woman compounds the problem for me. It is not false modesty, but I cannot help recognising the historical realities which have made it possible for me to be a pathbreaker in many areas of our society.

The choice of my first career was a product of historical necessity. My passion for independence was the major driving force, and a medical career was the ideal choice for an African woman at that time. It is noteworthy that my father did not question the suitability of my choice of career on grounds of gender, but on rational, domestic, economic ones. He had full confidence in my intellectual abilities, and often lamented my lack of application to do better. The only sexist remark I overheard my father ever make with reference to my ability was that he lamented the waste of brains on a female child, which could have been better bestowed on a son. But I was never made to feel that I could do other than achieve the best possible.

The self-confidence I developed as a child has served me well thus far. The fear of success which has been shown to plague some women has never been an issue for me. For such women, femininity and individual achievements which reflect intellectual competence or leadership potential are seen as desirable, but mutually exclusive, goals.

The double jeopardy of being black and female in a racist and sexist society may well make one less afraid of the sanctions against success. A non-subservient black woman is by definition a transgressive – she is the ultimate outsider. But political activism, with its infusion of a purpose higher than oneself, and the steeling effect of having had to break most of the rules in a society desperately in need of transformation, have added an important depth to my adult life.

My professional life has been marked by real enjoyment. I have never had the misfortune, after my internship period, of having to do work that has given me little enjoyment. I have almost always been fortunate to design my own jobs. But I also have enjoyed the relations with my colleagues wherever I have worked. I have had little difficulty finding a satisfactory basis for a good working relationship with people: male or female, educated or uneducated, white or black.

These working relationships have not come without cost and tough bargaining. But I believe in bargaining being done right at the beginning to avoid misconceptions and misunderstandings. I also realise that such open negotiations are not necessarily acceptable to people brought up in a different institutional culture from mine. My greatest difficulties have arisen with people coming from backgrounds where uncomfortable issues are not supposed to be raised, and differences remain unacknowledged. But in most cases I have found a resolution or a way of living with an open admission to agree to differ.

I have been able to negotiate good working conditions and thrive in circumstances in which I would not have expected to do so. For example, after I joined the UCT executive as a Deputy Vice-Chancellor in July 1991, some women colleagues at UCT were genuinely concerned about the impact my working environment would have on me. The all-white, male executive did not look like a supportive working milieu. They offered to form a support group for me in which I could unwind. But they were surprised and disappointed when I replied that I actually loved working with my colleagues, and needed no more support than they did as academics. I have no doubt that support groups are valuable for women finding themselves in hostile territory, and that the failure of the women's movement to make gains similar to those of organised labour stems in part from lack of solidarity action. But I have had to survive without them all my life. I was not going to have one simply to show that I was not being swallowed by the male culture around me.

This point raises an important issue. To what extent is the expectation that those who are outsiders to institutions will fail to 'fit in', the product of a self-fulfilling prophecy? What role does personal agency play in these situations? I hasten to add that I am not referring here to racist or sexist institutions which have no intention of changing; that would simply be like walking into a lions' den. I am referring to institutions that have made some declaration to change, however tentative.

My concerned women colleagues at UCT made certain assumptions. Firstly, that I was going to try to 'fit in' and would be frustrated – a reasonable assumption, given the many women who have been co-opted into honorary male roles. But I was employed in my executive job to take charge of the Equal Opportunity Policy Portfolio, aimed at changing the culture of the institution. Fitting into it the existing UCT culture would negate my mission. A second assumption was that as a woman I would find little support amongst my male colleagues. It is dangerous and limiting to exclude the possibility of real supportive relations with caring male colleagues wherever one goes, for they do arise. I have over the years developed a support network consisting of both men and women who are invaluable for my sanity.

Then again, my blackness in a white stronghold must have been an added concern to my women colleagues. One of the enormous benefits of having been steeled in the furnaces of Black Consciousness activism is that I have been liberated psychologically. I feel I belong in any part of my country, and I treat any major public institution in my society as part of my heritage. I do not have to apologise for being there for a legitimate purpose. This sense of belonging is particularly strong in my current job at UCT, where I was invited to come and make a contribution. The knowledge that UCT, despite its history, represents an important national asset is sustaining and makes the effort worth while.

It is interesting how many South Africans have failed to appreciate the importance of Black Consciousness in the historical struggle for justice in South Africa. The largest group of people in this category are those liberal white English-speaking South Africans who felt rejected by Black Consciousness activists in the 1970s. For them this was a slap in the face which they found hard to take. People like Dr Beyers Naudé, having experienced the humiliation of Afrikaners under English rule, had little difficulty in understanding and supporting the need for blacks to redefine themselves and their aspirations.

In contrast, Alan Paton died without overcoming his anger at being 'excluded' from the struggle by the Black Consciousness Movement. One also detects the same confusion in Nadine Gordimer's musings about her relief at 'the re-emergence of non-racial politics' in the 1980s.* What Nadine and others do not appreciate is the importance of the positive identity and self-confidence which Black Consciousness instilled in blacks, and its role in shaping the politics of the 1970s, as well as laying the foundations of the defiance politics of the 1980s.

Mongane Serote has aptly noted that the Black Consciousness Movement breathed oxygen into the moribund ANC operations in

*See Charles Villa-Vicencio's *The Spirit of Hope* (Johannesburg, 1993), p. 106.

exile, particularly its armed struggle, which benefited from the
young militants who had been nurtured by the BCM. One need only
look at those who have played a significant role in both the BCM and
the ANC to see the connection – Cheryl Carolus, Jay Naidoo, Frank
Chikane, Cyril Ramaphosa, Murphy Morobe, Terror Lekota and
Thenjiwe Mthintso, to name but a few.

The second group of South Africans who reject the importance of
Black Consciousness comprises some of the older generation of ANC
leaders, particularly those connected to the South African Communist Party. Mr Govan Mbeki, for example, was quoted in the *New
York Times* of 12 February 1994 as saying that whilst performing his
duties on Robben Island as a political educator during his imprisonment there, he had had to confront young political prisoners from
the BCM tradition with the meaninglessness of their talk about
'blackness' and move them to a higher level of appreciating the
importance of class analysis. The fact is that those young activists
needed to go through an understanding of racism in South Africa to
be able to integrate it with class analysis.

Mr Mbeki and others of his generation, who grew up as members
of a proud peasant class in the Eastern Cape, have never had to
doubt their own worth as human beings in spite of the racism
around them. But for those young blacks growing up in the squalid
townships of the 1960s, it was much more difficult not to have self-
doubt. A Black Consciousness perspective was essential for these
young blacks growing up in a racist country.

The same imperative applies to women, who have to integrate an
understanding of their 'womanhood' in a sexist society in order that
they may be able to develop an appreciation of the dynamics of race,
class and gender as these impinge on their lives. Belonging to exclusive women's organisations is a necessary step in the process of liberation and personal growth for most women. By the same token,
worker consciousness, an important part of the protective armour
against exploitation, is part of the same social reality.

The added depth which political activism gives to one's professional work has embedded within it the seeds of self-destruction. The
merging of one's personal professional life with the destiny of one's
own country is a powerful but deadly combination. One's entire life
becomes dedicated to national service and eventually one starts to
feel as if one is being treated as, or has indeed become, national

property. I had to face up to this sooner or later.

The journey to independence is long and hard. My body has an excellent early warning system which tells me to slow down when the going gets tough. But I often ignore it. I went through adolescence without a single pimple on my face, but have to contend with acne in my mature years as a sign of stress. I have had two major breakdowns as a result of not heeding the warning signals. It is as though the engine of my body just stops after running on over-drive for too long.

The first episode was in 1988 whilst at the Bunting Institute. After taking in the excitement of academic discourse, I went into over-drive trying to complete a major piece of work before going back to South Africa, where I knew the distractions would be many. I worked myself to a standstill. In the end I was admitted to the Stillman Infirmary at Harvard with viral meningitis. I had woken up one morning late in November with a high temperature and splitting headache. I kept hoping that it would pass. No amount of painkiller seemed to help. About midday, I realised that something was very seriously wrong with me and called a colleague to come and assist me. It took days for the doctors to diagnose my illness. The only treatment was rest, rest and more rest. I owe my recovery to the many colleagues at the Bunting and to friends who rallied around me.

Unfortunately, I had to go on yet another punishing schedule to promote our book, *Uprooting Poverty*, in February 1989, only eight weeks after this episode. It is not surprising that I was impatient with what I perceived as the American arrogance of some of the panelists at the launching conference at Duke University. I stood up during the last session of the conference and reminded American academics and foundation executives that South Africans had fought for their liberation, and would continue to do so, with or without American assistance. We do not need your help if it comes at the cost of our dignity, I declared. That dramatically spelt the end of the session and the conference. Some of my South African colleagues made apologetic comments afterwards, but I was unrepentant.

Francis Wilson captured the state of my mind when he bought me a coffee mug after the conference. The inscription on the mug read: Grant me patience, O Lord, but hurry! Clearly I had to do something to slow myself down and stop carrying the burdens of the world on my insubstantial shoulders.

The story of my internal battle for independence from the imprisonment of political activism, which burdened me with the duty of national service, is a long and complex one. As part of the process I have had to deal with critical questions in order to make the adjustment from passionate all-consuming activism to a lifestyle more suited for a woman in her forties with growing children.

It was the opening of political space after Mr Mandela's release from prison in 1990 that added momentum to the urgent need I felt to create a better balance in my life. At the same time, I began to feel that my worst fears regarding the shortsightedness of the anti-apartheid politics of the 1980s were about to become part of the reality of the 'new South Africa', which was announced with such fanfare.

My misgivings about the direction taken by the liberation struggle started in 1983 at the time of the launching of the United Democratic Front (UDF). I remember meeting enthusiastic activists who had been to the Mitchell's Plain launch of the UDF, saying how wonderful the occasion had been. Their response to my enquiry about what had been most striking about the conference was that 'It was just like the fifties!' For romantics this was a wonderful sign that the politics of the 1950s was back with us. I was dismayed. I feared that the lessons of the 1960s and 1970s would be lost in the romantic quest to recapture the past.

Observers of the South African political scene would know that much of the liberation struggle in the 1980s was to reassert the political authority of the liberation movements which had been driven underground by repression. It was thus inevitable that the politics of the 1950s had to be re-enacted in large measure, including the reinstatement of the old leadership in community structures and the opening of the road to the ANC-in-exile in Lusaka to seek political direction, legitimation and authenticity for internal programmes.

Much good came out of this cross-pollination between internal and exile politics. But there were major costs as well. The quality of long-term strategic planning for a post-apartheid South Africa suffered. For the exiled political leaders, the major thrust of their strategies was to make the country ungovernable so as to force the Nationalist government to relinquish power in deference to the liberation movement. A large number of internal political activists shared this goal, but there were differences in the choice of appropriate strategies. Tensions arose and intensified within communities between contending political ideologies, young and old, those working within the system and those outside it. Development of individuals and communities was sacrificed in the quest for 'the political kingdom',* in the hope that all else would follow its attainment.

Some of my friends and political peers from the 1970s often regarded me as a prophet of doom whenever I criticised the retrogressiveness of anti-apartheid politics in the 1980s. I lamented the failure to build on the positive gains of the 1970s when some foundations had been laid for liberation politics that put development of individuals and communities at the centre of political concerns. The 'bounds of possibility'† which had been extended in the 1970s with a positive definition of what the struggle was about, rather than what it was against, were largely ignored in the heady anti-apartheid activities of the 1980s. The chickens of political expediency began to come home to roost with a vengeance in the 1990s.

Most of my life in the last twenty years or so has been dedicated to the struggle for justice and freedom in my country. It has been an exciting time for me: a period of phenomenal growth, nourished by both joy and pain. It had its victorious moments as well as its frustrations. I have invested enormous psychic energy in 'the struggle'. This investment derived from a complexity of motives – idealism, altruism, the need for realising one's potential and, most important, the need for personal healing.

It was understandable that when the end of 'the struggle' seemed so seductively near, I would be compelled to stop and take stock. Would my country finally be free? What quality of life would accompany such freedom? Would one's ideals of living in a truly non-racial, non-sexist, egalitarian society be finally realised?

The signs around me gave me little cause for comfort. On the one hand, the Nationalist government of F. W. de Klerk did not seem to have made a final commitment to abandon the past and redress the injustices of the apartheid era. On the other hand, the liberation movement seemed to have been thrown into disarray by the sud-

---

*The call to seek first the political kingdom is Nkrumah's unfortunate legacy to Africa. It was made in good faith, but based on a superficial analysis of colonial power relations, ignoring the cushioning effect of colonised people on lower classes amongst colonial settlers. A simplistic linkage was thus assumed between political rights and material benefits.

†A metaphor coined by Barney Pityana to characterise the impact of the Black Consciousness Movement of the 1970s on South African politics.

denness and extent of the concessions by De Klerk's government. It was too good to be true! Not only did Mr De Klerk open up political space for the African National Congress and the Pan Africanist Congress, and agree in principle to the release of all political prisoners, but he legalised the South African Communist Party as well! There must be a catch somewhere, some activists ventured. There had been little strategic preparation within the ranks of the liberation movement for such an eventuality. Small wonder that valuable ground was lost in the first few months. The challenges of negotiation politics required a longer period of adjustment than most South Africans had anticipated. Questions began to be posed openly by concerned South Africans about the capacity of the liberation movement to transform itself into a viable alternative to the Nationalist government.

But there was also increasing tension between the demands of political activism and parenting. As a single parent I had to reassess the extent to which I was being fair to my children and myself in this regard. Hlumelo has been most affected by my relative unavailability. He was often teased by his teachers and friends about my many absences. He once said to me: 'It is not nice, Mum, when people ask you if your mother is away *again.*' Poor child. I have to remind him often that it may well be envy, rather than ridicule, which triggers the teasing. He does admit that there are many compensations in the lifestyle of our family. But it is hard for a teenager to remember that, when faced with cruel comments.

I had to suffer another breakdown before I could find a satisfactory resolution of the tensions which are inherent in my demanding life and which flowed from my failure to draw a clearer line between the personal and the political, so essential for a balanced life.

The following nightmare which I had one night in March 1990 was a mirror of my state of mind: I dreamt that I had been walking through a farming district in some unknown rural area in South Africa. Suddenly as I was passing a homestead, a pack of vicious dogs charged me. I tried to run, but they closed in on me. They pinned me against a thornbush fence. I resigned myself to being killed. Just before the dogs could maul me, an old woman whose sight I had caught with the corner of my frightened eye, came to my rescue. She was half person and half donkey. She asked me to get onto her back and then carried me to safety over the thorn fence by leaping over it. She vanished as mysteriously as she had appeared.

I told Carol Abramowitz, a psychologist friend, about this nightmare the very next morning. Being a practising Jungian, she smiled knowingly, but in her wisdom did not delve into the meaning of this dream at that stage.

I woke up that morning in bad shape. I had a splitting headache which was found to be due to high blood pressure – a new development signalling the level of tension within me. I was also very weepy and saw nothing bright in the world around me. Something was horribly wrong. I spent the next few days resting in bed with little sign of improvement.

On Tuesday I went to see Father Ted King, Dean Emeritus of St George's Cathedral, which he served for more than three decades. I have been entrusted to Fr Ted for spiritual direction by Archbishop Tutu since 1989. Fr Ted is a gentle giant physically, intellectually and spiritually. As soon as I told him how I felt, he realised what the problem was. He had been working hard since 1989 to get me to see my role in perspective as a person in my position, given my history and the complexities of South Africa. There had been little evidence of success. I had too much excess baggage which I was not yet ready to relinquish. In a sense this crash had to come. I had to hit the real bottom of the existential valley before I could be ready to take stock.

He ministered to me and recommended that I should go somewhere away from the pressures of my life and relax for a week or so. He armed me with C. S. Lewis's *The Lion, the Witch and the Wardrobe*, and reminded me with a touch of his dry sense of humour that St Paul had counselled that a bit of wine was good for the stomach. Thanks to the generosity of the Browne family I got free access to Watersedge, their holiday house on Seaforth Beach near Simonstown, to which I retreated that very afternoon.

I stood on the *stoep* of Watersedge and took in the views of False Bay and the gentle sound of the waves. The tide was still fairly low, but was slowly coming in. The salty smell of the sea was comforting. The sounds of the seagulls frolicking around were the only interruptions to the quietness which pervaded the atmosphere. I marvelled at the sea with its endless energy and rhythm of its own. It was very comforting.

My first evening alone at Watersedge was tearful but peaceful. I was in bed at eight and read a few pages from C. S. Lewis's wonderful story, which I found absorbing in a strange way. I fell asleep to the sound of the waves, by then splashing quite hard against the bottom of the *stoep*, creating a soothing, rhythmic lullaby.

The next day I went for long walks along the sea past the Boulders towards the southern edge of Simonstown. It was so restful to just be, without having to speak to a soul apart from greeting the occasional passer-by. I felt completely at ease on my own.

I realised that I was in the grip of a serious metaphorical post-natal depression. Had all the energy one put into the struggle been worth it? What if post-apartheid South Africa turned into a big disaster with violent conflict between the various contenders for power? I could not see myself living in such a society. I had invested too much physical and emotional energy in this society to countenance the possibility of a negative outcome of the liberation struggle. But what would I do if the worst came to the worst?

I spent ten days at Watersedge on my own, walking, sleeping, reading and reflecting. I could not see a way out of the historical trap in which I found myself. C. S. Lewis's story of the children playing in the wardrobe and landing up in a fantasy world was a helpful distraction from the feeling that South Africa was heading for impending doom. The story also had important symbolic messages for me. Like those children, I was also caught in a fantasy world with real and imagined problems. I had to find a way of making sense of my life in the unfolding historical drama.

A visit by my sons, Hlumelo and Malusi, during my first weekend away brought more sadness and tears. Anxiety was written all over their little faces. There was a great emptiness inside me, which made it difficult to nurture even my own children. It was too painful a situation to bear. It was as if I had given away their entitlement as dependent children, and now had to send them away empty. I had nothing to offer them emotionally. What pain they must suffer with a mother like me: a single parent, career woman, an idealist given to running out of energy and collapsing in a heap, sometimes in the most inconvenient of times and places.

I went to the Kalk Bay Anglican church that Sunday. I was moved by the simplicity and warmth of the parish Eucharist. I shed more tears – bitter-sweet ones this time. If only I could have the space to lead a simple life! History has unfortunately shaped a different pathway for me.

That Sunday evening I felt a little stronger. I went to stand on the *stoep* of Watersedge and watched the waves again. They have an inner energy and logic which no human being can alter. Their rhythm derives from a force beyond anyone's control. Who am I to think that I can change the course of history through sheer determination? Why should I think that my shoulders can hold up the sky above South Africa? The lesson of the waves was slowly sinking in, and having a therapeutic effect on my depression.

H. A. Williams, a theologian, once wrote some particularly apt words to capture this crisis: 'That is the agony, both as pain and the Greek *agon*, which people of the deepest vision have to endure in order to find life and to give it. If my devils are to leave me, I am afraid my angels will take flight as well.'* My angels had taken flight as I struggled to make sense of my role in the emerging 'new South Africa' and of my response to the euphoria which gripped South Africa after the release of Nelson Mandela in February 1990. I went back home frail, but a little wiser.

Travelling does have a beneficial effect on me. Whenever I am under enormous pressure I seem to benefit from stepping aside to get a better view of my country and my own role in it. At about the same time I have just described I fortunately had some overseas visits scheduled which enabled me to retreat further from the activism I was involved in.

I had a trip planned for April 1990 to go to Bermuda for an Aspen Institute seminar, which was part of Senator Dick Clarke's programme to educate American legislators on foreign policy questions. About twenty congressmen and one congresswoman, senators and their spouses, as well as a few foreign politicians, were brought together in a luxurious setting to be 'exposed to a variety of opinions from South Africa presented by participants from all the liberation movements, Inkatha, the South African government and parliamentary opposition parties'.

I took it as an extension of my time out from the intensity of my life, and really enjoyed the luxury and relaxed atmosphere. Bermuda is spectacular in its beauty. The houses are all painted white, each with a water-tank to catch rainwater, which is a scarce resource and the only source of drinking water. The place is clean, and great care is taken to service the tourist industry, which is a major contributor to the country's economy.

The trip also provided an opportunity for me to meet fellow South Africans. Cyril Ramaphosa, the ANC's Secretary General, and

* H. A. Williams, *The Simplicity of Prayer* (London, 1976), p. 38.

Chairman of the Constitutional Assembly in the new South African parliament, had been a passing acquaintance until then. I got to see a glimpse of the person behind the tough mineworkers' champion. He is a very private person. One is tempted to stereotype him, for this deep privacy is common amongst the people from his area of origin, Venda. I remember how some of the children I grew up with in that area would deny any knowledge of the whereabouts of their parents, fully aware that they were in one of the huts in their homestead. *Thidebe* (I don't know) was their first response to any question: an appropriate survival tactic in an uncertain world. Such a culture with its reverence for privacy must have had an impact on a person like Cyril Ramaphosa.

Colin Eglin also became more than just a public figure to me. A witty man, who is the strategist of the Democratic Party, he is also a typical South African male and became quite agitated by my frequent reminders to all and sundry that political transformation had to address gender inequalities seriously. He remarked that I sounded like a scratched record, whereupon I reminded him that the references to racism by South African politicians sounded equally repetitive, but were tolerated because they were seen as mainstream concerns by most opinion-formers, who were threatened by a gender analysis.

I also had the privilege to get to know Dikgang Moseneke, an advocate, and then a spokesperson for the Pan Africanist Congress. He is a charming, sophisticated person who had a hard time coping with my teasing about the PAC's 'One settler, one bullet' slogan. In fairness to him, though, he must have been struggling with the hardliners within his organisation, who were not yet willing to let go of the slogan. His resignation in November 1992, in the wake of the PAC's intensified terror campaign targeted at white people, came as no surprise to those who knew and respected him.

Koos van der Merwe was by far the most remarkable of all the participants. The righteousness of his cause did not seem to be in any doubt in his mind. He put up an impressive performance defending the Conservative Party line, and inviting all South African participants who voiced their disagreements with him for a meal back home to talk matters over: Neville Alexander of the Workers' Organisation for a Socialist Azania (WOSA) and Franklin Sonn, then Rector of the Peninsula Technikon, and currently South African Ambassador to the United States of America, were amongst the first to be invited. Koos also put up a well-orchestrated political show at a local cemetery where Boer prisoners of the Anglo-Boer War lie buried. He was armed with a video camera to record the ritual of his standing to attention, hat on chest, in deference to the departed Afrikaner heroes. I was even more amused when I heard him comment on Mr Ferdie Hartzenberg, a CP leader with whom he had differences that were to lead to his resignation from the CP: *Hy is so verkramp, jy weet, jy kan hom ploeg!* (He is so conservative, you know, that you can literally plough him).

Bermuda was the best possible setting for me to stop taking my country and myself too seriously. I arrived back home after ten days feeling much better. It was fortunate that my long-standing invitation to visit Australia as a guest of the government of that country was scheduled for about the same period. I requested that it be postponed from April to May to enable me to catch up with my children before setting off again.

The Australian trip advanced the healing process. An old friend, Bruce Haigh, was my tour director. Bruce met me in Perth after the long flight from South Africa and immediately took charge of all arrangements for my comfort. It was bliss. Bruce is a nurturer by nature and had been a great source of support for me during the most difficult time of my life during my banishment to Lenyenye. I relaxed and enjoyed myself.

The programme was organised to suit my needs and interests. I met a number of academics from universities in the cities we visited: Perth, Adelaide, Melbourne, Canberra and Sydney. I also visited interesting community and health projects in various parts of the country, including Alice Springs. I must confess that I was disappointed in the approach some Aboriginal leaders adopted to development for their people. Understandably, most of them have no faith in integrationist approaches, given the disastrous consequences of forced integration in the past. It is logical that they should have a consciousness-raising campaign to ensure that Aboriginal people develop self-respect and value their own culture. However, it was difficult to see how they could successfully pursue a 'homeland' strategy, as advocated by some of them. Some of the leaders had difficulty understanding why South African blacks were clamouring for the dismantling of homelands.

I was also dismayed to see the level of dehumanisation, alcohol abuse and violence which plagued Aboriginals in most areas, particularly in Alice Springs. The sight of groups of extended family members gathered under a tree with a five-litre box of wine was a common one. The level of inter-personal violence amongst Aboriginals was also a major concern to me. The approach of the Australian government to redress by providing free housing and welfare cheques to all needy Aboriginals seems to have exacerbated the feeling of worthlessness and dependency amongst most of them.

I also met some charming Aboriginal people. In Melbourne, there was an Aboriginal health centre which was run by a dynamic woman who prohibited any smoking or littering on the premises. It stood in sharp relief to other Aboriginal health centres I had visited. Her approach was that one had to set high standards of good behaviour, because people either rise or fail to meet expectations society has of them. Those treated like boys, behave like boys, as Anthony Barker once observed in the South African context. There were also wonderful young women in Alice Springs who were going about the business of development. They were thrilled by my observations about male dominance in their community leadership system. I remarked that it reminded me very much of my own country. The women do most of the grassroots organisational work and carry the administrative burden, yet have a limited part in decision-making and negotiating with the federal and regional governments.

I cannot do justice in this book to the complexities of the problems facing indigenous minorities globally. But I will only note the dangers posed by the devastating combination of guilt and deep-seated lack of respect shown by the white colonial authorities, and the role of victim adopted by the colonised. Coupled with this role is a glorification of indigenous culture which poses the greatest threat to the ability of indigenous people to transform their social relations. Modernity is a reality they cannot wish away, but engaging it creatively requires a critical appraisal of indigenous culture, and the retention of the good as well as the jettisoning of the bad.

The Australian landscape is extraordinarily varied and beautiful. It provided the nourishment of the spirit which I sorely needed. The coastal areas with their lush vegetation and rivers are given stiff competition by the central desert area with its ruggedness and vastness of space. It was in Alice Springs that I saw a double rainbow for the first time in my life. It was here that I also woke up to the sense of depth and distance represented by the different hues of mountains and hills, which I was convinced was a particular feature of

Australia. Bruce Haigh was amazed that I could have been unaware of this, coming as I did from a country like South Africa, which has many similarities to Australia. What kind of life was I leading that could have made me so blind to my own environment? This was a further indication of a lifestyle in serious need of balancing.

Sydney, my last port of call, was the highlight of my trip. It is a beautiful coastal city which has taken full advantage of its setting. The old harbour sports an imaginative waterfront development with wonderful restaurants situated in refurbished old warehouses. Boat rides to neighbouring coastal settlements provide spectacular views and relaxed entertainment. The famous Sydney Opera House graces the evening landscape as one rides back into the harbour.

We had a dinner party on the penultimate night of my visit in the old part of Sydney with its handsome Victorian and Georgian houses. What a pleasant environment to be in. I met some of the 1960s Australian activists who are all professional people, probably struggling with the same kind of tensions I have to deal with myself. We danced the night away – my first real dancing party since I left Lenyenye in 1984. It was wonderful to do the bump-jive and other energetic dances again.

I was sad to leave, but it was time. I spent most of the first part of the trip home gazing out through the window at the country below us. I felt ambivalent about going back home. But I knew then that if I wanted, I could uproot from South Africa and live elsewhere. I was free at last to get to explore a lifestyle beyond the 'bounds of possibility' which I had imposed upon myself.

It is symbolically significant that like many women caught on the horns of a dilemma, I too have suffered depression. As Apter so aptly noted, 'it is the very sensitivity of women to other people's needs that is likely to produce the appearance and the consequences of mental instability – women's instability stabilizes the world'.* But unlike most women, my depression was occasioned by too close a merger between the personal and the political. My 'instability' was a reflection of my over-sensitivity to the dangers which I felt lay in store for the future of the society I live in and love so passionately.

But like any growing child, further development is only possible when the child learns to distinguish itself physically, emotionally and intellectually from its parents and other family members. Interdependence then becomes not only possible but a joyous

*Terri Apter, *Why Women Don't Have Wives* (Basingstoke, 1993), p. 203.

human attribute. I had to learn that too much clinging is a sign of insecurity and not a source of strength.

The relationships which develop amongst activists are both supportive and stifling. Finding a healthy balance in such relationships is a major challenge. It is a life-long quest. I have taken heed of the injunction of St Bernard of Clairvaux to a new pope: 'You too are a man [I assume my exclusion is not deliberate]. So then in order that your humanity may be entire and complete, let your bosom, which receives all, find room for yourself also. So remember to restore yourself to yourself.' As an ordinary mortal I have an even greater need to 'restore myself to myself'. There is no other option for the sake of my sanity. I have to stop more frequently and smell the flowers.

In the whole process of establishing my personal boundaries I have also had to negotiate greater independence from my close-knit family. This has been relatively easier than the struggle at a national level. My family has been very supportive of me through all the pains and joys, as well as the triumphs and failures. But the process has been marred by many personal sorrows. There are many times when I have felt that I have had to deal with more losses than most people.

A big scratch to the scars left by previous bereavement was the sudden death of Morongwa, my elder sister's daughter, in April 1991, on the operating table at Baragwanath Hospital, during a routine operation to clean out her womb after a miscarriage. No one has yet explained the cause nor has an inquest been held into her death.

The loss suffered by her young husband, their daughter Mamphela, then only four years old, and my sister, who relied so heavily on her, is hard to describe. For me it was like losing a second daughter. She had been under my care for seven of the eight years I spent in Lenyenye, because my mother, who was her guardian, had come to live with me.

Morongwa's smiling face, her energy and sheer love for life were her strong features. I was shocked by the news but also angry that she should have died such a death, which suggested negligence on the part of her care-givers. I flew to Johannesburg the very next day after her death, and dealt with the pain of the loss by immersing myself in practical arrangements for the funeral.

I spent many fruitless months afterwards trying to get a definitive statement of the cause of her death from the hospital. No official pronouncement has been made to date. Only an emptiness remains. But more was to come.

Dominee Maphoto's opening prayer captured the feeling of all those present in the Westernberg Dutch Reformed Church on a morning in June 1993 for the funeral service of Sethiba, my 43-year-old brother. 'Lord, you have reaped when the field was still green, before the corn was ripe.' This admonishment of the Lord was an attempt to communicate the overwhelming feeling of disappointment at the turn of events. It is difficult to come to terms with the death of someone as young and energetic and with as bright a future as Sethiba. His wife, Mamakiri, and his four-year-old son Letladi attached an even greater meaning to the words of this prayer. Their life plans lay in ruins in the wake of this untimely death.

Sethiba's life had all the features of a middle child. His childhood was uneventful except for his remarkable physical strength: he was capable of both delivering devastating blows to bully boys, and wrecking my father's tools, which earned him many a spanking. He was always interested in things mechanical and tried to understand how they worked.

He was unfortunate in being taken to my paternal grandparents at the age of 12 to help the ageing couple look after their livestock. It was a cruel decision by my father, who like many of his contemporaries viewed children as part of their possessions with no independent voice. The decision did not enjoy my mother's support, but women at the time were given little choice in such matters – the children belonged to their fathers. My grandparents were not nurturers by any stretch of imagination. My father's younger brother added insult to injury by the manner in which he and his wife made Sethiba feel unwanted and unloved. His pain must have been immense then, but as a child he was not given a hearing, and my mother's pleadings for him to come back to the family home fell on deaf ears.

It was only after my father's death that my mother brought him back and sent him to Setotolwane High School to finish his Standard 8 and to commence matriculation. Tragically because of the financial problems my mother experienced in paying for both Sethiba and Phoshiwa, his younger brother, the burden of sacrifice had to fall again on Sethiba, who was forced to leave school. He subsequently registered at a technical college. After qualifying he began an unsuccessful struggle to find a job as an apprentice.

My mother's brother, Malesela, on whom she relied heavily for support, offered to help. Sethiba moved to Sibasa to live with my uncle, who got him set up as a self-employed all-purpose car mechanic. He became quite proficient, and attracted a lot of business. Sadly, my uncle let him down by not managing the finances properly. Even though Sethiba worked very hard, he had little money to show for it.

It was not surprising in my view when I learned that he had become quite ill with what sounded like migraine headaches. The traditional healers to whom my uncle took him interpreted these as signs that he was experiencing a 'call' to become a healer himself. I felt quite unhappy about this turn of events. I was already convinced in my own mind that Sethiba was showing the strains of the many burdens which fate had forced him to carry in his youth. His abandonment by his own parents to the uncaring custody of our paternal grandparents, the disappointment of having to leave an academic school career and later his exploitation by an uncle who was supposed to help him establish himself as a tradesman, were all too much for one young person to bear, however resilient he may have been.

I took advantage of our meeting at my grandmother's funeral in 1975 to discuss my concerns with him, and to offer to send him back to school. He was well prepared to rebuff me. He said his ancestors had warned him that as a medical doctor I would attempt to dissuade him from his chosen path, but he should and would resist. We parted on an understanding that should he change his mind, my offer stood.

It was with great joy in January 1977, when I visited my mother in Maupje after my release from detention, that I found him at home. He admitted that he had come to the end of the road with both my uncle and his unsuccessful struggle to get a job elsewhere. We agreed that he would go to Mafeking and do an instructor's course at the technical college there in 1978. It was a privilege to finance his education: his was an uncomplaining, gentle and yet hardworking nature.

His teaching career started in 1981 at the technical college in Hammanskraal, where he met his wife, Mamakiri Moleba. It was with pride that I arranged his wedding from my house in Lenyenye. Sethiba was promoted to the headship of a division at Shikoane-Matlala Technikon in Pietersburg in February 1992. He commanded respect from all those who got to know him as a meticulous worker, an excellent teacher, an active practising Christian, and a loving husband and father. Amongst my brothers and sisters he was an anchor for all of us.

It was thus with shock that I learned on 20 June that he had alveolar cell cancer of the lung, which was likely to be rapidly fatal. I had just got back to my house from a trip to Pietersburg to see him, when I received the news from my sister Mashadi, who had also been with me during that weekend. He had been unwell for a number of months but in his usual uncomplaining way he had brushed aside my concern at the length of the illness.

I suspect that the shock of the diagnosis must have contributed to Sethiba's rapid deterioration and death. He was, however, true to form to the very last. He spent most of his last day, just hours before his death, with his wife helping her to get to grips with life without him. He even planned his own funeral programme, emphasising the least amount of fuss. His greatest regret was having to abandon his four-year-old-son, Letladi, who was particularly attached to him.

Coping with such a loss is extremely difficult. It was harder for his wife and son, who were just recovering from the loss of their daughter and sister, Matlala, who died in August 1992, of brain damage occasioned by pneumococcal meningitis, contracted at the age of two months which reduced the beautiful lively child to a floppy sad shadow. It is not inconceivable that the stress of Matlala's illness and death may be linked to Sethiba's own illness and death. After all, his was a very rare cancer, seen mainly in elderly people. Stress is suspected by many analysts to be a factor in the loss of the body's capacity to deal effectively with potential cancer cells.

Each loss has its own individual meaning, but also invokes the meanings of past sorrows. Wounds inflicted by these sorrows start to bleed again after each new one. The resilience which enables one to accept the loss and to give up clinging to what is irretrievably gone is diminished by each additional loss. Nevertheless, the finality of death, which makes physical clinging impossible, forces one to accept that the lost object of one's love is irretrievable. It is not as if one has an opportunity to negotiate the terms of the loss – one is presented with a *fait accompli*.

In all this my mother has been a tower of strength for all of us. At 76 years of age she is still active and maintains her sense of humour. She has borne many pains in her life time but also known much joy.

# 8

# Stretching Across Boundaries

An important part of any process of transformation has to be transgression of social boundaries which made sense in the past but which stand in the way of creative responses to a changing environment. South Africa has many transgressives who have brought the country to its current historical position: all those who have died in the struggle for liberation, those who have more recently been involved in negotiations at various levels, whether constitutional or socio-economic, and the many unsung heroes and heroines who continue to lead lives which stabilise society. But it is fair to say that Nelson Mandela is by far the most important transgressive at this moment in our history. Without his willingness to talk to his gaolers at a time when doing so was tantamount to mixing the profane with the sacred, our history would have been very different.

I am fortunate to have got to know this remarkable man. I first visited him at his invitation when he was still in prison. This was too crucial an appointment to miss, so I took no chances. I set the clock for 6 a.m. to make sure that I would be on time for my 7.30 appointment. As I drove along the highway towards Pollsmoor on Sunday morning, 31 July 1988, I could hardly contain the excitement. Many questions raced through my mind. How was I to respond to this living legend? What kind of person was he in real life? Why was he interested in meeting me at this stage? I had to wait to find out.

I was at the gate by seven o'clock. I was shown into a living-room by a friendly looking warder, who sat down at a makeshift desk at the entrance of the room. Soon Mr Mandela's tall, trim, well-built frame, oozing authority and grace, appeared. His face had a softness and gentleness enhanced by his beaming smile. He was wearing an immaculately clean prison outfit – a long-sleeved khaki shirt, gabardine pants and spotless boots.

His sensitivity to others shines through in every encounter he has with people. The mark of greatness in people often manifests itself in the respect with which they treat others irrespective of social status. Mr Mandela's respect for his captors as human beings was also obvious in the manner in which he acknowledged the warder at the door and requested him to warn him in case we overstepped our time limit. This respect was in turn rewarded in most cases by the deference which they showed him, and which became more obvious to me during my visits to him between 1988 and 1990.

On my first visit, Mr Mandela's major focus was on establishing a relationship of trust between us as one human being to another. He chose to greet me in Sesotho, my mother tongue, *Dumela Kgaetsedi yaka* (Hallo, my sister), to signify his wish to engage the human being in me. His great social skills were in evidence at every turn – he put me at ease without patronising me. He could see that I was in awe of him.

Our conversation centred on trivia but was peppered with penetrating questions which indicated his curiosity about the real Mamphela. He enquired about my career aspirations, my hobbies, the books I was interested in, and the well-being of my children. I was amazed at how well informed he was about events in the country, people in different walks of life in our society, international politics, and the world of arts and music. There was hardly a book published over the last few years that he had not read or heard about. I was in the presence of a giant.

Just before we parted he urged me to ensure that the history of the Black Consciousness Movement was properly documented, and that the place of Steve Biko was properly delineated. He said earnestly: 'Steve Biko must take his rightful place in the history of the liberation movement in South Africa. He has made an enormous contribution. We must not allow that to be forgotten.' I made a promise to him which I kept. The publication in 1991 of *Bounds of Possibility: The Legacy of Steve Biko and Black Consciousness* is testimony to that.

Writing the book was itself part of the process of healing which I have had to go through. I had to record that part of my history as objectively as I could. The participation of former fellow activists in the project, particularly Barney Pityana and Malusi Mpumlwana, made it more meaningful as a collective process of healing. But like all collaborative projects, it took time and energy to keep it on course. Barney's methodical approach helped a great deal in facilitating the completion of the book.

There was also pain involved in the project. AZAPO, which see themselves as the custodians of Steve Biko's legacy, publicly opposed this project. They asserted that we, who were not members of AZAPO, had no right to record and reflect on that history. They put pressure on people such as Harry Nengwekhulu, who had agreed to contribute a paper and attend a seminar in Harare where draft chapters were discussed, to withdraw. It was to me a sad reflection of a failure to grow beyond parochial boundaries. Steve was larger than any one organisation – his life was dedicated to the struggle for liberation of the whole person, which includes the freedom from being constrained by ideological or organisational straitjackets. It could in fact be argued that AZAPO's parochialism has done a disservice to Steve's vision of society and his memory as an important player in the liberation struggle. By claiming sole ownership of this man, they have made it difficult for others to acknowledge his contribution to the struggle. Those of us who were determined to let Steve take his rightful place in history refused to be deterred.

Subsequent visits to Mr Mandela between 1989 and 1990 were made under very different circumstances. His accommodation at Victor Verster Prison, in Paarl, near Cape Town, was luxurious by any prison standard. Major Gregory, his personal warder, was gracious and made sure I felt at home during the visits. Gone was the prison garb. Mr Mandela wore smart casual clothes with soft slippers to ease his swollen ankles – the aftermath of many years of hard labour in the cold Robben Island climate. He sat in an easy chair with his feet elevated on a stool. I got to know a little bit more about the person behind Mandela the symbol.

On one visit in December 1989, my two sons, Hlumelo and Malusi, accompanied me at his insistence. He took time to engage them around their own interests – tennis in the case of Hlumelo, and starting school and favourite TV programmes in the case of Malusi. It was the closest my sons have ever been to relating to a grandfather. They liked him enormously and valued his interest in them as persons. Their respect for him has grown over the years as he continues to take an interest in their development.

With each subsequent visit, our discussions moved from the initial polite trivia to important issues confronting our society. We found great areas of agreement, but also agreed to disagree about a few questions of strategy. One question related to the role of traditional leaders in a democratic society. The first time I broached the subject I could see that he was deeply troubled. I asked him how the ANC reconciled its espousal of democracy and its commitment to non-sexism with the resuscitation of the Congress of Traditional Leaders of South Africa (Contralesa). Traditional leadership by its very nature is hereditary and leaves little scope for the democratic election of leaders. Male dominance is an ethos deeply embedded within African traditional authority structures. Mr Mandela's face darkened. He sat up in a regal posture, and said: 'The issue you have raised is too complex to be dealt with cold in the short space of time we have available during this visit. We have to defer it for discussion during the next visit.' I could see that he was troubled.

Two weeks later when I arrived, he went straight to the heart of the matter. He acknowledged that he had been upset by my raising the difficult issue of traditional leadership, but also that he had not until then reflected on the contradictions I had pointed out in my question to him. He took his time to explain the complexities of mass political mobilisation in a country where traditional leadership is part of the political and social landscape. Mobilising people entails taking them from where they are, and that may be an uncomfortable place for one's sensibilities, to where one would like them to be. The ANC also had to face the challenge posed by the National Party government's continued use of traditional leaders for the perpetuation of apartheid. The resuscitation of Contralesa was part of the ANC's strategy to bring traditional leaders into the fold of liberation politics. I could fully understand the logic of his approach but pointed out the long-term costs of such a strategy.

I have over the years noticed the extent to which Mr Mandela has taken gender equity seriously. It was one of the issues he highlighted in his inaugural address in May 1994 as the first democratically elected President of South Africa. He acknowledged the difficulties of changing the male-dominated culture of South Africa, but insisted that everyone has to learn to live up to the commitment to gender equity – 'starting with the President'. Listening to that made me glow all over with pride and admiration. I feel incredibly privileged to have been able to share more than just a casual acquaintance with this remarkable man. Our friendship continues to grow.

Mr Mandela's presence makes the task much easier of lowering boundaries in our divided society. This involves both stretching across well-established boundaries and transgressing them, because some parties that have retreated behind barriers are too far to be reached by merely stretching to them from the safety of one's comfort zone. But transgression also brings with it the danger of incurring the disapproval or rejection of people – one's own camp – who may be harmed by the breaking of pollution taboos. It is a risky enterprise, but one which is driven by such compelling historical imperatives that one feels privileged to be part of the process.

My transgressive activities have been focused on one central goal: transforming the major institutions of our society. Unlike many post-colonial societies in Africa, South Africa has a viable and extensive infrastructure: transport and communications, finance and banking, tertiary education, science and technology, and so forth. The major problem area is the development of human resources, which have been sacrificed on the altar of racial bigotry. The major task ahead of us in South Africa is making human development the centre of a process of reconstruction which will create a better fit between the infrastructure and the people whom it is intended to serve. Such a better fit will also enhance the infrastructural base and make for its more effective and efficient use.

My areas of engagement are those shaped by my competencies: higher education, social policy, and uprooting poverty. My training as a doctor and anthropologist enables me to stretch across the boundaries between natural or medical science and social science in interesting ways.

The danger of medical doctors being treated as, and behaving like, demigods has been the subject of many analyses, particularly by medical anthropologists. But the mystique lives on, because it serves an important psycho-social function related to the ultimate vulnerability of human beings – the fear of our own mortality. However, it is also fair to acknowledge the enormous psychological advantages which a doctor derives from being a member of a powerful, respected profession. It gives one enormous self-confidence, over-confidence in many cases. It is the ultimate proof of how the expectations others have of one influence and shape one's own expectations of oneself.

My membership of this powerful club has stood me in good stead throughout my life, beyond the naïve expectations which lay behind my initial decision to become a doctor in my quest for independence. I had no idea how right my childish instincts were in choosing a medical career. Security police in both King Williamstown and

Tzaneen, conservative farmers and traders in Tzaneen, strangers everywhere, all change their response to me because of my profession. They could easily dismiss me as a black person, a woman, but not as a medical doctor. This was strategically important, and remains so in my current engagements.

My anthropological training has given me insights into my own behaviour as member of a complex society, and tools for ongoing exploration. I can stand back as a participant observer in the many complex settings I find myself in, and try to learn from the social dynamics I see around me. The capacity to switch roles, and become a visiting anthropologist, is essential for my survival in some of the conflict-ridden settings in which I often find myself: there are often people with such differences in outlook that it does not pay to try to argue with them. Listening with empathy becomes a valuable step before taking decisions about the need for, and nature of, further interaction.

I stopped practising medicine in 1988 when I went to the Bunting Institute at Radcliffe College. I tried to go back to my part-time work at Guguletu Hospital towards the end of 1989, but after a few sessions it became clear to me that it was time to move on from the clinical practice of medicine. I found the endless problems of diseases of poverty exhausting. But even more distressing was the regular appearance of sexually abused children. I could not cope with my impotence in the face of such symptoms of social disintegration. I felt that I could perhaps make a better contribution by involving myself more actively in shaping creative social policies which would provide a safer environment for children. It was the right decision to make at the time. I do not miss medical practice at all.

It is difficult for me to imagine a better place to be at in the higher-education sector in South Africa than the University of Cape Town. Its physical setting makes it tower above its surroundings – an interesting symbolic statement which even Cecil John Rhodes, who bequeathed the land, could not have fully comprehended. It also has a solid infrastructure which puts it in a good position to make a significant contribution to higher education not only in South Africa but in the entire continent. It fulfils the criterion I have alluded to, being one of the major institutions in our society which I believe need to be harnessed for the better service of humanity. Without a vibrant higher-education system capable of producing the best in high-level human resources, the development of South Africa in the context of the competitive, technologically based global economy will be at risk.

Even in my wildest dreams I did not, however, ever imagine myself as an executive officer at UCT. Not because I did not think that I had the ability to play such a role, but because after settling into my new-found position as a social science researcher, I was content. I enjoyed the space to read, reflect, write and interact with colleagues across disciplines, both nationally and internationally. What more did I need? The little I had seen and heard about the lifestyle of UCT executives and the demands on them was enough to make me believe that one would have to be self-sacrificial to accept such a job.

In the second half of 1990 I was riding on the crest of a wave after coming out of the depression I have already referred to. It is to the credit of the Vice-Chancellor, Dr Stuart Saunders, that I eventually succumbed and agreed to serve. But I was not ready to give up my research base, so I negotiated a 50 per cent engagement. Anyone with experience of executive jobs would have known better. There is just no way one can do an executive job part-time, for it is more than a full-time commitment. One's whole lifestyle is shaped by it, however hard one tries to prevent this happening. I had to learn this lesson the hard way too. The part-time arrangement lasted only a few months. They felt like years. Doing a full-time executive job whilst still attempting to pursue my research was a recipe for burn-out. I reluctantly came to terms with the fact that my research work had to be put on hold.

The naïve side of my nature had led me to believe that I could pick and choose aspects of my new job which suited me and leave out the rest. It is perhaps true that unlike many of my colleagues, past and present, I have had greater flexibility to shape my own job. As the first woman ever to occupy an executive position at UCT, there was clearly scope for flexibility. Similarly, as the first black person in this position, one could take certain liberties.

My task as the executive officer in charge of the Equal Opportunity Portfolio presented me with both space for creativity and major challenges. UCT had until 1990 responded to its environment and its heritage, as part of apartheid South Africa, by changing aspects of its operation to become more open and accessible to blacks and women in South Africa. But it had not systematically set out to alter course radically. The emphasis of the leadership policies was on blacks gaining access to the UCT they had come to love and respect. Black advancement was the primary focus – a problematic approach, which implied that blacks were to be advanced by whites to where the latter already were.

The shape my portfolio took reflected my philosophical orientation, forged over the years, as well as my social analysis of the interrelationships between the various markers of power in society and my understanding of what was possible within the institutional framework of UCT. I thus placed emphasis on equity as the goal which should shape the vision of a transformed UCT. But equity could not only be seen in terms of blacks and whites, but had to include gender and class as important determinants of inequity in our society. It was also vital to ensure that whatever process of change my portfolio promoted should take cognisance of the realities which make UCT what it is and motivate those within it. People function at their best when they feel that their own interests are not being compromised and, if they are, that such compromises should be seen to hold long-term benefits for them.

My approach to equity is informed by the research carried out with my research colleague, Carla Sutherland, through the Equal Opportunity Research Project, which I established as part of my portfolio. The creation of greater equity in higher education, and indeed in all areas of our inequitable society, has to involve three thrusts: greater access, opportunities for personal development, and a change in institutional culture. Firstly, increasing access to UCT for blacks and women means more than just simply welcoming them. It has to do with reaching out to them wherever they are, addressing their perceptions of UCT, which often lead to self-exclusion, and then facilitating their application to come, which may involve putting extra resources at their disposal. Access also involves assessing individual potential to succeed, which is a difficult issue, given the paucity of reliable measures and methods of measurement.

Once people are on board, their ability to succeed depends not only on their own efforts and skill but on how much support is provided for their development, and how much value the institution places on the time and energy expended in developing human resources. An essential part of the nurturing which helps people succeed is the setting of developmental goals early on. People need to know what is expected of them, and to negotiate goals which they feel are achievable. Nothing succeeds like success. This open goal-setting process is particularly crucial when one is dealing with people who are 'outsiders' in terms of traditional positions of power in society, namely women and blacks.

Another important goal of this exercise is to ensure that the student takes responsibility for his or her own personal development and success. The institution has a responsibility to create a nurturing environment with opportunities for growth, but the individual is the one who holds the ultimate key to success or failure. The encouragement of human agency is crucial to breaking the victim image blacks and women often adopt.

Thirdly, however well one selects people and tries to encourage their development, if the institutional culture remains unaltered, the chances of long-term success are low. Institutional cultures reflect the collective and cumulative customs, rituals, symbols and preferences of the people flowing through them over time. It is not surprising that most institutions in South Africa, including UCT, have a dominant white male culture. It would be surprising if that were not the case. The problem is not the existence of the culture but the need to acknowledge it, examine it and change aspects of it that prevent its members from realising their full potential.

Therein lies the rub. A lot of what constitutes institutional culture is not often articulated and acknowledged. It could be argued that the power and mystique of institutional cultures lie in the very fact of their being interred in habit and beyond normal discourse. Discourse may, and does, strip it of the veil of mysticism, which makes it intangible and beyond the reach of any potential pollutants or detractors. The attraction people often feel to belonging to exclusive clubs is precisely the sense of being privy to something no-one else can fully explain – one has to belong to be able to know.

But people who are 'outsiders' in the broader society are not well placed to negotiate the mystique of institutions in which they find themselves. Nor are they necessarily inclined to do so. Young white males may have some romantic notions of such exclusive clubs which their own fathers belonged to, but blacks and women may find some aspects of the very cultures offensive. Failure to address this problem openly lies at the heart of many failed programmes of affirmative action and black advancement.

Affirmative action as it has been pursued in the United States and in many other parts of the world assumes that 'outsiders' have to be brought into the mainstream to ensure their participation, without there being any fundamental questioning of that mainstream as a desirable social framework. When blacks or women fail, it simply proves to conservatives that 'they do not have what it takes to make it'. At the same time failure raises uncomfortable feelings in liberals, who are troubled even to admit the reality of the failure, lest it play into racist hands. But they too have not questioned the assumption that one has to succeed according to the terms of white male institutional culture.

I must hasten to add that there are certain basic fundamentals about knowledge, science, work patterns and behavioural approaches which are common across cultures. It would be difficult to function in the increasingly unified global village if such assumptions were not possible. One has to trust that certain fundamentals are in place in all similar institutions, whatever the country: trains must be on time, planes must be flown by competent pilots, phones must work, and time must mean the same to all people.

But I am referring to the frills that serve to exclude others or depict them as subordinate or invisible: manner of dress, accents, the etiquette of eating, names of celebrated heroes and so on. It is amazing to observe the ease with which people who can't speak English, or speak it with a non-standard accent are often dismissed as unintelligent by white South African English-speakers, who more often than not have made no attempt themselves to master an African language. The fact that they live in Africa has not had any impact on them. But even more damaging than these frills, as I call them, are invisible practices that create circles of privilege and access to information crucial for promotion within the hierarchical system.

Needless to say, an agenda such as the one I have set out to pursue at UCT is bound to generate a lot of conflict and to please very few people. In anticipation of the difficulties ahead, I decided to conduct visits to individual faculties and departments throughout the entire University to engage people in the process of transformation. The aim of the visits was to get individual deans and heads of departments to set their own goals based on what they perceived to be achievable within the constraints of their particular circumstances. Such goal-setting is essential if key players are to take ownership of the process of change. The role of my portfolio is a facilitatory one. I have been amazed at how willing many people are to change if they see that their own best interests are served in this way, if not in the short term, then in the long term.

It is too early to judge how successful the transformation of UCT is likely to be. But it is noteworthy that the people who stand to benefit from greater equity at UCT are often still sceptical of the motives behind the University's equal opportunity policies. Their past experiences have conditioned them not to expect much from liberal institutions. The danger of the self-fulfilling prophecy looms large. Success in transforming this institution depends on the involvement of all to move it in new directions.

There are also fears, on the part of blacks particularly, that their hard-earned achievements will be devalued if they are lumped together in the University's affirmative action basket. The attacks levelled at affirmative action by conservatives have clearly had their desired impact. My approach to such attacks is to point out that most, if not all, white people in South Africa have been recipients of affirmative action at many levels, and it does not seem to have hurt them. White males in particular are the greatest beneficiaries of that excellent affirmative action programme, the old boy network. It would be folly for black people, and women, to reject well-targeted affirmative action programmes simply because they fear being labelled by people who ought to know better. Carefully designed and applied affirmative action programmes are essential to the establishment of greater equity.

The criticism directed at me earlier on in my career for joining UCT had died down by 1990 as more black South Africans realised the importance of academic work as real work, and its contribution to social policy and the general development of society. But some people thought that my joining the UCT executive in 1991 was going too far. Was I not allowing myself to be used by white liberals, who had no intention of changing, but needed to protect themselves by having a token, high-profile black woman? 'They are using you,' said someone whom I respect, and who really cares for me. I was troubled by this perception, but remained convinced that my decision was the correct one for me.

I have no other way of knowing the real motive behind Dr Stuart Saunders's invitation to join his executive team, but feel quite comfortable taking his stated motives at face value. But if he was indeed intending to use me, as some people say, then he has a major problem on his hands. UCT can never be the same after the process it has been through over the last few years. It would have had to change anyway, with or without me. But I would like to believe that the strategies for which my portfolio staff and I have sought acceptance at UCT, and which I have had the pleasure of seeing put into operation, will have far-reaching consequences beyond UCT, and indeed will help shape the way in which South Africans tackle equity issues generally. The Equal Opportunity Research Project, through its outreach programme, has played an important role in helping other institutions of higher learning, the private sector as well as nongovernmental organisations, to develop policies and programmes around issues of race and gender equity.

Not all aspects of my job are enjoyable, however. Nor is it possible to change all the things I find irritating and uncomfortable. There is no escape from interminable committee meetings, appointments, and dealings with bureaucrats. These are all part and parcel of working with people anywhere in the world. But the only time I really felt uncomfortable and ill at ease, if not downright embarrassed, was the first occasion I had to wear the robes of office at an inaugural lecture. I had naïvely thought that I could elect to be part of the audience. It dawned on me later that in the same way that I enjoy the pomp and ceremony of High Mass at St George's Cathedral, I too had to make academic rituals come alive for those participating in the life of the University.

I have learnt to relax and see the funny side of donning robes designed for the cold weather of the Northern Hemisphere, and wearing hats which could only have been designed with men in mind. One does become willy-nilly an honorary man in these situations. The awkwardness of a woman in my position shows up more starkly in public ceremonies. At the first graduation ceremony I presided over in December 1993, the Dean who was to present candidates to me for graduation had to establish how he was to address me. When he said he did not want to use a sexist form of address, I asked him how he would have addressed my male colleagues. 'Mr Acting Vice-Chancellor,' he stated confidently. 'Well,' I said, 'I am Madame Acting Vice-Chancellor!' One has to learn to laugh at oneself in order to remain sane.

Another important institution in the transformation of South Africa is the Independent Development Trust. I was invited to sit on the board of the IDT in 1990 as one of its founding trustees and was appointed its third chairperson at the end of 1994. The IDT was launched with R2 billion from the National Party government. Many people correctly pointed out that this was blood money. But what money in South Africa or anywhere else in the world is clean? Are the large American philanthropic foundations not the beneficiaries of the bequests of robber barons of old? Of greater symbolic significance is the Nobel Peace Award, which derives its legacy from a successful armaments industry.

In setting up the IDT, the South African government was for the first time trying to acknowledge its responsibility for the poverty which it and its predecessors had deliberately created amongst the majority of South African citizens. The grant of R2 billion was one of the initiatives of a party trying to reform itself. I was initially hesitant to be part of this initiative, for different reasons. I did not want to be over-extended, and having just emerged from a personal crisis, I was not ready to take on new commitments. But with the encouragement of Eric Molobi, the Executive Director of Kagiso Trust, I agreed. Here was an opportunity to implement a major development programme drawing on my previous experience and social analysis. My past involvement with development efforts had been at a local level; here was a chance of engaging in meaningful macro-level work. More important, this time the problem of the job would not be about where the money would come from, but how to spend the considerable resources judiciously to maximum effect.

But I had under-estimated the scale and the nature of the problems. In spite of enormous energy and careful planning by the executive directors of the IDT, a key problem remains: how to create capacity amongst the poorest of the poor to enable them to participate meaningfully in major development efforts. The IDT has set itself the task of promoting the development of the poorest people of South Africa, who are the victims of apartheid. It has four main areas of focus: housing, education, rural development, and health.

The capacity of the poor to engage effectively in the development process and to use substantial resources has been found to be extremely limited. The most devastating impact of apartheid on poor black South Africans has been the destruction of people's faith in themselves as agents of history. Their life experiences are scarred by survival strategies which destroy trust and faith in their fellow human beings. Moreover, their dealings with development agencies have in many cases merely reinforced their mistrust of systems and their fellow human beings. They have been taken advantage of for so long that they have stopped trying, and have become apathetic.

Some people who read *The Mountain People* by Colin Turnbull may find it offensive, and accuse the writer of exaggeration or lack of empathy with the subjects of his study, and there may well be justification for the criticisms. Unfortunately, some communities in South Africa show patterns of behaviour which are not dissimilar to those Turnbull describes in his book on an African community living on the edge of survival in the mountains between Uganda and Kenya.* Their desperate poverty has led to the development of extremely utilitarian behavioural patterns: parents are even prepared to abandon their children to ensure their own survival. Mistrust is the guiding principle in their human relations. This extreme poverty almost makes them unreachable for development purposes.

Phola Park, a squatter camp on the East Rand, presents similar features. It has deteriorated from being, in 1990, a model of resilience and creative self-governance to a wasteland ravaged by war in which criminals and opposing political tendencies fight for control. Ironically it is their extreme need for development which makes the people of Phola Park unreachable. Because of their focus on today's battles they have become losers in the war on poverty. What once made for good oppositional politics in the late 1980s constrains these people's ability to take a long-term view.

The problem of reaching the poorest of the poor is complicated by yet another problem in the development field: gatekeepers. Development is a highly politicised process everywhere in the world. This politicisation takes on new meaning in a situation where people have been deliberately under-developed and have waged a liberation struggle around the issue of development.

The South African liberation struggle has moved through many phases over the last three decades. The 1970s was a developmental phase under the Black Consciousness Movement. In those years development became a tool for conscientising and organising oppressed people. Some people criticised the BCM for this approach and charged that we were delaying the struggle by getting poor communities to believe that they could develop themselves out of their misery. For these critics the answer lay in the overthrow of the apartheid regime. They were substantially correct in their analysis, but failed to take cognisance of the historical fact that chronic pover-

*C. Turnbull, *The Mountain People* (New York, 1972).

ty has rarely fired people to rise against their oppressors. It is acute change for the worse or for the better, which creates a crisis of rising expectations, that may lead to revolution.

The 1980s brought in the season of development. Almost everyone in the liberation struggle began talking of, or doing, development. Development became not only politically correct, but lucrative as well. After the repression of the 1970s the international community had been shocked out of its complacency about apartheid. Support for the anti-apartheid struggle assumed global dimensions, and resources to support victims of apartheid became widely available. The European Economic Community established the Victims of Apartheid Fund with considerable resources at its disposal. This was a welcome change from the struggle for funding which had previously been experienced. But it was a double-edged sword.

In the 1980s development became more politicised than it had ever been in South Africa. One had to be 'cleared' for funding by political organisations, which found themselves in enormously powerful positions to direct resources where they pleased. The whole business became iniquitous. As is often the case, the development gravy-train, which picked up steam in the 1980s, travelled along the rails of existing privilege. If one had the right political affiliation, lived in an urban area, was male and well connected, one was made. Scholarships, self-help project money and more, often went to enrich people who were well placed to take advantage of these opportunities.

The industry also generated jobs for many politically correct people, some of whom were advanced beyond their level of competence. Funders were often too embarrassed to ask searching questions. Huge bureaucracies were established and flourished. At the same time it would be unfair not to acknowledge the good work done by many South Africans during this era. They took advantage of existing resources and applied them effectively and efficiently. They laid the foundation for continuing creative work which fills one with hope for the future role of non-governmental development efforts in South Africa.

The 1990s is the era of transformation and nation building. Some of the development workers of the 1980s have been able to transform themselves into nation builders and have creatively engaged the negotiation process at local, regional and national levels to ensure that the death of old institutions does not create a hiatus before new institutions are born.

But some of the politically correct activists of the 1980s h.
to make the transition from the politics of opposition to the po.
of engagement. They have become gatekeepers who hold poor communities to ransom and thereby demonstrate their power in the
wider scheme of things. The anti-apartheid gravy-train has also
ground to a halt, adding to their frustrations, and making them more
vicious in their attacks on others who have adopted a different and
more successful approach. They decry 'independent development'
as a myth, and are always seeing themselves as the protectors of hapless 'masses' who would be cheated but for their vigilance.

The 1990s has also brought other dangers. As the scale of operations has moved from the micro- to the macro-level, and resources
have become available to big operators, a new breed of person has
surfaced in South Africa – the development consultant. Many are
white and male, and some have 'done time in the struggle politics'
of the 1980s, thus acquiring credibility and legitimacy. They com-
mand high fees and are part of the fastest-growing sector of the
economy. Some of them are doing really valuable work, but not
enough are interested in transferring their skills for the benefit of the
people with whom they work. It does not make economic sense for
them to lower their scarcity value. But successful development is all
about the transfer of skills.

The IDT has been caught in the development maze I have
sketched. It has had to learn to negotiate directly with communities,
and to undercut gatekeepers by helping establish authentic community-based organisations. It is a laborious task, but it has enormous
long-term benefits. The IDT has also fallen victim to the consultancy
industry, which descended on it like vultures on a carcass. It has
taken effort and courage for those leading the IDT to create a better
balance between the enabling contributions of consultants and the
danger of exploitation.

The biggest obstacle to development in South Africa after 1990
was the policy vacuum into which the country was thrust. The
National Party government not only lacked the legitimacy to create
a supportive policy environment, but had elements within it which
were determined to undermine any independent development
effort. These elements still wanted to use taxpayers' money to gain
political credit for the National Party. Moreover, there was sheer
bureaucratic incompetence, which held up many programmes.

The liberation movements were also caught in a bind during the political transition after 1990. They did not want to give their blessing to development processes for which they could not claim political credit. However much they understood the importance and urgency of tackling poverty, they did not want the National Party government to benefit politically from development. In consequence the IDT was caught on the horns of a dilemma. On one hand, the government's detractors accused the IDT of being an instrument of the liberation movements, particularly the African National Congress, its main rival in the power game. On the other hand, some ANC operatives charged the IDT with failure to respond to ordinary people's needs because it was tied to the apron strings of the National Party government and big capital.

The annual reports of the IDT tell a different story. It is establishing important models of sustainable development which are indigenous to South Africa, whilst learning from the mistakes of other countries. It has chosen to work with community-based groups and non-governmental organisations in relationships that are mutually empowering and promote public accountability. It has commissioned studies to explore alternative policy approaches to the problem areas in South Africa: education, housing and rural development. It has forged partnerships with Kagiso Trust, the Development Bank of Southern Africa, and the private sector, to maximise development resources. It has also made many mistakes, but has acknowledged them and hopefully learned from them.

The fact of the matter is that without large indigenous development agents, such as the IDT and Kagiso Trust, any government in South Africa will have great difficulties tackling the development challenges ahead. There is a sizeable resource base accumulated over the last few years, both material and intellectual, which no sensible government can ignore. One can only hope that as the political temperature cools down, and the real work of reconstruction and development is tackled, the importance of independent development agents will be recognised as partners of government, not as opposition.

With the adoption of the Reconstruction and Development Programme (RDP) by the Government of National Unity soon after its inauguration in May 1994, a national framework has been created for development. It is interesting to see the extent to which former activists who were highly critical of the IDT for failing to deliver development at grassroots level are finding themselves confronted by the realities of working with disempowered people. The capacity to absorb the development resources of the RDP has to be created – it cannot be wished into being.

Mr Jay Naidoo, Minister without Portfolio, who is in charge of the RDP, has had to swallow his pride in this regard. His unhappiness with being allocated only R2.5 billion in the 1994/95 budget turned into an anxiety to prove that even though not much had been spent on the ground, most of the money had been allocated for projects on the basis of business plans. He too has had to come to terms with the fact that development is a process and not an event. The poorer people are, the less able they are to take advantage of development resources. This is most frustrating, but it is the price one has to pay for transforming a system which destroyed development opportunities for people.

Some of the new bureaucrats in the government have yet to learn that the government can only deliver the goods in partnership with the private sector and the non-governmental sector. Their eagerness to be seen not only as liberators of the people but as the providers of development resources, is a major constraint on development.

In the last few years I have been increasingly involved in the corporate world in South Africa. In South African political parlance there are degrees of pollution attached to institutions and processes. At the extreme end of the profane sits the corporate world. The Big Five or Six, who have major control over the Johannesburg Stock Exchange, are the 'untouchables': Anglo American Corporation & De Beers, Rembrandt, Sanlam, Old Mutual, Liberty Life. The antipathy of political activists towards the big corporations is understandable. Not only did they remain silent at crucial points in the history of South Africa, but they decidedly benefited from the political environment provided by racial discrimination.

The iniquitous migrant-labour system enabled the mining industry to make high profits without the added problem of social responsibility for the families of black workers. It is true that the sending countries of these migrant workers also benefited from the system, and that it cost the mining industry lost opportunities in not being able to have a stable work-force. But the fact of the matter is that the system of migrant labour, and with it the despicable hostel compound system, were introduced into South Africa by the mining industry. It was not a system imposed on the industry by the government of the day.

Nor did big business play the creative role in the development of human resources it could have played. It followed the policy of job reservation for white workers with little effective protest. It did not invest in the education of its own workers, let alone that of other underprivileged people. The money that trickled down for social responsibility projects was too little and unfocused to make any real impact. Even when the Sullivan Code obtained in the 1970s and 1980s little progress was made because most institutions played the game of tokenism. Those that did not failed to understand the importance of the need to tackle access, human development and institutional culture. Thus the few blacks who found their way into managerial positions became frustrated and angry.

It is understandable that my former activist colleagues and some friends were dismayed at my decision to accept invitations to sit on the boards of Anglo American and the Old Mutual.* Why should I step into such profanity? One could have knocked me down with a feather five years ago if it had been suggested that I would find myself sitting in the boardrooms of these corporations today. But history is full of ironies. I made the decision to engage the large institutions in our society which play an important role in the economy of the country, because they have to be harnessed for the good of the entire population. They cannot be wished away. I have no illusions about their conservative history and their likely resistance to change. But I also have faith that at some stage their proven economic prowess can be made to serve the majority, when they realise that their long-term interests will be best served only if they intersect with the developmental interests of the majority of South Africans.

Some could argue that legislative compulsion is a better, cleaner and surer way of changing the behaviour of big business than wasting one's time in boardrooms. I have no doubt that major legislative initiatives are required to compel all business enterprises to fulfil basic social responsibilities. But there are limits to what can be done without the risk of triggering a panic flight of capital. Whatever the legislative environment, I believe that most South African institutions will need assistance to grapple with change in institutional culture, wherein lies the successful transition to a new operating envi-

*I resigned from the Old Mutual board at the end of 1994 because I felt my input was not making the impact I had hoped for.

ronment. To the extent that I feel I can influence the key players in this regard, I will continue to risk pollution.

My part in the 1990–1 scenario exercise sponsored by the Old Mutual–Nedcor group of companies to examine future options for changing South Africa was crucial in shaping my decision to become involved in the world of big business. The major conclusion of our study was that a successful transition from authoritarian rule to a prosperous democratic order would only be possible if political and socio-economic transformation received equal attention. The study also concluded that the complexities of the problems are such that no single sector of society can meet the challenges ahead. Social compacts between the government, organs of civil society, including trade unions, and the private sector were the only sensible approach for South Africa.[†] I believe that my role in the major corporations will make some contribution towards that end.

It is interesting to see the extent to which some of the approaches suggested by the Old Mutual–Nedcor scenario have been incorporated into the RDP, including the rhetoric of 'kick-starting' the post-apartheid economy. I could not resist the temptation on one occasion in October 1994, after Jay Naidoo had spoken at a seminar I was chairing, to warn him not to assume that everything had to be 'kick-started', because there was a real danger of kicking some existing programmes to death. Government has to engage other parties who have been in the development business before the official RDP was launched in order to ensure maximum collaboration and the effective delivery of development goods to all. The establishment of Nedlac, the National Economic, Labour and Development Council, is another concrete outcome of the impact the scenario had on South Africa's transitional politics.

But there is more to the reconstruction of post-apartheid South Africa than socio-economic development. The moral fabric of our society has been seriously damaged by apartheid and by the struggle against it. While atrocities committed by the South African security forces in the name of 'national security' were legion, the anti-apartheid struggle, like any war, has also left scars – abuses of power and brutality – in its aftermath. A process of national healing is required to put us on a firmer footing as a new democracy.

The proposed Truth and Reconciliation Commission is an impor-

[†]Bob Tucker and Bruce Scott, *South Africa: Prospects for Successful Transition* (Kenwyn, 1992).

tant development. If healing is to occur, the abscess lying under the skin of our new nation has to be incised. One cannot have reconciliation without acknowledging past wrongdoing.

But there are serious questions which are likely to make the work of the Truth Commission complex. How far back in history does one go to ensure that justice is done to all those affected? What definition of atrocity is one to apply? Is the Commission to focus only on overt political crimes, and if so, how are these to be defined? Who is to be held accountable for past atrocities: the officer who pulled the trigger or the general who gave the order to shoot? What about the politicians who presided over the policies which created the environment for the commission of atrocities?

The issue of compensation is also important. Who is to compensate the victims of past atrocities? The state? Past government officials? Individual officers, some of whom received generous golden handshakes for services rendered? Compensation is crucial, particularly for those left destitute as a result of past losses. But where are the resources to come from? There is also the question of the extent to which one can compensate for loss. How much and what form should such compensation involve? Can material compensation make up for the pain one has suffered through loss?

These and many other questions have prompted some people to caution against the dangers of opening old wounds and the risk of further pain which our society can ill afford. Some have urged us to let bygones be bygones. I personally feel that we cannot avoid the pain of having to incise this festering sore and letting it heal from the base. There can be no healing without pain. Some of us have already gone through our own painful journeys to find healing, and can therefore afford to let bygones be bygones. But for the countless destitute widows, mothers who have lost children, children who have been orphaned, and many others whose loved ones disappeared without trace, the Truth Commission has an important symbolic healing role to play. Their pain has to be publicly acknowledged, and some restitution has to occur in order to allow them to pick up the pieces and move on.

My own healing has been assisted by my most important mentor and spiritual counsellor, Fr Ted King, who helped me to negotiate my independence from my political activist past and to deal with the painful process of healing. He helped me to develop a healthier historical perspective, whilst nurturing me in the context of a caring

Christian community. Through his encouragement I am able to enjoy myself without feeling guilty, to go on retreats to 'restore myself to myself', and to trust my own conscience in making difficult decisions. There are others who have played larger or smaller roles, and continue to be there in times of need – and there are plenty of them.

The company of caring friends and family has been important to me. Both male and female friends have enabled me to laugh at myself, and many have been there when I needed them most. My friends come from a wide range of backgrounds and are a source of important insights into worlds which would have been otherwise closed to me. I remember with particular fondness Moira Henderson, who died in May 1989 from stomach cancer. She had a beauty which was deeper than her obvious physical attraction. Her wisdom and caring nature shone through, adding a particular character to the ever-present twinkle in her eyes. The age and class differences between us did not impede our enjoyment of each other's company. She introduced me to the beauty of the wild spring flowers around her Langebaan holiday house. The splendour of the varieties of colour, shape and size was overwhelming for me on my first visit in 1985. It became a spring ritual to spend a weekend in Langebaan. Moira also introduced me to regular walks and an appreciation of the beauty of nature. Her wit and keen intellect were a joy to share.

My family has been particularly supportive, even when they had no way of understanding why I was doing the things I did. My sons in their own way have aided my personal growth. They hold me to whatever word I give them, thus forcing me to be more honest with them about my abilities and vulnerabilities. They also cut me down to size when I take myself too seriously. Hlumelo, my elder son, sometimes reminds me that I am not a model of how society functions. On the contrary, he reminds me, our family transgresses many of the accepted norms. I have to remember this even under difficult circumstances.

I have found my life as a transgressive a constant challenge. The most frightening aspect of it is coming to terms with the need to rely on one's own conscience to guide one's decision-making in critical areas of life. It is unnerving to have to go ahead with decisions with which all one's friends and colleagues disagree. It is even more troubling when one is vindicated in those decisions, because such vindications distance one even further from them. The danger of arrogance and conceit is real.

There are many ironies of history which strike one as one stretches across boundaries. The most riveting for me was finding myself in the Cabinet Room in Tuynhuis, Cape Town, at the beginning of 1991. I was a member of the Old Mutual–Nedcor scenario team that presented our findings to the National Party Cabinet. One could not but note the irony of sitting in the same room with some of the politicians who had participated in making decisions to repress political dissension and activists like myself. My own banning order in 1977 must have been discussed in that very same room.

In my role as a UCT executive, I am often reminded of the irony of being a former activist having to deal with present-day student activists. I sometimes feel a deep empathy for their naïveté, but also get irritated by it. I have to confess a tinge of pain when I am not trusted by students simply because I am a member of 'the administration'. The taste of exclusion by those for whom one cares so much hurts, but it is part of the reality with which one has to come to terms. I am also often used as an accessible target by angry black and women staff and students, who vent their anger at me. I accept this role with all its pain because it is a bridge to a better future.

But there are many compensations in my life. The small changes you are able to bring to the institutions in which you work are like fuel which keeps you going. It is also exciting to engage the minds of people who do not ordinarily cross your path. The more boundaries you stretch across, and even transgress, the more opportunities you have to meet with interesting people. My ever-growing global contacts also afford me the opportunity for broadening my perspectives. In many ways I feel at home in the global village. And global citizenship is the ultimate in transgression.

Recognising that you are a member of the global village is essential to lifting you above the narrow nationalistic interests and concerns of your own country. The perspectives which global citizenship affords are of particular value in situations of momentous change such as we are experiencing in South Africa. South Africa is not inventing new problems nor is it likely to invent entirely novel solutions. The one novelty it could do itself the favour of inventing would be to learn from history.

I have enjoyed international travel and meeting new people in this way. Donna Shalala, Secretary for Health in the Clinton Administration, was responsible for my first trip to the United

States. She invited me in 1983, at the suggestion of Desmond Tutu, as part of an international campaign for the lifting of my banning order. I was invited to come as a commencement speaker at Hunter College, where she was President at the time. I was able to travel to New York with Hlumelo in May 1984.

It was a remarkable visit. We were generously hosted by Bernice Powell, another Tutu connection, in her comfortable home in Harlem. A major tension point was the tight schedule which left little time for Hlumelo and me to explore New York together without the presence of strangers. He got so frustrated by being entrusted to baby-sitters that he started heckling me in meetings which I addressed. On one occasion he decided to repeat what I was saying at every turn until I invited him to come and sit next to me on the podium. It was quite an experience to have brought a personal heckler all the way from South Africa.

Donna and I became good friends. Her diminutive physical stature belies her inner strength. She is an energetic, creative political strategist, attributes which the Clinton Administration has sadly not fully used. She adopted my sons and me as part of her family and encouraged us to visit her as often as we could. On my second visit to New York in 1985, she looked at me mischievously and said: 'Mamphela, I am going to introduce you to American decadence.' She then took me to a place where she regularly had her weekly manicure and pedicure. What bliss! I have never looked back. I have learnt to enjoy paying attention to my body. This I believe is a necessary part of the healing process I personally have to undergo. That healing process has finally begun in earnest.

I want to conclude by acknowledging how privileged I feel to have been part of the most exciting period in the history of South Africa. The struggle to find the most meaningful way of engaging with this exciting history is not likely to end soon. The theologian H. A. Williams reminds us that 'The vocation of being human is a vocation to enter into . . . creative conflict and make it our own.'* For as long as one is human, one is destined to deal with conflict. A good dose of humour and some willingness to take risks give one the chance not only to transcend artificial boundaries but to derive deep pleasure in doing so.

---

*H. A. Williams, *The Simplicity of Prayer* (London, 1976), p. 20.

# Index